FREEDOM AND FEDERALISM ★ Congress and Courts 1861–1866

Patricia Allan Lucie

Garland Publishing, Inc.
New York & London ★ 1986

Library of Congress Cataloging-in-Publication Data

Lucie, Patricia Allan, 1946–
Freedom and federalism.

(American legal and constitutional history)
Bibliography: p.
1. Courts—United States—History. 2. Federal government—United States—History. 3. Afro-Americans—Civil rights—History. 4. United States—Politics and government—Civil War, 1861–1865. 5. Reconstruction.
I. Title. II. Series.
KF8719.L83 1986 347.73′1 86-22944
ISBN 0-8240-8285-0 347.3071

All volumes in this series are printed on acid-free, 250-year-life paper.

Printed in the United States of America

FREEDOM AND FEDERALISM,

CONGRESS AND COURTS, 1861-1866

Patricia Allan Lucie

Table of Contents

Preface and Acknowledgements

I wrote this dissertation in 1972. Since then a period of time has elapsed which is almost as long as it took Americans to fight their Civil War and reconstruct their nation. During that time, some of the historians I admire most, among them Harold Hyman, Michael Les Benedict, Herman Belz, William Wiecek, Philip Paludan, Kermit Hall and Donald Nieman have been unlocking doors, some of which I was knocking on and some I didn't even know were there. Their work continues to revitalise the history of the period and the Constitution. This dissertation was a modest tributory of a larger stream.

It begins with Congress confused about the nature of the war and doubtful about the adequacy of the Constitution to the task at hand. It ends with their growing legislative expertise and confidence, especially in the deployment of the federal courts to underpin the restored Union. Experience is its theme. As Republican legislators struggled with the immediate problems of designing a confiscation policy and taking their first stumbling steps towards emancipation, they began to discover resources within the Constitution which promised not only the preservation of the Union but a more perfect Union.

Their voyage of discovery took them into areas of federal relations which apparently had nothing to do with the future of the South or the Negro. When they debated the Habeas Corpus Act in 1863 the immediate problem was to do something about the literally thousands of suits pending against federal officers in the state courts of Kentucky, Indiana, Pennsylvania and New York. They discovered the truth of Albert G. Riddle's observation that, "The Government is a unit, it cannot exist in broken parts; and whoever strikes it down in South Carolina strikes it down in Massachusetts. If you cannot enforce its laws in New Orleans, it is idle to adjudicate them in New York." The truth was that unpopular federal law was no safer from resistance in the name of States rights in the North than it was in the South, and that until it was there was little chance of it being obeyed in South Carolina. Reconstruction was national in a very real sense.

So it was too with citizenship. Republicans discovered how little was known about what it meant to be an American citizen when they were forced to define the status of freed slaves. Debates on proposed emancipation and Reconstruction laws in the Thirty-eighth Congress reveal that they expected much more from freedom than the absence of slavery, but when they used white men's rights as a yardstick for black they discovered that the nation lacked the tools to protect any of its citizens in the states. They changed that.

The tools they used were the federal courts. There was not much choice in the absence of a large, effective bureaucracy or a willingness to pay for one. If Republicans still smarted from the sting of Roger Taney's Dred Scott opinion, they nonetheless distinguished between that outrage and the continuing relevance of the whole federal court system to the enforcement of the nation's laws. The resolution of that dilemma dated from the Confiscation debates. Republicans worried that federal courts might confuse persons and property, but decided to make the distinction in the law rather than by avoiding the courts. Still they went warily, expanding federal court jurisdiction to in rem proceedings for the confiscation of property which minimised judicial discretion. At the same time they considered judicial procedures for guaranteeing personal liberty to slaves freed under the acts but drew back because it was coupled with a requirement which made emancipation itself dependant on the courts.

It took time to work out how the federal courts could serve them most effectively and at least risk. In response to a range of new legislative demands the Republicans expanded and refined court roles. The experience they gained from providing federal officers with procedure to remove cases against them from state to federal courts under the Habeas Corpus Act of 1863 was central. It taught them that the need for pathways into the states to enforce the law was not confined either to the South or to slavery-related matters. It also prompted them to discuss the relationship between process and substance and to explore how things actually worked at the interfaces of state and nation. Lessons learned were applied to securing freedom and guaranteeing the equal protection of the laws. The experience of early setbacks in making removal procedures work led to stiffer formulae in the removal procedures of the 1866 Civil Rights Act.

After the Habeas Corpus Act it became a habit for the Republicans to include the federal courts in the design of laws which attempted to cross state lines and weather possible unpopularity. The Wade-Davis Bill was an attempt to combine new state political arrangements with federal judicial guarantees to secure freedom. The Thirteenth Amendment put the freedman's right to a writ of habeas corpus in a federal court beyond doubt and did much more. Chapter 5 surveys its political and judicial history, arguing for a broad substantive approach to its original meaning and a planned capacity for growth both by judicial interpretation and "appropriate" legislation.

Democrats accused Republicans in all these matters not only of planning but of plotting. It seemed to many of them that the Republicans were designing legislation to affront legitimate State rights and avoid the consequences in state courts. Their use of the federal courts offered convincing proof. Cases between citizens of the same state on matters of state law were to be snatched from the states and re-tried *de novo* in the federal courts; those who executed federal laws on confiscation, emancipation and Reconstruction were to be shielded from the consequences of flouting state laws and made unaccountable. The Confiscation Acts, the Habeas Corpus Act, the Wade-Davis Bill, the Thirteenth Amendment, the Freedmen's Bureau and Civil Rights Act were all inter-locking pieces in the one plot.

There were indeed links, but there was no plot to undermine the states and place federal officers above the law. The links were in the problems and hence in the attempted solutions. The Chapters which follow will suggest that the Republican response had more of an element of planning and overlap than perhaps has been realised. Plans which looked tidy in Washington, however, had to take their chances in a very untidy real world. In 1866 the Freedmen's Bureau and Civil Rights Acts together with the amended Habeas Corpus Act constructed a sophisticated machinery for protecting not only freedmen but the Bureau and army agents who protected them. Chapter 7 contrasts that tidiness with the continuing chaos out in the field.

Laws which made courts their linchpin relied upon bench and bar to keep faith with their intentions, give or take an honest disagreement. What happened when state courts simply refused to allow cases to be removed to federal courts or interpreted the laws in ways which undercut their purpose is also explored in these Chapters. State courts in Reconstruction have not received the attention they deserve and time and distance have prevented me from fuller investigation of some of the questions raised in Chapters 3 and 7. We need to know a great deal more too about the lower federal courts in order to understand how legislative intentions and judicial interpretations parted company in the 1870's after hopeful beginnings in the 1860's. Whether the failure to achieve racial justice may be attributed to an original design flaw or to later drifting, deliberate sabotage or dwindling will remains of interest, the more so since the machinery is still in use.

My own interest in these matters dates from Peter Parish's stimulating seminars on the American Civil War at the University of Glasgow in 1968. William R. Brock supervised my dissertation there and I thank him for many insights. Rice University, Houston, Texas very generously provided a graduate studentship for a year and the privilege of joining Harold Hyman's seminar. His infectious enthusiasm for constitutions and laws has been with me ever since and survived the attempts of my three children, Karen, Alison and Philip to impede the pursuit of knowledge. Margaret Fewson typed from a messy manuscript with great patience and good humour and I appreciate her help.

CHAPTER 1 INTRODUCTION

Freedom and Federalism, Congress and Courts

Successful reconstruction of the Union depended on somebody learning something from the American Civil War. To have adopted the conservative slogan of restoring "The Constitution as it is, the Union as it was," would have been to stand still, to wait until the next crisis rent both asunder. More thoughtful Americans addressed themselves instead to a study of what had gone wrong, and began the long, slow process of putting it right. In many ways it was a new experience for them to speak of the Constitution's flaws and defects. Americans, as E.L. Godkin wrote in 1864, seemed to believe that, "when the Federal Constitution was framed, the canon of political revelation was complete.[1]" They congratulated themselves on having secured their liberties in wise political arrangements, but never stopped to analyse the component parts, or watch how they grew and changed. As a Kentucky lawyer put it in 1861:

> They have sailed upon a smooth sea, without the experience of a single storm to waken serious apprehension for their safety, and have never examined the vessel which has borne them, to understand the great timbers and braces that hold it together[2].

There had, of course, been occasions in the past which might have suggested the need for close study. But the fact that a political compromise was reached before the Hartford Convention or the South Carolina Nullification controversy led to disunion, delayed the nation's education. Slavery was the one issue explosive enough to defy compromise and bring the constitutional edifice to the point of collapse[3]. The questions it had posed for federalism for a generation could no longer go unanswered.

In all these strains on the federal system, a common factor might have been revealed. Federalism had become dangerously state centred in its politics, its laws, and its daily routines. So much thought had been given to avoiding the possibility of overmighty central government that the balance had tipped in the other direction. What was missing in the federal system was a bridge across state lines to enable both the individual citizen and the federal government to make some claims on each other. Both liberty and effective government depended upon it.

There could be no effective government unless the law was obeyed even when it was locally unpopular. In the wake of the Nullification controversy the federal government found great difficulty in protecting its own revenue officers from harassment and prosecution in state courts for offences allegedly committed in the course of enforcing an unpopular law. Slavery produced more examples of how states could resist federal authority, when Northern state court judges issued writs of *habeas corpus* to release prisoners held under a federal law, the Fugitive Slave Law. Old habits persisted after the war and threatened the effectiveness of the military effort. State court judges released conscripted minors on *habeas* writs. Union officers were hounded in state courts for alleged offences against state law.

If effective government depended on creating a federal presence in the states, so too did freedom. In *ante bellum* America the nature of freedom was not much studied - less so than slavery. But like slavery it was state business. Antislavery agitators who fell foul of state laws while exercising their right to speak, experienced a little of what slaves lived with all the time. They were at the mercy of state and municipal law, frustated by being cut off from the rights which they believed belonged to them as men and as citizens of the United States. States rights could be as damaging to liberty as it was to Union.

It was not quite true that no thinking had been done on the subject. The trouble was that the people who had developed a constitutional case for a bridge remained outside the pale of constitutional orthodoxy and political reality, at least for the moment. They belonged to the anti-slavery movement. Even within that movement there was no consensus. Garrisonians in the 1840's moved towards a position which rejected the Constitution as a corrupt instrument, proslavery in text and intent. While believing that freedom was God's law they did not instruct judges to interpret the Constitution by its standards. Rather, where a judge found his conscience in conflict with positive law, his duty was to resign rather than compromise. It was not an argument for analysing the Constitution's defects and setting them to rights within the existing system[4]. Moderate antislavery opinion, as it was developed by men like Salmon P. Chase and Arnold Buffum, was absorbed in the mainstream of the Liberty Party and later the Free Soil coalition. It relied upon the view that since slavery was the creature of positive municipal law, the withdrawal of all federal support for it would ultimately be a death blow. The Constitution, it was argued, restrained the federal government from establishing slavery, but it also tied its hands from interfering with it. Although Chase and his supporters had originally laid more emphasis on the Constitution as the home for equal rights of citizenship, the price of increasing Western political support was that they rallied behind the more limited anti-extension platform of "Freedom national, slavery sectional," which allowed the disaffected of all parties to unite on common ground without taking a more advanced view on the race issue than Western sentiment demanded[5].

More creative and interesting arguments were offered by a minority of radical antislavery men, notably Alvan Stewart, Lysander Spooner, James G. Birney, and William Goodell. From the late 1830's they began to develop and slowly mature an argument which obliged constitutional law to draw its life from natural law. At the heart of their case was the argument that governments exist in order to secure liberty. Natural law, the common law, and the Declaration of Independence all recognised the primacy of man's right to life, liberty and property. Antislavery theorists stressed that since these rights were held equally by all men, government owed them equal protection. According to Jacobus TenBroek, who along with Howard J. Graham first explored the dimensions of anti-slavery constitutional ideas, equal protection was understood to be a double-edged concept; first, the negative duty of government not to pass laws abridging fundamental rights; second, and more important, the positive duty to guarantee full and equal protection[6]. This duty was the federal government's. Implicit in all their thinking was the idea that all Americans were citizens of the nation and entitled to the fundamental rights of citizens. Both the substance of these rights and the powers to protect them were to be found in the Constitution.

At this point they ceased to sermonise about the moral imperatives to read the Constitution by the light of its higher law purposes and kinship to the Declaration of Independence, and attempted to anchor their ideas more squarely within the specific provisions of the text, to the privileges and immunities clause, the guarantee of republican government, and the Bill of Rights, especially the Fifth amendment's due process clause. Their case was not self-evident, as Chapter VI will make clear. Apart from the ambiguities of language and the contradictions of historical evidence, they flew in the face of orthodoxy. While they argued that the Bill of Rights was a source of national citizenship, binding on the states, Chief Justice John Marshall ruled in Barron v Baltimore that it was a limitation on the federal government, though not on the states[7]. No self-respecting constitutional lawyer would have entertained a claim that the

Fifth Amendment was a substantive guarantee of individual freedom, though property was perhaps a different matter[8]. No court would have given a sympathetic hearing to the view that the federal government had any interest in the right of a citizen of Massachusetts to speak his mind in South Carolina.

The dominant style of judicial reasoning in the 1840's and 1850's was not one which invited natural law concepts to dictate constitutional interpretation. The Constitution was to be discovered by the application of logic to the text as illuminated by the intentions of the framers, precedent and settled law. The exercise of will was no part of judicial business. It is true that in the 1820's and 1830's judges at all levels had taken more risks and used the common law creatively and to some extent self-consciously to alter the economy in favour of the entrepreneur or give effect to majoritarian will. But there was a difference between private and public law, and a difference between 1820 and 1850. By that time, instrumentalism, in the sense of acknowledged judicial policy making, seems to have been waning as those who had gained economic benefits from it sought more formalist defences of their interests[9].

But the Supreme Court never acknowledged that judicial will had any part in its decisions on slavery. Both proslavery and antislavery constitutional arguments ruled out overt judicial policy-making functions. Radical antislavery theorists would have made natural law a limitation on judicial will, naively ignoring the processes of construction and interpretation of value laden concepts. At the other extreme, proslavery Justices on the Supreme Court affected to simply apply the constitution as it was[10]. Prigg v Pennsylvania, Latimer, Jones v Van Zandt and above all Dred Scott testify that this was a delusion[11]. The dedication of the majority of Justices on the Taney Court to some of the same goals of expediency underlying instrumentalist decisions in the economic sphere, namely national unity and expansion, leads some historians to describe these decisions as instrumentalist[12]. But even proslavery judges would not have admitted that there was any need to add to what the law already said. Justices like Story and McLean who personally disliked slavery accepted the constraints of positive law and believed that they had a duty to subtract will from their judgement. These judges "squirmed" as conscience collided with law, but they found room within a shared judicial style to differ from proslavery colleagues. There was some freedom to manoeuvre at the margins of interpretation, in the construction of statutes and the choice of law in conflict of law cases. The choice, as

Roger Cover says, amounted to this, "He may apply the law against his conscience. He may apply conscience and be faithless to the law. He may resign. Or he may cheat." This he could do by introducing his own sense of "what ought to be" interstitially, where no "hard law" yet exists[13]. For McLean and Story it was enough to make a difference, but at some distance from radical antislavery constitutionalism.

The isolation of radical antislavery thought from the mainstream of practice at the time is hardly an appropriate standard by which to judge its contribution to the eventual absorption of the trilogy of privileges and immunities - due process - equal protection into the Fourteenth Amendment. Their theorists had an audience. However imperfectly argued and open to criticism their ideas were, they were in touch with the instincts of many outside the ranks of believing abolitionists who believed that as Americans they surely had rights in the nation's trust. John Bingham's career testifies to how ideas travel and adapt when their time comes[14].

But all that was in the future. The Republicans who met in Washington for the Thirty-seventh Congress certainly did not transplant a tidy constitutional formula from its antislavery background to the Fourteenth Amendment with a cry of "Eureka." While abolitionists could set their sights on perfectable man's future, Congress had to deal with it a day at a time, most often with dreary and obstinate problems of organising for war which seemed less than visionary. They faced a complex task of preserving the Union, a task which could not be accomplished by the recitation of constitutional shibboleths of any kind. Nor were they engaged in discovering academic solutions to constitutional problems in a manner appropriate to Harvard Law School. They were politicians, responding to public opinion, leading it, acted upon by events and shaping them, engaged in a present-minded political contest for party advantage, but deeply concerned for the quality of the Union and Constitution they left to the future.

The most striking feature of the Republican party in Congress was its ability to "grow." Not only is there a distance in understanding between the Crittenden-Johnson resolutions and the Fourteenth Amendment, but also a distance in legislative expertise. E.L. Godkin was highly critical of the lack of attention which Americans had paid to legislative science:

> The study of the law as it is has attracted all the keenest intellects in the country, while the consideration of what the law ought to be have been left, strangely enough, to newspaper men and clergymen - two classes singularly ill-fitted for the task[15].

The Thirty-seventh Congress began with no clear idea of where it was going and no claim to expertise. But it got through a staggering amount of business, ranging from equipping an army, to Homestead and Pacific Railroad legislation. Where did their expertise come from? A glance at the composition of the Thirty-seventh Congress reveals that about half the Republicans had experience in state legislatures, perhaps a doubtful commendation. Interestingly, fifty-four percent of the "young" Republican party, compared with only thirty-one percent of the Democrats, had previous experience of a national Congress. A high percentage of both parties were lawyers - approximately sixty-four percent in the House, eighty percent in the Senate[16]. Whether or not this was an asset is open to question. Standards of legal education were very variable, ranging from high professional standards to a mere nodding acquaintance with Blackstone's Commentaries. But the Thirty-seventh Congress provided a crash course in constitutional law for those whose background was deficient. It may be true that Congresses were soon to delegate much of the work of drafting and painstaking detail to specialist committees, but this Congress was in transition[17]. A great deal of time was spent on the floor of both House and Senate on details and amendments. Certainly there was no skimping on attention to constitutional principle, which occupied much debating time and called upon great reserves of verbosity as well as learning!

At the same time, committees were becoming much more important. They were the real schoolhouses of legislative expertise. During the war their numbers rose to thirty-seven in the House and twenty-two in the Senate. It was in committee that much of the real business of shaping and drafting legislation proceeded. Power bases were made there. Charles Sumner's importance was as chairman of the Senate Select Committee on Slavery and Freedmen and the Foreign Relations Committee, rather than as an eloquent Pied Piper for Radicalism on the floor. For the same reason, their status on powerful committees, John Bingham, Lyman Trumbull and William Pitt Fessenden were prominent architects of Reconstruction. This was not always so. The comparative failure of Senators Anthony and Foot to make their mark on legislation from important committee chairmanships suggests that personality, oratorical skills, and intra-party allegiances also had a part in determining leadership[18]. We need to know a lot more about the role and structure of committees, and parliamentary skills in these Congresses.

Continuity of both problems and personnel must have added to Congress's growing expertise. This carry-over is more evident between the Thirty-eighth Congress (1863-1865) and the Thirty-ninth (1865-1867), than between the Thirty-seventh and Thirty-eighth. Only thirty-seven Republicans who served in 1861 were returned in 1863. Nevertheless, even that small group contained a nucleus of twenty-five who would go on to serve in the Thirty-ninth Congress. It included the important parliamentarians John F. Wilson of the Judiciary Committee, Schuyler Colfax, Speaker of the House in the Thirty-eighth Congress, Henry Dawes of the Election Committee, Thaddeus Stevens of Ways and Means, Thomas Eliot, architect of the Freedmen's Bureau, George Julian of the committee on Public Lands and James Ashley from the important Committee on Territories. Of real importance for continuity were the seventy-five Republicans who sat in both the Thirty-eighth and Thirty-ninth Congresses which produced the Wade-Davis Bill, the Thirteenth Amendment resolution, the Freedmen's Bureau Acts, the Civil Rights Act, and the Fourteenth Amendment. Legislative lessons were not self-contained. Problems encountered in freeing slaves were relevant to securing them civil rights. Problems encountered in securing civil rights for freedmen in the South were relevant for all Americans wherever they lived. Problems which apparently had nothing to do with freedom, like indemnifying Union officers from harassment in state courts, yielded valuable lessons about the relationship between state and federal authority, state and federal courts. Congressmen became receptive to legislative patterns designed to meet familiar problems. What they learned about protecting Union officers in Kentucky courts, they would apply to the business of protecting freedmen and loyalists in Alabama courts. Their technical grasp improved, albeit within the limits of their commitment to a Union in which state power was to be made biddable rather than radically altered.

Growth in understanding is elusive to measure. The flanks of the party moved at different paces and embraced a spectrum of opinion on the nature of the Union, the Constitution, slavery and the priorities of relationships among these things. It is beyond the scope of this dissertation to analyse these differences in terms of answering the question, "who were the Radical Republicans?" The old view of an easily identifiable, cross-eyed, club-footed core of Jacobins presiding over a spiteful Reconstruction has been interred[19]. The application of roll call analysis has produced a more intriguing party profile.

Quantative methods do confirm that there were Radicals, Moderates and Conservatives within the Republican party and careful scholars begin to offer a model of the dynamics of interaction. The most discerning computer users have left room for variables which include not only ideological differences but also personality issues, constituency in-fighting, seating arrangements, boarding house friendships and legislative log-rolling[20]. The labels appear to have more validity with respect to slavery and Reconstruction issues rather than economic or geographical interests. One of the most important issues to emerge from these studies, however, is that although Radicals may be identified, that is a very different thing from attributing Reconstruction to them. The major pieces of legislation went through with a remarkably high degree of party unity on the day.

Of course this unity was the product of compromise and negotiation, and two roll calls votes on the same side may conceal an ideological gulf. Republicans at the time were conscious that some were "purer" in motive than others. After a brush with Thaddeus Stevens, Representative Abram B. Olin remarked that he knew he was "more than suspected by my friend from Pennsylvania of not being in regular standing in the Republican Church[21]." In the same way, Lyman Trumbull's temperament and zeal differed from Charles Sumner's. The editors of the Liberator who reported their legislative performance for a committed abolitionist readership were as sensitive to the subtleties as any computer, if not so systematic. But much remains to be learned about the art of bridging factions and straddling principle and expediency to explain what kept the party together and moving in the same direction. Certainly, as Michael Les Benedict suggests, parliamentary procedures themselves may have shaped a misleading unity[22]. Where committees were unified and efficient they could often ensure that debate on the floor was brisk and contained. Skilful managers of bills could avoid opportunities for amendment and debate by manipulation of the rules, especially in the House. But readers of the Congressional Globe will lend only cautious acceptance to the notion that committees falsely harmonised the work of Reconstruction. Most major measures ran the gauntlet of challenge through committee conflict, substitute bills, floor amendments, extensive debate and often House-Senate adjustment. Committees coped with intraparty conflict rather than masked it. They could rely on some important common ground among Republicans.

They did begin with a common belief that Republicanism was more than a political "mixed bag," flung up from the wreck of parties in the 1850's to meet the crisis of disunion. It was a party with ideas and ideals. As George Julian put it in 1863:

> Republicanism is not like a garment, to be put on or laid aside for our own convenience, but an enduring principle, which can never be abandoned without faithlessness to the country. It is not a succession of "dissolving views," brought on to the political stage to amuse conservative gentlemen, or to dazzle and bewilder the people, but the fixed star which should guide us through the shifting phases of American politics and the bloody labyrinths of war[23].

"Progress," "enlightenment," "humanity," "democracy," "Christian civilization," "free institutions" and "liberty under law" are a few of the ingredients which Republican speeches claimed for their party. Professor David Donald suggests a cruder common factor of "simple antislavery zeal[24]." But really, it wasn't so simple. To understand the larger tasks of Reconstruction they undertook, their antislavery position should be understood, as they themselves understood it, in the wider set of notions which shaped their course of action when their ideas took shape in wartime.

President Lincoln regarded his paramount duty as the saving of the Union. His reply to Horace Greeley's Prayer of Twenty Millions in August 1862 is well known:

> If I could save the Union without freeing any slave I would do it, and if I could save it by freeing all the slaves I would do it; and if I could save it by freeing some and leaving others alone I would also do that[25].

The idea of apparently making such a priority of a mere form of government, relegating freedom to "military necessity" seems puzzling. But to Lincoln, the Union was more than a form. It was "the last, best hope of earth[26]." If democracy failed in America, if its critics were right and it was unworkable in so large a territorial unit, the disappointment would be one for "the whole family of man[27]." The Union was everything. It was symbolic and spiritual, but at the same time it was because it was a cherished workaday place that it was worth fighting for. It was a real place, where economic opportunities bound men of property and free labourers in a common cause – the expansion which would make men of property out of the propertyless. It was a land full of resources and people with the energy to develop them. Looking to the day when America would be the foremost of nations in industry, commerce and power, Lincoln said, "The struggle of today is not altogether for today - it is for a vast future also[28]." Attaching emancipation to survival did not seem to Lincoln to be a debasing mix-up of priorities. Nor did Union seem such an ethereal concept to the ordinary people who were prepared to fight for it. Philip Paludan scotches the myth that the Union was not real enough to march to war for[29]. The daily experiences of most Northerners as participators in local decision making attached them to the Union as the embodiment of stability and order. Secession threatened violence and disorder, the loss of real benefits. Lincoln was not alone.

The Republican party shared this attachment of values as well as tangible benefits to Union but travelled more quickly to the point where there could be no choice between freedom and Union as a matter of consistency with what the Union was. Republican speeches are full of associations between the ideas of "free institutions," democracy, and Union[30]. Free presses, spreading education to the masses, along with free expression, were the cornerstones of democracy. Debate, participation and representativeness were its essential conditions. As Representative Lansing said, slavery did not only deny these things locally where it existed:

> The system cannot live in the midst of free speech and a free press. Wrong is ever aggressive and violent. Slavery is a great wrong, and can only sustain itself by warring upon free principles and free institutions[31].

Free labour, the right to the fruits of one's work, the dignity of choosing what to do, and the independence of mind which was the essential corollary of that freedom was an important part of Republican thinking[32]. Slavery degraded all labour by degrading that of black men and women. Lest the white labourer should feel that a community of interest between black and white labour was a little sentimental and remote, Henry C. Wright among others reminded them of the South's aggressive attitude towards labour in general, quoting George Fitzhugh, "Make the laboring man a slave and he would be far better off[33]." Instead, the Republicans would elevate all labour, make consumers of former slaves, and expand man's mastery over his environment, anticipating the millenium when Henry Winter Davis "would give each laborer, not a human, but an iron slave[34]."

It was not the war which caused the Republicans to fuse their Unionism with antislavery in a hasty marriage of expediency. War was the most explicit demonstration of slavery's aggression on free institutions, but most Republicans had already come to that conclusion anyway. Their belief grew that the Union's preservation depended on a shared commitment to free institutions among all its members. Breaking down what Frederick Douglass called the "Chinese wall" at the South was the precondition of survival in a much more important sense than military victory[35]. Within that growing consensus, Radical Republicans may have been distinguished in drawing more of an antislavery commitment from the genuine pain they felt for its black victims. It would be wrong to suggest that the degree to which individual Republicans' motivation sprang from predominantly black or white concerns did not matter. There were differences in ideological commitment although for the duration of the war they often resolved themselves into questions of timetables. The many demonstrations that moderates and even conservatives could arrive at the same point as Radicals, even if they were just getting ready to leave, must have bred a certain patience within the party. By the middle of the war Unionism and antislavery seemed so much of a corollary that Radical Martin F. Conway stood alone in posing them as a choice when he declared, "I would sacrifice the Union to freedom any morning before breakfast[36]."

These were not the sentiments of his party or the constituencies who elected them. Representatives were affected by public opinion, the size of their majorities, and the complexities of political in-fighting amongst factions in their home states and districts. Except in the safest seats some account would have to be taken of marginal or hesitant voters[37]. Many constituencies, especially in the Northwest, were both antislavery and anti-Negro[38]. The last thing that they wanted was an influx of freed blacks from the South, and because of geography this was a more controversial issue in the West than in the Northeast. Against this background Republicans had to emphasise "necessity" and go cautiously on "equality." Those to whom the argument of the dignity of free labour was directed had to be convinced that their jobs would be safe from black competition[39]. Emancipation was therefore presented, even by Radicals like William Kelley and Thaddeus Stevens as a means of keeping blacks in the South. Their love of the sun became proverbial as the Republicans sought to reassure their constituents that freedom secured in the South was the best insurance against mass migration[40].

But public opinion not only responded to arguments for emancipation out of military necessity. It clamoured for it. The quashing of General Fremont's first, limited proclamation of emancipation in August 1861 brought a storm of popular disapproval. Whatever fine points about the relationship between slavery and federalism went unobserved, the public did understand that there was a connection between emancipation and winning the war. The North found a new, and less embarrassing public image for emancipation, based on patriotism rather than philanthropy[41]. The people discovered that "salus populi est suprema lax" while Republicans sought ways of harmonising that rule with the provisions of the Constitution.

Inside Congress the same arguments were rehearsed. As early as Bull Run in July 1861 some Republican Congressmen asked whether it was not like fighting with one arm tied behind their backs not to strike at slavery. The immediate result was the Confiscation Act of August 6, 1861, which took the first, hesitant steps towards emancipation, freeing slaves actually used in the rebellion. But the argument became still more compelling as the Northern armies blundered through the first two years of war without much to show for their superior numbers and resources. Emancipation was urged to strike at the power of the rebellion, to lift Northern morale and win European sympathy by dignifying the conflict with a cause. Whatever arguments went on in Washington as to the constitutional powers of Congress to do anything about it, the advance of the army into parts of the seceded states disrupted the relationship between master and slave and sent thousands of slaves flocking behind Union lines. The relationship between the army and emancipation did not remain accidental. The first proclamations of emancipation for military reasons issued from the generals - Fremont in August 1861, Hunter in May 1862. The army became a powerful complement of the party which cared about winning the war and lending them every support to do it - the Republicans. Not that the Republicans were simply buffeted by the breezes which blew in from the military fronts. While they were prompted at every stage by the need to respond to events they did so from the ship's bridge rather than a life raft. Civilian control over the military was an article of faith[42].

They had a Constitution, to which all Republicans were committed by both oath and conviction. Perhaps at the beginning there was some apprehension as to whether it was equal to the task. Representative Albert G. Riddle expressed it this way:

> I revere and venerate the Constitution, but I love my country a million times more. The one was formed and may be dissolved by the breath of men. The other is the creation and the growth of God; and rather than that mere constitutional names should stand in the way of the nation's salvation, better a thousand times solemnly roll the Constitution up and lay it reverently away[43].

He accurately added, "These too are not the sentiments of my party." For they were not. Even Riddle was really talking about what he would do if the possibility ever arose of the war leaving behind it an empty document and no nation. Most Republicans recognised that conditions of war must involve some risk to cherished peacetime liberties. George Julian predicted that "cases may arise in which patriotism itself may demand that we trample under our feet some of the most vital principles of the Constitution[44]." But such were the exceptions. In the matter of internal security, arbitrary arrests were held to a minimum, habeas corpus suspensions regularised by statute, and loyalty oaths applied without excessive zeal[45]. It was not necessary to roll up the Constitution. It was not a straight-jacket.

Far from that it contained a prescription for its own survival, power enough to save and reconstruct the Union[46]. The Constitution the Republicans invoked, however, was not that from which slavery drew its power and which had been venerated for its limitations. The power to suppress insurrection was clearly constitutional and clothed with express provisions on raising and supporting armies and calling forth the militia. So too was the power to "make all laws which shall be necessary and proper" to execute these express powers. Republicans who in 1860 foreswore the constitutional power to interfere with slavery where it existed by 1862 found the power implied in the battery of these survival powers. When it came to Reconstruction theory, whether they believed that the states were "in the grasp of war," or had committed suicide, reverted to the status of territories, or were merely out of their proper practical relation to the Union, the Republicans had one thing in common. They derived the power to set conditions for the return of the states to the Union from a perfectly adequate Constitution.

Survival and emergency was one thing however. The commitment of the Republican party to freedom and the equal protection of the laws as the basis of a more perfect Union demanded a permanent alteration in constitutional thinking. It could not, like emancipation, be achieved as an event or even like Reconstruction, as a process limited by geography, goals and time.

Controversy surrounds the meaning of the changes wrought by three constitutional amendments and the several civil rights acts in effecting national responsibility for the permanent protection of freedom and citizenship. Increasingly, the changes are described as conservative[47]. The failure to accomplish racial justice is attributed as much to the inherent limitations of Republican thinking about traditional state roles as to dwindling political and judicial will in the 1870's.

Did they not realise that freedom would take radical federal policing? Frederick Douglass predicted as early as 1865 that states rights would not be easily disciplined:

> That spirit will still remain, and whoever sees the Federal Government extended over those Southern States will see that government in a strange land, and not only in a strange land, but in an enemy's land. A post-master of the United States in the South will find himself surrounded by a hostile spirit, a United States marshal or United States judge will be surrounded there by a hostile element[48].

Freedom would take more than a hope and a prayer in this environment. The Report of the Joint Committee on Reconstruction confirmed their worst fears. Always responsive to new information, the Republicans responded, as they would until 1875, by expanding their perceptions of what a person needed to be free - from civil rights to political rights and ultimately social rights. This thesis will argue that Republicans' concept of the rights of citizens which states must respect was substantively broad. It will also admit that Republicans did indeed hesitate at state boundaries and wrestled with the "self-imposed constitutional dilemmas" that sprang from a deeply ingrained respect for state rights[49]. Prepared as they were to build a bridge into the states to protect individual rights, they expected that traffic would be light when states fulfilled their responsibilities. They were not prepared for a massive enforcement operation. They created no permanent bureaucratic machinery. There was no question of stationing a federal officer at every crossroads. The federal civil service remained small[50]. The Freedmen's Bureau was temporary and staffed mostly by regular army officers. Immediately after the war the army itself was reduced to its peacetime size of 16,000 men - a mighty occupation force! That left the federal courts - the only permanent presence of the nation in the states. Reliance on courts however does not betoken a lack of seriousness of purpose.

Until recently historians were satisfied with the traditional interpretation of the Supreme Court's loss of prestige among Republicans. According to Charles Warren and others, the Court never recovered from the self-inflicted wound of Dred Scott. Republicans came to power determined to get their own back by packing the Court and reducing its influence. So successful were they that the Court played a weak and submissive role in Reconstruction[51]. Stanley Kutler, Harold Hyman and William Wiecek offer a convincing reinterpretation[52]. Of course Republicans were angry with the Court over Dred Scott but they distinguished between Taney's opinion and the institutional relevance of the Court itself.

The Taney Court in the long perspective was a creative Court, at least where slavery did not taint its decisions. Among its achievements these may be numbered; it laid the foundations of national uniformity in commercial law, developed admiralty jurisdiction, succeeded in holding a balance between vested property interests and state police power, and created the political questions doctrine. Its decisions on the scope of judicial power "constitute some of its most enduring monuments[53]." Roger Taney's own contribution, argue Hyman and Wiecek, should not be underplayed because "the intensity of his devotion to the welfare of slavery forced lapses in his judgment, aberrations of an otherwise sure instinct for constitutional statesmanship[54]." The irony is that in the political questions doctrine Taney had fashioned the very tool which could have avoided the self-inflicted wounds of the 1850's[55].

But wounds they were, no more to be forgotten than Taney's achievements. Few Republicans wanted simple vengeance. John P. Hale and Thaddeus Stevens did not carry a majority with them in venting hostility on the Court. What most Republicans wanted was to make the Court more responsive to their own interests and representative of the regions they served, freeing it from the time-served Southern dominance which had led it to disastrously partisan behaviour. Change would not happen overnight. Even as the North mobilised for war and began coping with problems of internal security, Roger B. Taney was still alive and well, still Chief Justice on a bench which included Nelson, Grier, Wayne and Catron who concurred in Dred Scott, along with Nathan Clifford, appointed by Buchanan and regarded as something of a "doughface." But Republicans shared a sense that it wouldn't be forever and that life and law go on in wartime, taking their chance with judicial tribunals. They fought to save the institutional fabric of the Union - their case was that it was the South which defied the law. Republican Representative Albert G. Riddle put the priorities this way:

> I know it (the Court) needs reconstruction. I believe it answers pretty well the purposes of a common-law law and commercial court - or would, with an addition to its force. It certainly has, through some misfortune that I care not to discuss, fallen below the respect of the nation. Do you propose now to reconstruct the Federal judiciary? Why, sir, the very map is dissolving about us. The Government is a unit, it cannot exist in broken parts; and whoever strikes it down in South Carolina strikes it down in Massachussetts. If you cannot enforce its laws in New Orleans, it is idle to adjudicate them in New York. I know that by common consent we may continue to obey them; but the essential sanction, found only in national sovereignty is gone; so that a patriotism limited to the narrow boundaries of a State binds us to the inexorable necessity of restoring all the States under the national sovereignty; for it is only through that means that the integrity of our own States can be preserved[56].

The Supreme Court might not be perfect but it had its place in the things they fought for. In the natural course of events, the Lincoln administration would have its chance to fill vacancies. And that happened quickly. Between January 1862 and December 1864 Lincoln made five appointments. The choice of Noah Swayne, Samuel Miller, David Davis and Stephen Field, all of whom were in sympathy with Republican war aims, encouraged returning faith in the Court, or at the very least helped neutralise Republican suspicions. When Roger Taney died unlamented in October 1864 his replacement by longstanding antislavery campaigner Salmon P. Chase added symbolic confirmation to real changes in the Court's make up[57]. Congress intervened to secure these gains by reducing the size of the Court to nine in 1866, leaving vacant the place made vacant by Catron's death in May 1865. A decade after <u>Dred Scott</u> the Court had stepped out from its shadow.

Meanwhile, legislators not only assumed that what they did would be passed upon by courts and ultimately the highest one, but they actively took courts into partnership to implement their policies. It was the lower federal courts which became the real workhorses of Reconstruction, and the Republicans began their education on how to use them as early as the Confiscation Acts of 1861 and 1862. Thereafter expansion of their jurisdiction became a regular feature of legislation. Twelve acts were passed between 1863 and 1875 removing certain classes of cases from state to federal courts. It was not so surprising that Congress should react to conflict within the federal system by enlarging the jurisdiction of the federal courts. Article III Section II of the Constitution contained a potentially broad grant of judicial power, extending "...to all cases, in Law and Equity, arising under this Constitution, the Laws of the United States and Treaties made or which shall be made, under their Authority..." The surprise perhaps was how little of this power had been used. The circuit and district courts dealt mainly with admiralty, and diversity of citizenship cases. In times of crisis, however, the government's response had been to enlarge their jurisdiction. In 1815, at the time of the Hartford Convention, Congress passed its first removal act since the Judiciary Act of 1789. Under it, revenue officers prosecuted in state courts could remove their cases to the federal courts. A similar act was passed in 1833, again in response to the crisis in federalism brought on by the Nullification Controversy. Once again in 1855 a removal act was proposed, though not passed, to deal with violations of the Fugitive Slave Law. In the past, when federal officers were unable to receive a fair trial because of state hostility to the laws they represented, the government made its courts the alternative. And this is exactly what they did in 1863 to protect Union officers under the Habeas Corpus Act and to protect all persons in the exercise of certain civil rights in 1866. The Removal Act of 1875 consolidated the work of bringing vastly increased business to the courts to the point when they "ceased to be restricted tribunals of fair dealing between citizens of different states and became the primary and powerful reliances for vindicating every right given by the Constitution, the laws, and treaties of the United States[58]."

War and Reconstruction put the federal courts in the front line. But could they cope? The Republicans it seems were prepared to expand the business of the courts but not to reform the judicial system, to create the new courts and increase their personnel sufficient to meet the kind of demands which could be expected if removal legislation was activated enough to make any impact on state justice. Kermit Hall argues that no nationalisation of the lower federal courts took place[59]. Republican priorities were to ease pressure on the Supreme Court docket by reducing circuit riding and to ensure that circuit organisation achieved the desirable political results of reflecting dominant regional interests. The Judiciary Act of 1862 was a modest reform increasing the circuit representation of the Northwest at the expense of the South, where a strong federal presence mattered most. Because it was important not to give the South the opportunity to increase its representation on the Supreme Court by creating new circuits there, the most that could be done was to increase the amount of circuit judgeships rather than additional courts. Besides, it was cheaper. Despite accumulating evidence that federal justice was neither sufficiently available nor inexpensive to benefit blacks in the South, the Republicans shrank from expanding the resources of the judicial system at its most important point, by creating many more district courts. As a result, says Professor Hall:

> At least in their institutional structure the federal courts proved resistant to the impact of the Civil War and the first years of Reconstruction. For their part the Republicans emerged as at best reluctant nationalizers, willing to extend the jurisdiction of the courts but unwilling to break from more traditional notions of parsimonious government and judicial representation that emphasized local and regional diversity over the assertion of national or central authority[60].

The reluctance of the Republicans to undertake a radical remodelling of the judiciary need not be taken as evidence that they were somehow not serious about federal protection of civil rights. In the short term they put more reliance on the Freedman's Bureau and the army. In the long term they optimistically believed that the role of the federal courts throughout the Union would be corrective of occasional state lapses rather than a broom to sweep up an earthquake.

Lack of resources was not the only problem which faced the federal courts in their expanded role. Earlier crises had come and gone without leaving tried and tested tools for co-ercing reluctant state courts. The history of relationships between state and federal courts had been one of avoiding rather than joining conflict. The courts of nation and state had generally refrained from interfering with each other's processes and officials. Federal courts observed limitations when they did become involved with state judicial systems, observing the prohibition on issuing writs of injunction to stay proceedings in state courts and respecting state laws where they applied in federal proceedings[61].

There had to be mutual forbearance while the judicial systems were so inter-related and the federal government relied on state courts to do so much of its business. In 1884 a writer in the American Law Review looked back to a time when:

> the doubtful policy of the founders of the government and of their successors, until a period comparatively recent, committed the execution of the Federal laws in part to the judicatories of the States; made the justices of the peace of the States the examining magistrates in criminal cases for the Federal tribunals; made the judges of the States Federal magistrates for the purpose of executing extradition treaties with foreign countries, for the purpose of naturalizing aliens, and in some cases for the purpose of executing the criminal statutes of the United States; and made the jails and prisons of the states the jails and prisons of the Federal Government[62].

The removal acts of the 1860's, however, potentially brought into federal courts matters which the states had always considered exclusively their business. Federal responsibilities for citizenship rights touched on sensitive state faiths. By 1866, officers of state courts who refused to relinquish jurisdiction legitimately claimed under the acts could be prosecuted - after eight decades of courtesy! Of course there was no question of war between two jurisdictions. The nation could not afford to lose the services of state courts in doing its business. But some state courts put a severe strain on tolerance.

Too little is known about state judiciaries. Professional journals lamented their lower standards and tutelage to the electorate who voted them into office. In 1870 a writer in the Saturday Review commented, "Few things are full of uglier omen for the future of the United States than that growing disrespect for the judicial body which seems to be spreading itself through the country." Where original state constitutions mostly provided for the appointment of judges for life, or "during good behaviour" by the Governor or legislature, by the 1880's only New Hampshire, Massachusetts, Rhode Island and Delaware retained such methods. The rest had succumbed to popular election. John F. Dillon found that the effects of this change on the standards of the state judiciaries was one of the few blemishes in a century of American law[64].

Not all comment was unfavourable. The Yale jurist Simeon Baldwin had enough faith in the people to think that although they might not choose more wisely than the legislature they might choose more honestly[65]. James Schoular believed that the direct election of judges made them more independent and more efficient by freeing them from the influence of the legislature. By the time he wrote, however, in 1897, some states had begun to remedy one of the most common complaints about direct election, that it encouraged short, precarious careers. New York's 1873 constitution extended the tenure of judges to fourteen years, and Pennsylvania's constitution the same year to twenty-one. It was an attempt to temper accountability with independence[66].

State appellate courts were the aristocrats of state judiciaries. In the South before the war they were far more likely than lower courts to maintain high standards of procedural fairness in cases where slaves were accused of crimes[67]. Their willingness to do this does not necessarily mean that they risked running against the tide of public opinion. In the absence of a separate codified law of slavery, justice for whites depended on its observation for blacks, at least at the level where intellectual rationales for doing otherwise would be of some account. It mattered to the South that their most public adjudications of traditional notions of fair process should not be vulnerable to attack from outside[68]. If Southern State appellate courts were responsive to any public opinion it was to that of a landowning, upper class from which they were drawn. Judicial quality and integrity do not seem to have been the casualty of democratisation when posts became elective in the 1850's[69].

A recent study of state appellate judges in the midwest by Kermit Hall also challenges the notion that they were lacking in competence and quality[70]. Their social and economic background was similar to that of federal judges. A higher percentage of federal judges had college educations, and more had attended law schools, but state judges compensated by having generally accumulated more judicial experience before they reached appellate courts. The study produces no indicators which suggest any obvious disparity in levels of technical competence. It does confirm that state judges were necessarily more continuously active in state politics and suggests that this made their career patterns different from federal judges in terms of past experience, age of appointment and length of service. But there has been no proven correlation between partisan affiliation and judicial record on the bench.

Typically their experience - educational, judicial and political - was local, though local need not be shorthand for seedy or subservient. New federal laws to cement the Union had to transcend localism, however, and it was in this department that federal judges were, perhaps unjustly, presumed superior. Kermit Hall's study of the background and recruitment of the lower federal judiciary in the nineteenth century reveals the extent to which local constituencies shaped the federal bench[71]. Politics played as much a part in their selection as in the election of state appellate judges, though in a structurally different way. Nevertheless in rewarding and representing local interests, the federal government had a mind to its own interests, which included judicial quality as well as political suitability. Institutionally the federal government was bound to accept the distance which independence of life tenure put between judges and their political debts. Perhaps that, and being on the federal payroll, may also have attenuated political connections between judges and their local constituencies.

The enforcement of the Habeas Corpus and Civil Rights Acts, outlined in Chapters 3 and 7, suggest quite an uneven picture of judicial reactions to the enlargement of federal authority and the assertion of federal court jurisdiction. There was no simple pattern of alignment with state courts on one side of the fence and federal courts on the other. In the South the picture is complicated because the war disrupted the judicial system, closing courts and causing vacancies which were filled initially by appointment rather than election. During Reconstruction judicial offices were filled by a mixed bag of scalawags, perjurors to the loyalty oath, and carpetbaggers. As yet we have no collective biography. The lives of some outstanding carpetbag justices have been documented however. George Andrews served on the Tennessee Supreme Court from 1869 to 1870 and briefly struggled for impartial justice[72]. Albion Tourgee served on the North Carolina Supreme Court from 1868 to 1876, later describing his stand against the dominant political currents there as a "Fool's Errand.[73]" Carpetbaggers by no means dominated Southern state judicial systems, but, like scalawags, they deserve closer study for their albeit brief impact.

The task of securing equal justice in law involved the bar as well as the bench. Yet, argues W. Raymond Blackford, the crisis of the mid-century found the legal profession "demoralized" and ill-equipped to meet it[74]. Standards of admission to the bar, which were high in the Revolution period, were eroded in the first half of the nineteenth century. Jacksonian democracy, with its optimistic faith in the capacity of all men to understand and apply the law was in reality a "cult of incompetence," destructive of professionalism. Property, age and educational standards for admission to the bar were lowered. By 1860 only nine out of thirty-nine states had any educational requirements. Lawyers meddled in politics. They had a poor public image, and seemed incapable of improving it by imposing standards on their own profession. Bar associations dissolved or dwindled into social clubs in the 1830's. Blackard concludes that "the lowest ebb in the downward course was reached shortly after the war between the states."

As with state court judges, such a judgment conceals variable standards. Perry Miller notes the rising standard of the law schools from the 1820's and the fine leadership of Kent, Story and Hoffman in legal scholarship[75]. The law schools continued their rise, and although a majority of lawyers would still learn their law in traditional office apprenticeships they may not have been immune from books.

Maxwell Bloomfield looks behind formal organisation for evidence of standards and discovers that in this period of presumed stagnation lawyers were promoting a new self-image, proclaimed in the obituaries and descriptions of office practice in proliferating law magazines[76]. Lawyers who combined politics with personal advancement were deprecated. The preferred image was one of hard work, technical competence and self-made success. They attempted to shake off the aristocratic elitism which de Tocqueville had observed as characteristic of American lawyers and which had inspired reformers in the Jacksonian era in efforts to lower qualifications and codify the laws. Their object was to open up the profession to new social groups and interests. It was not an exercise in malignant anti-intellectualism. When lawyers organised the American Bar Association in 1878 and their new professional pride manifested itself in state bar organisations it did not signify a sharp break from previous gloom[77]. The profession had already made adjustments to some of society's demands of them.

War would make more and different demands, but it found them in introspective mood, getting on with business and foreswearing politicking. Certainly the war generated plenty of business both North and South. Maxwell Bloomfield offers us the marvellously adaptable William Pitt Ballinger as an example of the old adage that it's an ill wind that blows nobody good[78]. This ex-Confederate lawyer first turned his professional skills to the task of securing pardons for himself and many business associates as a prerequisite for reconstructing his own legal practice. Then it was business, not just as usual, but better. He reactivated cases he had pending in the Supreme Court docket before the war. By 1866 his firm was employed in 192 suits at district level alone. He went on to become a successful corporation lawyer, oiling the wheels of returning economic life and living with the modest amount of racial change which Reconstruction brought.

Lawyers interested in social justice were much thinner on the ground. Some were black. Howard Law School opened up in 1869 and under John Mercer Langston's guidance produced a crop of black lawyers, most of whom remained in the South. Many may have faded into the daily obscurity of private practice or clerical work but others made a contribution to civil rights[79]. Like the white attorneys who worked for the Freedmen's Bureau until it was dismantled in 1868, they represented a different ideal of law practice and a concept of law as the instrument of social justice which was well in advance of contemporaries.

There were just too few of them. Gilbert Pillsbury wrote about the state of the legal profession in South Carolina when he asked Salmon P. Chase for his advice abour drawing up a constitution. The convention, he said, "will be composed, no doubt, mainly of loyal men; but we do not know a single loyal man of the legal profession in the state, who will be likely to participate in the deliberations of that body.[80]" Surely it was not because they had all forsaken politics for legal professionalism. Another correspondent of Chase's wrote that the bar of Maryland was "generally disloyal," - in a state which never left the Union![81]

Policies conceived in distant Washington had to take their chance with bench and bar all the way down the system. Implementation of the law depended on so many parts of the system working on its behalf that Congress's legislative expertise and good intentions could quite easily be frustrated or perverted by legal personnel who were ignorant of the law, hostile towards blacks, or disloyal in spirit. Aware of the possibilities, the Republicans sought ways of trumping state justice if need be. By expanding the jurisdiction of the federal courts, they gave the litigant an alternative means of securing justice, and the government a bridge across state boundaries to see to the execution of its laws. The education of the Republican party to legislative possibilities and judicial realities began quite soon after the first shots of war.

CHAPTER 2

Confiscation: Constitutional Crossroads

The Confiscation Acts of 1861 and 1862 have not stirred the imagination of historians. The debates were turgid, legalistic and neverending. The results were unimpressive. Republican Senator John Sherman recalled that they had "little influence upon the result of the war.[1]" Very little property was actually confiscated. The emancipation sections of the acts were quickly overtaken by Lincoln's Proclamation and the Thirteenth Amendment. James G. Randall's view of the acts as ill-considered, vindictive and ineffective prevailed[2].

Yet it is precisely because the acts were so clumsily and painfully cobbled together from old constitutional dogmas and new possibilities that they deserve close attention. It was the first winter of war. The debate on confiscation and emancipation focussed thoughts on beginnings, on how to proceed most effectively and quickly against a rebellion based on land and slaves. But it also involved asking questions about whether they were fighting enemies or subduing traitors, persuading them back to a familiar Union by offering them their old constitutional liberty or reaching for a new constitutional freedom for all men as the fruits of victory. So early - and yet they were talking about Reconstruction[3]. Republican Representative Albert G. Riddle recalled these first halting steps:

> Already the two Houses, twin giants, congenitally bound to act together, helpless when divided, all powerful when in harmony, were beginning to awaken and but half-seeing in the twilight, were clumsily fumbling about for the unaccustomed weapons, which they felt must be within reach somewhere[4].

But the way was not clear. Confiscation was a belligerent right, exercised during the Revolutionary War with Britain, confirmed by the Supreme Court under Marshall, and expounded by the publicists of the law of nations[5]. Yet to admit that the United States was at war with an independent Southern Confederacy meant recognising secession and undercutting the objective of restoring these states to a Union from which secession was argued impossible. On the other hand if the Union was confined to using only its sovereign power over traitors it would be reduced to conducting a feeble judicial operation, a grand assize to bring individuals to justice. To get a bill at all, Republicans straddled these two positions by anticipating the "dual status" theory later expounded by Justice Grier in the Prize Cases, that the United States possessed both belligerent and sovereign powers over the rebels[6]. The apparent simplicity of the theory does not reflect the confusion of Congress in combining the two legal concepts in the one piece of legislation, as they did in the Confiscation Act of 1862. They did not blend.

Supporters of a vigorous confiscation policy, like Lyman Trumbull in the Senate and Thomas Eliot in the House had no difficulty in advocating confiscation and emancipation as war measures, retaining sovereign power to deal with traitors by ordinary judicial process when and where courts were open[7]. They designed procedures which did not depend upon convicting traitors. Conservative Republicans and Democrats took a different view of the Constitution's dictates, however. It was not that they denied the power to confiscate both property and slaves in times of military necessity. But the power belonged not to Congress but to the Executive as commander-in-chief of the armed forces, thus ensuring that confiscations made under his authority were temporary, the title reverting to the owner when the emergency passed. Beyond these limited circumstances property could not be seized without due process, or compensation, or a jury trial over a certain amount. Rebels were subjects who retained their constitutional rights. If caught and found guilty of treason, then by the 1790 law they forfeited their lives, but not their property beyond the grave. The Constitution gave this assurance to a traitor's heirs that ".... no attainder of treason shall work corruption of blood, or forfeiture except during the life of the person attainted." Conservative Republicans did appreciate that the law's rigid penalty was inappropriate to the dimensions of the rebellion. Looking to a forgiving peace, they sought to provide alternatives to the gallows by changing the law of treason to mitigate its penalty by providing alternatives of imprisonment and fines for lesser crimes. But since this was an exercise of sovereign power its enforcement would have to wait until that power was re-established and its courts open. It was no war measure. Thus, while armies were raised to shoot down rebels, compromise had to be made with those who would take lives but not land and slaves without due process and the benefit of common law[8]. The price of housing these changes side by side with what survived of a more vigorous confiscation measure was the piecing together of an unsatisfactory patchwork of two constitutional understandings which came to be confused in the minds of those whose duty it was to enforce and interpret it.

A second area of confusion and conflict arose from the association of "confiscating" property and persons. The right to do both could be argued under Congress's war powers of raising and supporting armies, making rules concerning captures on land and water, and doing all things necessary and proper to make these powers effective. Solicitor of the War Department, William Whiting argued that there was no legal distinction between different kinds of property, including slaves, in their liability to confiscation[9]. Some Republicans would argue from expediency that if an ox could be confiscated why not a slave?[10] Nevertheless the acts made no attempt to transfer title in slaves to the government and they employed quite different machinery in the case of persons than property. In 1862 the House argued emancipation in a separate bill from confiscation and the title of the original Senate bill was one "to confiscate the property <u>and</u> free the slaves of rebels." While moderate Republicans knew the value of associating slaves with contraband in order to persuade people whose path to emancipation was not along the high road of justice, nevertheless it was only conservatives who believed they were the same. Senator Garret Davis complained that the Confiscation Act of 1862 employed a double standard. "All that the Union slaveholders ask for slave property," he said, "is that it shall be treated by Congress and the Government and the Army impartially and equally like other property[11]."

But it wasn't. Although property used in the rebellion was subject to condemnation in the federal courts under the August 6th Act, owners forfeited their claim to slaves so employed without any mention of the judgment of a court. Although slaves could be declared free by courts as part of the punishment for treason under the July 17th Act there was no mention of transfer of title, or sale as there was for other property. No other part of that act relating to procedures in federal courts for "in rem" proceedings against property applied the same procedure to slaves. Most Republicans believed that the appropriate standard of equality before the law was between persons and not between persons and property. The debate reveals that they intended emancipation under the acts to be irreversible. At a time when Congressional power to emancipate at all was deeply controversial it is hardly surprising that they lacked the confidence, the cohesion, and even the legislative skills to translate that intention into workable guarantees of personal liberty. In this first contest between freedom and slavery they were breaking new ground in a highly sensitive area of nation-state relations. Slavery existed under state law, until now immune from federal interference. As yet there was no alternative relationship between freedom and the nation's laws and courts. Congressmen of all persuasions were often confused about the legal implications of the emancipation sections of the Confiscation Acts. When an owner 'forfeited' his title where did it belong? Against whom would an owner bring suit? More important, once freed could a former slave defend and maintain that right in a court of law? What is important is not just that the questions were asked in 1862 but that numerous bills on the subject provided an opportunity to experiment with some legal procedures for guaranteeing personal liberty, even if they were for the moment left out of the final version.

Few Congressmen grasped the complexities of these issues when they passed the first Confiscation Act which became law on August 6th, 1861. Most Republican members could accept the limited objective of confiscating property and divesting the title of owners to slaves actually used for insurrectionary purposes. There was no debate on the little-known judicial machinery which the act employed. After the President had caused property, anywhere in the Union, used for such hostile purposes, to be seized, its condemnation and forfeiture was to take place in federal district and circuit courts. Thereafter it could be sold, the proceeds going to the Treasury. The proceeding was to be _in rem_, and not _in personam_, in other words an action against guilty property, not resting on the actual criminality of the owner. No jury trial was necessary to establish his guilt. The court was only concerned with the predicament in which the property was found. This machinery, drawn from revenue acts, was to become a major cause of disagreement in the debates on the second Confiscation Act. But in 1861 it passed unnoticed, perhaps because Congressmen foresaw no difficulty in the courts identifying the guilty predicament of property actually used in rebellion, or perhaps because they were so unfamiliar with the procedure[12].

When Trumbull introduced the bill from the Senate Judiciary Committee on July 20th, it contained no reference to slaves. The fact that his amendment to the bill, emancipating slaves employed in aiding or promoting insurrection, was adopted by 33 votes to 6 on July 22nd by a Senate deliberating the Johnson resolutions, can be partly attributed to the impact of the Bull Run disaster the previous day. Ten Eyck said that although he voted against the amendment in committee, the recent reverse had caused him to change his mind. Representative McClernand argued that if Confederate horses could be confiscated, why not slaves?[13]

But the judicial machinery for freeing a slave differed from that for seizing a horse. The House did not adopt Representative Kellogg's amendment to put the two on the same footing by "confiscating" claims to service or labour, rather than "discharging" the slaves in Senator Trumbull's original wording[14]. Section four of the Act, as finally amended by the House and accepted by the Senate narrowed the scope of emancipation by confining it to slaves used in Confederate military service, but it neither "discharged" nor "confiscated" them. It provided that when slaves were employed in any military or naval services whatsoever the owner would forfeit his title to the slave, state or United States law to the contrary notwithstanding. Where the title went, was left unsaid. The slave, it seemed could not bring suit against his owner to establish his freedom under the act. It presumed escape. After that, the slave's guarantee of defending his freedom rested on the provision that it was sufficient answer to an owner's claim to establish the use of the slave for the such hostile and insurrectionary purposes described in the act[15].

Conservative Senator Pearce noted that emancipation did not involve the legal sentence of any tribunal, and doubted what good it would do the slave. He argued, quite perceptively in the light of later experience of conflict between federal and state law:

> The state courts would undoubtedly set it at defiance. If you could cause the individual to be discharged in such a State, it is most probable that the State laws would immediately be put in operation against him and that he would be subjected to a procedure by which he would again be remanded to the condition of servitude[16].

Against such odds the section of the act making the fact of the use of the slaves for insurrectionary purposes an answer to the owner's claim for his services seems a poor guarantee. In the priorities of the special session of Congress in the summer of 1861 the business of effectively suppressing the rebellion took precedence over emancipation and much more so over a quest for legal guarantees to the freed slave. The act passed both Houses with near-unanimous Republican support and became law on August 6th, 1861. It was a limited undertaking, confined to places where the United States could assert its authority and even there rarely enforced[17]. Senator Ben Wade later referred to it as "a scoff and by-word of contempt throughout all rebeldom.[18]"

But events between August 1861 and July 1862, when Congress passed its second Confiscation Act, moved in favour of those who advocated sterner measures. Increasing military involvement meant that more slaves were coming behind Union lines. General Butler's use of the term "contraband" to describe those slaves the army had captured at Ft. Monroe, helped popularise the connection between emancipation and confiscation as twin war measures. Edward L. Pierce wrote thus in November 1861:

> The venerable gentleman who wears gold spectacles and reads a conservative daily prefers confiscation to emancipation......His whole nature rises in insurrection when Beecher preaches in a sermon that a thing ought to be done because it is a duty, but he yields gracefully when Butler issues an order commanding it to be done because it is a military necessity.[19]

At a time when public opinion was clamouring for action from General McClellan it seemed that he and Halleck were using the army for little more than rounding up escaping slaves to return to their masters. By contrast the generals like Fremont, Butler and Hunter, who freed slaves and confiscated property, won popular approval. They also won the tacit support of the War Department. Indeed, General Townsend claimed that Secretary of War Stanton had prepared a proclamation declaring forfeit all slaves and other property of persons engaged in rebellion. Because of confusion and friction over such military orders, however, he "instigated the Second Confiscation Act" instead.[20]

If the North was slow to take the war seriously the South was not. In August 1861, the Confederate Congress passed a Confiscation Act which was less sensitive towards Northern property rights than the Union Congress's policy proved to be towards the rebels. Confederate Attorney-General Judah P. Benjamin proceeded to enforce it vigorously against loyal men.[21] To the North the policy of confiscation and emancipation, as weapons against a rebellion based on land and slaves, commended itself more and more. It would also help to raise money to defray the cost of the war - though this was only a secondary argument.

Responding to these events, and the rising tide of public opinion in favour of emancipation, both Congress and the President moved to a more vigorous policy. Republicans in the second session of the Thirty-seventh Congress passed an act for the emancipation of slaves in the District of Columbia, an additional article of war prohibiting the armed services from returning fugitive slaves, and a resolution to aid emancipation in the border states. Though Lincoln's interest in emancipation was tempered by his concern for border state opinion and his fear that confiscation measures might jeopardise it, he acknowledged Congress's right to legislate on confiscation. Republicans Loomis in the House of Representatives and Wilkinson in the Senate could point to the fact that although Lincoln asked General Fremont to modify his proclamation of August 30th it was to make it conform to the Confiscation Act of 1861.[22] Writing to Senator Browning of Illinois, the President objected that Fremont's confiscation of property and slaves went far beyond the temporary orders justified by military necessity. He said that he was not denying the propriety of Congress to pass a confiscation act or even saying that as a member of Congress he would not vote for it, but "what I object to is that I, as President, shall expressly seize and exercise the permanent legislative functions of the government.[23]" But of course Lincoln was cautious. By March 1862, he was making moves towards the border states to persuade them of the benefits of gradual, compensated emancipation. Although he revoked General Hunter's emancipation proclamation of May 19th 1862 he took the opportunity of appealing to the border states to emancipate in the light of these "signs of the times.[24]"

It was against this background that Congress debated the second Confiscation Bill. Despite public opinion in favour of stronger measures, it took six months of debate, two Judiciary Committees, two Select Committees and a Committee of Conference of the two Houses to produce the act. The final compromise was the bill which became law on July 17th 1862. The first four sections modified the law of treason, providing alternative, lesser penalties at the court's discretion for the crime of inciting, assisting or engaging in rebellion. This section, dealing with persons convicted of crime by regular judicial process, was an exercise of the sovereign power. It was also the contribution of a divided Senate to the bill. Sections five to eight were about confiscation. They set out procedures for the condemnation and forfeiture of property belonging to designated classes of rebels immediately after the passage of the act, and of all rebels who did not return to their allegiance after sixty days. As in the August 6th act upon which it was modelled the jurisdiction of the federal courts was extended to *in rem* proceedings against property. The guilt of the owner was not to be judicially ascertained. That part of the act rested on the war powers, later confirmed by the Supreme Court in *Miller v U.S.* in 1870[25]. It also represented the House contribution to the act. Sections nine to twelve dealt with slaves. Slaves of persons thereafter engaged in rebellion, escaping behind Union lines, deserted or captured were to be deemed "captives of war" and declared "forever free." Owners reclaiming their services were required to prove not only the validity of their claim but past loyalty to the Union. A further section authorised the President to make provisions for the voluntary colonisation of slaves freed by the act. These sections, and an authorisation to the President to grant amnesty to rebels, represented areas of compromise between House and Senate. The act concluded with a grant of full power to the federal courts to carry these powers into effect.[26]

Senator Trumbull never intended such a patchwork affair. On January 15th he reported a bill from the Senate Judiciary Committee, to which seven confiscation proposals had already been sent in the opening week of the session. Explaining this bill to the Senate on February 25th, Trumbull stressed that it was a measure for the vigorous suppression of rebellion based on powers derived for this purpose from a quite adequate Constitution.[27] But it had nothing to do with treason. Respecting the constitutional limitation against attainder of treason working corruption of blood or forfeiture beyond the life of the person attainted, the bill proposed to leave traitors to the judgment of the courts when and where they could be tried. Where they could not be reached he invoked the right of confiscation - by the army in disloyal areas, and by <u>in rem</u> proceedings in federal courts where their property was situated in the loyal states. This procedure, already used in the August 6th act, was borrowed from revenue laws which extended admiralty jurisdiction over seizures of smuggled goods, without trial of the owner for crime. In the case of <u>The Palmyra</u> in 1827, Justice Story made just the distinction between the concept of guilty property and the trial of persons which Trumbull now made between confiscation and treason proceedings when he said:

> The practice has been, and so the court understands the law to be, that the proceeding <u>in rem</u> stands independent of, and wholly unaffected by, any criminal proceeding <u>in personam</u>.[28]

Although Trumbull now proposed the extension of federal court jurisdiction to the condemnation, forfeiture and sale of property under a confiscation law he foresaw no enlargement of the courts' discretion. There were to be no trials of persons, and the bill mentioned no crimes. It was for Congress, not the Executive, the courts, or the army, to get a law on the subject. Trumbull concluded:

> It does not lie in the mouths of the courts to question the right of the sovereign power to confiscate property. Then it resolves itself into a question of policy.[29]

There was a war on. This was essentially the case of those who ranged behind Trumbull as he opened the six-month struggle for an efficient law. Immediately, it became clear that the issue was a divisive one for the Republican party, as the debate opened out to a conflict over the nature of the war, rebel status, the relationship between Executive and legislative powers, and reconstruction.

Conservative Senators Edgar Cowan of Pennsylvania, Jacob Collamer of Vermont, and Orville Browning of Illinois, were the most prominent opponents of the bill - though not, they claimed, of confiscation. They agreed that under certain circumstances it was necessary to confiscate under the _jus belli_. But to legislate on the subject was to interfere with the President's sole power as commander-in-chief to authorise such seizures by the army. Titles to property, of course, remained unaffected by temporary confiscation.[30] A writer in the _Monthly Law Reporter_ argued that all "respectable writers" recognised a broad distinction in the law of nations between the capture of real and personal property. Only the latter could be seized under the power of the commander-in-chief. Title to land could not be extinguished without the constitutional safeguards of due process, jury trial and compensation.[31]

The proposed _in rem_ proceeding violated the constitution on all these grounds. Senator Browning referred to "this newly-invented, India-rubber _in rem_ proceeding." His colleague Collamer called it "hocus pocus." Garret Davis and Edgar Cowan both argued that the property itself yielded no clue to its guilt from appearances without the trial of persons. Trumbull's bill, they said, was _in fact_ about the guilt of persons - but it was a legislative assumption of this guilt, Congress having taken upon itself the functions of judge and jury.[32] Senator Carlile added that, in so reducing the discretion of the court:

> It would seem as if the authors of the bill, conscious of the unconstitutionality of the proposed measure, purposely framed it so that its constitutionality could not be pronounced upon by the Supreme Court.[33]

It did, he said, what the Constitution prohibited - it executed itself.

The conservatives foresaw a different role for the courts. Clever _in rem_ proceedings, they said, could not disguise the crime they were talking about. Only the courts could try the guilt of traitors. The accused was entitled to the safeguards of criminal law, and if convicted, to the constitutional prohibition on forfeitures of real estate beyond life.[34] It was not that they proposed a mass hanging. Since their reasoning was based firmly on the idea of not offending future neighbours by taking their property or their lives, they distinguished always between the guilty few who led the rebellion, and the "deluded masses" who followed.[35] To all they would offer their constitutional rights! This view would of course have negated confiscation as a policy for fighting the war. The courts in most rebellious districts were closed.

Supporters of a vigorous policy met these objections point for point. Though they claimed the right to confiscate was a legislative rather than executive power, it did not necessarily imply conflict with Lincoln. To avoid the problems of each commander on the spot formulating his own policy, and to ensure the permanent transfer of title, Republican Senators like Trumbull, Howard and Morrill wanted a law on the subject. Indeed, Senator Howard saw the bill as coming to the rescue of the President in putting down the rebellion.[36] Solicitor William Whiting of the War Department recognised the powers of both branches of the government to confiscate and saw no need for conflict.[37] Senator Henry Wilson of Massachusetts, expressed a familiar Republican sentiment when he said he would "not allow any discrimination anywhere but in the law[38]."

The procedural guarantees of criminal law to the individual had to be weighed against the business of putting down a rebellion which threatened to destroy all law. They were at war and the Constitution did not restrict them to fighting it according to common law. If that were the case, wrote William Whiting, the President ought to convert his armies into lawyers and juries and send "Greetings" instead of rifle shot.[39] Neither did the Constitution have to be thrown overboard. As a writer in the _Monthly Law Reporter_ put it, the "_salus populi suprema lex_ applies to constitutional as to all other law." Whatever safeguards the Constitution contained as to treason trials, due process, jury trials and so on, these existed side by side with specific powers to put down rebellion. The document, he said should be understood as a whole, concluding, "cry not peace, peace when there is no peace. Let us not hear the special pleading of the courts of judicature in the counsels of war[40]."

Besides, Charles Sumner, Radical Senator for Massachusetts, was one of many Republicans who defended _in rem_ proceedings as quite proper procedural due process in courts of law, and claimed that the rights which the federal government exercised against enemies did not negate their rights towards them as criminals, where common law safeguards would apply[41]. But, they insisted - _this_ bill was not about treason.

If less sensitive towards the peacetime constitutional rights of rebels in time of war, supporters of a vigorous confiscation policy were no less aware than the conservatives of the future role of rebels as neighbours and of the distinctions between the leaders and the led. Malice was not their intention. As Senator Howard said, "We conquer but to save[42]." To the bill's supporters it was a question of policy to accomplish a "democratisation" of the South which would benefit those with no active interest in preserving the rule of a privileged class. It was a rebellion led by landowners and slaveowners with vested political and social privileges. Although there were many white Southerners with no such interests or privileges, they could not take advantage of the technical democracy of having a vote where traditions or political leadership were firmly rooted in the hereditary ownership of land and slaves. Discussing the relationship between the war and democracy, Senator Morrill proposed breaking the power of the ruling class by confiscation, and all other means. But to the people who had simply been misled he would "give the assurance of amnesty, protection, and the privileges of free institutions, free schools, <u>homesteads</u>, even-handed justice and equality of political rights, privileges that enable and elevate the masses into the dignity of a sovereign people, and give to popular government a secure support[43]." Senator Howard also talked about the possibility of parcelling out of huge estates to small proprietors, drawing a comparison with confiscation during the French Revolution in teaching the world "that liberty and equality are no dream, and that there is no patriotism so strong as that which arises from a sentiment of brotherly kindness, and a consciousness of equality before the law[44]."

But these homestead suggestions bore little fruit. Republicans like Charles Sumner later regretted that confiscation had been a lost opportunity for making lands available to freedmen. On this subject he wrote in 1865, "From the beginning I have regarded confiscation only as ancillary to emancipation[45]." But, quite apart from the way in which confiscation measures were watered down before they became law on July 17th 1862, Sumner's idea of land for the freedmen was never crucial to the debate. It lingered as the vision of a number of Republicans.

It was difficult enough to get a consensus on emancipation. Senator Browning would go so far as to admit that slaves could be confiscated, where military necessity demanded it.[46] But like temporary seizure of property, there would be no transfer of title. State laws and state institutions were inviolable on any more permanent basis. Yet the Senate Judiciary Committee's bill was drafted with a view to the non-return of the slaves freed by it. After the commission of the act of forfeiture by the person claiming service, slaves were to be "discharged therefrom, and become forever thereafter free persons." The onus was put on the slaveowner to prove both legitimacy of his title, and his loyalty during the rebellion. Once again, while confiscation and emancipation were argued together for the sake of self-preservation, urged under the same powers to suppress rebellion, and uttered in the same breath by supporters of both, the connection was deceptive. Senator Collamer charged that confiscation was being used only as a vehicle for abolition and went on to draw attention to the difference in procedure between persons and property under the proposed bill:

> It is not provided that these slaves are to be taken or brought into any court or in any way adjudicated upon. There is not any proceeding _in rem_ required upon them nor any other proceeding. If that is not depriving a man of his interest in a slave without any conviction of himself, and without any process of law, and operating as a punishment on him, and yet leaving him to be hanged, I do not understand it.[47]

He was right. The government was not assuming title to the slave, and there was no question of proceeds from his sale going to the Treasury. Clumsily, Republicans were striking at state law, the support of slavery, without defining clear alternatives in federal law. What was emerging in the debate, however, were two quite different philosophies of constitutional law. Against what Browning, Cowan, Collamer and others were saying about depriving rebels of land and slaves without due process other Republicans were posing a different interpretation of due process and deprivation of rights. Senator Howard argued that slavery existed under local law which the government need not observe in time of war. The slave was free, he said, "for the local law having ceased he resumes his natural right of freedom, of which he cannot afterwards be deprived by the Government of the United States[48]."

Although some Republicans would argue from Vattel, that whether slaves were considered property or men made no difference in their liability to "confiscation" in practice it made a considerable difference as to whether the owner or the owned had the benefit of due process. Charles Sumner put the case for the slave:

> The slaves of rebels cannot be regarded as property, real or personal. Though claimed as property by their masters, and though too often recognized as such by individuals in the Government, it is the glory of our Constitution that it treats slaves always as persons: At home, beneath the lash and local laws, they may be chattels; but they are known to our Constitution only as <u>men</u>.

And, Sumner concluded, "Being men they are bound to allegiance and entitled to reciprocal protection[49]."

Yet, what flimsy 'protection' they were being offered - hardly enough to justify the conservative response that the federal government was trampling state laws and constitutions underfoot.[50] Any owner seeking to enforce his claim to an escaped slave's service had to establish his title and loyalty. There was some confusion in Congress as to the precise effects of this section of the act. In April 1862, writing of the effects of martial law, the distinguished jurist Joel Parker argued that if a slave availed himself of the opportunity to escape, the master's claim would then be against the government whose military operations terminated the relationship, rather than against the slave. He could make no claim under the Fugitive Slave Law. But, he concluded, if the slave remained and martial law ceased, emancipation would be temporary. The slave could assert no right of freedom under the laws of the United States.[51] But there was confusion. Unlike Joel Parker, Senator Jacob Collamer saw it as "a part, an addition, an amendment, of the fugitive slave law[52]." Charles Sumner, however, had insisted on including the words "the <u>trial</u>" of the owner's claim to service, deliberately to avoid recognition of the Fugitive Slave Law.[53] Like the August 6th Act it presumed escape and the disruption of the master-slave relationship. It seems unlikely that a slave who did not escape could have brought an action for freedom under the act. The lack of judicial procedure was the necessary price of avoiding the delays and impracticalities of making emancipation itself dependent on the decision of a court, as property confiscation was.

Many would have preferred to remove the problem out of sight altogether. One section of the proposed measure contained a provision which was recurrent in nearly all the other emancipation measures under consideration - the voluntary colonisation of slaves freed under the act. Colonisation was enjoying some support in Congress and an appropriation for that purpose had been included in the act to emancipate slaves in the District of Columbia in April 1862. The President's support was well-known. It had, too, a practical advantage in drawing some moderate and conservative Republican support, both because of antipathy to blacks in their constituencies, and because it seemed less of an interference with the institution of slavery when state laws requiring the removal of freed slaves beyond their borders were at least partly respected. More altruistically Trumbull suggested that abroad, Negroes would enjoy the rights and privileges of free men denied them at home.[54] But there was a good deal of opposition from Radicals on the grounds of principle. Senator Pomeroy argued it would be more sensible to deport the slave-owners, whose presence would be least missed![55] Democrats took the opportunity of accusing moderate Republicans of hyprocrisy and the radicals of a more sinister design to amalgamate the races! But on the whole their antipathy to taxation almost rivalled their antipathy to Negroes. Two attempts by Senators Willey and Doolittle to provide sufficient funds for the project were unsuccessful.[56] An Act, passed on July 16th 1862 did include slaves freed under the Confiscation Acts in a general appropriation of $500,000 for the purpose of colonisation. Nevertheless it did not seem that Congress in 1862 was seriously willing to finance what would have been an enormous task. But what were the alternatives? They were not ready yet to analyse freedom, to enumerate and define the rights of citizens or to create a legal framework to support it. Most Republicans at this time, including those who voted for colonisation, believed that the title of the slave belonged to the slave as a man, that as a man he possessed natural rights of life and liberty and that the government had a duty to protect him. But there was a war to be won, before the need for more positive definitions would have to be met. None of the many substitute bills offered to the Senate in April proposed any firmer guarantee for freedom.

By April the Senate was reaching deadlock. It seemed that every Senator who dissented from Trumbull's bill had written his objections in the form of a substitute bill, varying from Harris' moderate proposal extending _in rem_ proceedings to areas in rebellion as well as in loyal areas, to Cowan's proposed outlawry procedures, and Collamer's bill imposing alternative punishments for treason, including the forfeiture of lands through fines.[57] Of this last proposal, around which conservative Republican support was crystallizing, Trumbull objected, "...just call it a fine, and you may take the real estate forever." Treason proceedings, he argued, were not what was needed to fight a war. The enforcement of such a bill as Collamer's would await peace and the opening of the courts in rebellious districts. He went on:

> I believe that no bill is worth the paper on which it is written that hesitates to take the property of traitors and rebels before they are convicted in your courts of justice. Why, sir, it is because you have got no courts of justice in the South that this war is upon us.[58]

Such was the confusion in attempting to cope with alternatives, and Trumbull's frustration with his conservative colleagues, that the Senate finally accepted Clark's motion to refer all the proposals to a select committee. Attempts to do this had begun as early as March 14th, but Browning recorded in his diary that this move had been defeated in caucus by the "ultras[59]." A further attempt by Cowan was defeated on April 30th, and agreement on May 6th to Clark's proposal was reluctant.[60] Trumbull's refusal to serve on the committee deprived it of the leading advocate of an effective bill. The new committee was chaired by Clark, who had distinguished himself by saying almost nothing on the subject. On May 14th, the battle for an efficient confiscation measure was finally seen to be lost in the Senate when Clark reported the Select Committee bill.

It was no war measure, no confiscation bill, but one to modify the punishment for treason through imprisonment, the loss of slaves, and fines, which on non-payment could result in forfeiture of property beyond life - the choice of penalty being left to the discretion of the court. Though property could be seized, transfer of title had to await judicial proceedings against the owner when he was caught and the courts opened. An emancipation proclamation could be issued at the discretion of the President.[61] To Trumbull, Wade and others, this was a poor substitute for an efficient bill, not designed to be executed, and only to be voted for as a last resort.[62] It raised the problem of finding loyal judges and juries in rebellious districts, both problems avoided in Trumbull's bill by <u>in rem</u> proceedings in loyal areas. Trumbull asked:

> And do you want to put it in the power of the judge of the district of Georgia, who yet holds his office, as I was informed to-day, and who has probably done no act for which you can impeach him - do you want to put it in his power to say whether he shall fine and imprison Mr. Toombs, or whether he shall make him answer to the scaffold for the atrocious crimes he has committed against his country?[63]

The question derived added force from the fact that Congress was at the same time impeaching a United States district court judge, West H. Humphreys of Tennessee, whose crimes included enforcing the Confederate Confiscation Act.[64] Debate on the substitute bill continued sporadically until May 21st.[65]

Meanwhile the House of Representatives faced the same issues during these months of debate, in a separate attempt to legislate on confiscation and emancipation. Where the Senate Judiciary Committee had at least succeeded in reporting a bill, the House Judiciary Committee, to which several proposals had been referred in December 1961, reported only their disagreement on March 20th.[66] John A. Bingham then attempted to get House consideration of two substitute bills, one to institute _in rem_ proceedings in federal courts against rebel property, the other to emancipate the rebels' slaves. The scant debate does illustrate a little of the confusion in Congress regarding the relationship between confiscation and emancipation proceedings. Though Bingham resisted the efforts of his colleague Porter to have the slaves included in the _in rem_ procedure, doubts were expressed by Schulyer Colfax of Indiana that the courts would nevertheless associate property and slaves in the one process.[67] Recalling the shame of the Supreme Court's pronouncement on slave status in the Dred Scott decision, he argued that such a construction should be settled by Congress and clearly put beyond the scope of the Court's jurisdiction.[68] When the Democrat McKee Dunn took up the argument, Bingham replied simply that although he regretted the Chief Justice's opinion it was only an opinion, _obiter dicta_, not law - and it marred the career of a fine judge. Bingham was "...willing to forgive, and would, if I could, forget his error of judgment" - but he would not make it an excuse for not legislating.[69] Republicans refused to be paralysed by the memory of Dred Scott at a time when they needed to utilise the courts. The House accepted Bingham's separate confiscation bill on April 22nd 1862. The following day, it was unexpectedly tabled by 56 votes to 49 in a half-empty House.[70] The emancipation bill was not brought to a vote at the same time.

Like the Senate, the House had reached deadlock. Representative Olin's resolution to refer the matter to a select Committee was adopted by 90 votes to 31 on April 24th. Olin declined to serve as chairman, and Thomas Eliot of Massachusetts became the chairman of what Wickliffe described as "a well-selected committee," which in contrast to the Senate Select Committee, bore a more radical tinge than the original Judiciary Committee.[71] Thus, on May 14th, the same day that the Senate produced its weak substitute for

Trumbull's bill, the House committee presented from the twenty bills under consideration two separate measures for emancipation and confiscation which revived hopes for an efficient bill. They were debated together, confused with each other, and voted on separately.

The Confiscation Bill attempted a tactical distinction between the leaders and the led. It designated certain classes of rebels whose property would be immediately subject to forfeiture, wherever found. For the rest there was a 60 day period of grace. If they had not returned to their allegiance after that the President was authorised to confiscate their property too, anywhere in the Union. Forfeiture was again to be accomplished by in rem proceedings in the federal courts.[72]

Eliot and Noell, of the select committee, led the debate along Senator Trumbull's well-worn path, disclaiming the bill as one to punish persons for treason, or any other crime. It was no attainder, simply a procedure - due process in its own right - against property. It was justified under the Constitution and the war power and in no way interfered with the power to try traitors. The ground by May of 1862, was so well-worn, a fact which neither deterred Congressmen from a relentless duplication of arguments, nor made in rem proceedings any clearer for them. To Babbitt, a friend of the bill, it meant the exclusion of a jury from the proceedings. His colleague Noell claimed that, according to Brightley's Digest, a jury trial was allowed if a man made a personal appearance.[73] One way or the other, the arguments did not convince conservative Benjamin F. Thomas that justice would be done. As a member of the Judiciary Committee he had voted for the August 6th act which included the same procedure, but had now awakened to the scope of it, lamenting:

> Magna Carta is soiled and worm-eaten. The Bill of Rights, the muniments of personal freedom, habeas corpus, trial by jury, what are they all worth in comparison with this new safeguard of liberty, the proceedings in rem?[74]

Congress may have been influenced by the coincidence of the debate with the publication in May, of the Report of the Joint Committee on the Conduct of the War. Representatives Loomis, Arnold and others used atrocity evidence to back up their arguments for sterner measures.[75] On May 26th 1862, the measure passed the House comfortably by 82 votes to 68.[76]

The bill to emancipate, perceived as too radical perhaps in reaching the slaves of all who voluntarily supported the rebellion, was narrowly defeated on the same day by 78 votes to 74.[77] Though there was mounting emancipation sentiment in both Congress and the country, more conservative Republicans were still hesitant on the question of interfering with an institution for so long surrounded by constitutional taboos. Again, the House measure differed from its companion bill on confiscation in that there were no judicial proceedings for divesting the owner of his title to the slave or transferring it elsewhere. It simply declared the slaves of those engaging in rebellion forever free and guaranteed that freedom only by the provision making the insurrectionary activities of the owner an answer to suit for re-enslavement and requiring him to prove both ownership and loyalty.[78] Again there is evidence that Republicans intended that this law should permanently supercede all other law on slavery, and that the black man's title to himself should be inalienable. The Constitution, said Republican Hanchett, was the means of executing the Declaration of Independence so that "American liberty is the rightful, God-given heritage of man, not because he is an American citizen, but because he is a man[79]." By whatever means the slave might win his freedom out of war, Samuel Fessenden was equally sure that it could neither be taken away nor regarded as anything less positive than freedom with rights and responsibilities. He said:

> We propose to let them know that every husband may have his own wife, that every wife may have her own husband; that all parents may have their own children; that they may earn wages, and receive and demand wages, if withheld, which their labor entitles them to receive; that they may have all the benefits accruing from living under the administration of just laws, and that they may breathe God's free air as white men breathe this air.[80]

John A. Bingham was another who maintained the right of <u>any</u> natural born citizen to protection in his fundamental rights - as an American future.[81] Not all Republicans believed it possible, and would have preferred that the freedmen be left to secure these rights in Africa or Central America. As in the Senate, an attempt was made to shelve the issue of race relations by authorising the President to colonise slaves freed by the act, on a voluntary basis. But such a scheme, promoted by Francis Blair, and which included putting freedmen under a system of protective regulations until such arrangements could be made, was defeated by 95 votes to 52 by a combination of Radicals and Conservatives.[82]

As in the Senate, however, the time had not come for serious consideration of civil rights. Behind the rhetoric lay confusion on the more pressing question of how to make emancipation effective against the owner's claim. Democratic Representative Clements insisted that since state laws remained in force, only the courts, not Congress, could take a decision on the validity of title. He asked:

> The question will arise as to where the title to the slave exists. Is it in the rebels, in the Federal Government, or in the slaves themselves? This is a question, as the laws now are, that can only be decided by our courts. The Government cannot own slaves, and has no right to sell them. Then has a slave a right to bring suit against his rebel master for his freedom, or what right has the rebel master to claim his return under the laws he has taken up arms to destroy?[83]

The House did consider these questions more fully than the Senate, and E.P. Walton proposed a bill which included a legal guarantee of freedom. But it was attached to a confiscation measure which was more conservative than the select committee bill preferred by the House. Walton's bill provided that slaves freed under judicial proceedings for treason or by a proclamation issued at the discretion of the President, should have a remedy in the federal courts against re-enslavement. The court was to issue the slave with a certificate, valid in all courts, state or federal. Any person thereafter illegally seized was to have his release on a writ of <u>habeas corpus</u> issued by any court or judge of the States. The judge acting on the writ was to commit the would-be claimant for kidnapping. Without such a guarantee, Walton said, "Emancipation will be in vain if every slave state may again fasten the chain we have broken." But the conservative bill to which it was attached was defeated on May 26th by 121 votes to 29, the same day on which the Select Committee's emancipation bill was defeated.[84]

On Representative Porter's initiative, however, the bill was recommitted to the Select Committee on June 4th 1862. The new bill reported by Eliot on June 18th narrowed the scope of emancipation to conform to the property section of the confiscation bill they had just passed thus affecting only military and civilian personnel. But it drew its enforcement procedures from Walton's bill, and a similar proposal by

Representative Morrill. The President was to compile lists of the slaves affected by the act and return them to the federal district courts. If owners did not appear in court to claim their slaves, or if they failed to prove their loyalty, the court was to issue certificates of freedom, valid in all courts. Conscious of the lack of guarantees in the August 6th 1861 act, slaves and their descendants freed by that act were included in the right "always" to be entitled to release on a writ of habeas corpus in a federal court. The price of this judicial remedy to the slave was of course that the giving as well as the defending of his freedom was linked to procedure in court. The President was also authorised to negotiate lands for voluntary colonisation. The bill was adopted on June 18th by 82 votes to 54.[85]

Five days later, the Senate took up the House confiscation bill for consideration. Opponents of an efficient measure, like Browning, reiterated the principle of their original criticisms of Trumbull's bill, rarely touching on the specific provisions of the House bills. Wade, Trumbull, and Sumner, for the same reasons, urged the House bills. There was nothing new to be said.[86]

On the question of security for freedom, Sumner did propose an amendment allowing the testimony of Negroes in federal courts on all confiscation and emancipation proceedings. But it was defeated on June 28th by 25 votes to 14, without debate.[87] On the same day, Trumbull attempted to persuade the Senate to adopt the legal safeguards contained in the House emancipation bill. On June 30th, he said that he would withdraw his proposal to substitute the House emancipation bill for the Senate confiscation bill if someone proposed an amendment which included these legal guarantees against re-enslavement. But no one did and he withdrew his proposal.[88] On June 30th, the Senate agreed by 28 votes to 13 to the Select Committee's weak treason bill in preference to the House bill. Trumbull voted "yea" because it was better than nothing, Sumner because he hoped the House would stand firm.[89]

The House did stand firm, and on July 3rd refused to concur with the Senate amendment. The Senate having refused to recede and agree to the House bill, a Committee of Conference was appointed. The result was the Confiscation Act of July 17th.[90] Its weakness came from the inclusion of the treason section from the Senate bill. It drew whatever strength it had from those sections borrowed from the House bill authorising the confiscation of property by in rem proceedings in the federal courts and from its positive declaration of freedom to the slaves of rebels. (The Senate version only authorised the President to issue a proclamation of emancipation). The judicial guarantee of freedom was the now familiar requirement that the claimant should prove both ownership and loyalty. The Conference Committee report yields no clue as to why the House guarantee of a writ of _habeas corpus_ in a federal court was not included. The final section of the act, however, gave to the United States courts full power to institute proceedings, make orders and decrees, issue process and do all other things necessary to carry the act into effect.

James G. Randall argues that this was never intended to extend the judicial machinery of the federal courts to emancipation under the Confiscation Act.[91] There were, he says, no provisions for issuing certificates of freedom, the federal courts in the South were closed, and even when they opened the courts could not hope to deal with the volume of complaints or the slave afford to make them. Yet the provision does apply to the whole act. Another section - section 8 - gives the federal courts specific powers over the forfeiture and sale of property. It is unlikely that the Conference Committee would attach a second grant of power to the courts over the whole act if they did not mean the whole act. The House at any rate had demonstrated its willingness to use the federal courts in the emancipation bill they had just passed. It is true that their proposals had presented considerable practical and administrative problems. But the reason for rejecting them was that they had made emancipation itself dependent on process. That was very different from offering a forum for the resolution of any conflicts which survived what they intended to be a _fait accompli_. As for over-running the federal court dockets, there were no more slaves affected by the act than there were traitors!

This is not to say that the Republicans deliberately designed that part of the act with a view to carrying actions under the emancipation sections into the federal courts. It was quite usual for Congress, faced with a crisis, to adopt a loose form of wording, leaving the responsibility for a more specific construction to the courts if and when an individual case came up to test the law.[92] Clearly there was a duality in the Republican attitude to the courts. Lyman Trumbull had been troubled at the thought of leaving discretion to judges and juries in disloyal districts. Yet he understood quite well and accepted the key role of federal courts in the legislation which he and his colleagues were designing. Schuyler Colfax and others in the House had expressed some fears that in the confusion over the relationship between proceedings involving property and slaves, the latter might be held as property. Nevertheless, by comparison with the presumed fate of the freedman under state law and in state courts, the federal courts held out the greater probability of sympathy for national law. All that can be said at this stage in Congress's education was that they had not yet learned how to use the courts most effectively, and at least risk. But use them they must.

They may have had no clearer idea of the meaning of the last section of the Confiscation Act granting full powers to the federal courts, than Joshua Tevis, the United States Attorney for Kentucky. In January 1865, he wrote Attorney-General James Speed, asking for a construction of that section. He wanted to know whether it authorised a proceeding in the federal court to establish the freedom of a Negro emancipated under the act, or whether his protection was left to the general laws of the land for the protection of other free Negroes. Did it mean that an original action or suit could be brought to secure any right granted by the act?[93] Unfortunately, the Letterbooks of the Attorney-General contain no reply. This is not surprising, in view of the volume of enquiries from district attorneys and private citizens on a wide range of matters. Generally, the Attorney-General declined to answer, both because of the amount of business, his lack of enthusiasm for confiscation and because his opinion could be sought officially only by government departments, since it carried some legal weight. Nevertheless, the questions asked by the District Attorney for Kentucky are worth the historian's asking, even to come to the same position as he did when he ended his letter with another question - "Ought not the act to be amended so as to secure the freedom of the slave?" The question of security for freedom was a recurrent one until the ratification of the Thirteenth Amendment.

After six months of debate, the final hurdle for the bill's supporters was to escape President Lincoln's veto. Scheduled to finish the session on July 15th, Congress agreed to remain for a further two days at Lincoln's request. The President wrote Solomon Foot in the Senate, and Galusha Grow in the House to explain that he was considering the confiscation bill, and went on, "I may return it with objections, and if I should, I wish Congress to have the opportunity of obviating the objections, or of passing it into a law notwithstanding them[94]." Senator Browning had discussed the bill with the President on July 14th and expressed his view that it ought to be vetoed.[95]

Knowing Lincoln's views, several senators took advantage of the fact that the House was now considering an explanatory resolution on the bill, to attach a modification along the lines of Lincoln's objections. On

July 16th, claiming that he was "authorised" on the nature of these objections, Clark moved the amendment, "Nor shall any punishment or proceedings under said act be so construed as to work a forfeiture of the real estate of the offender beyond his natural life[96]." This objection had been advanced to every proposal by opponents of confiscation. Trumbull had recognised it. But it was the insistence of conservatives on having a treason bill that made the explanatory resolution necessary. Both Trumbull's original bill, and the House bill, had sought to avoid such objections through bills proceeding against property and not persons.

Apart from weakening the act, Trumbull thought that the circumstances surrounding the adoption of the amendment provided a bad precedent for relations between the executive and the legislature. Some signs of dissatisfaction with the Executive's use of power had become apparent in the last days of the debate on confiscation. Lincoln's appointment of military governors to Tennessee, Louisiana and Arkansas without the advice and consent of the Senate had occasioned some criticism.[97] Now Trumbull objected to the Executive shaping policy in Congress through conversations with its members.[98] But the resolution passed on July 16th and Lincoln signed the bill on July 17th, sending Congress a copy of his proposed veto message.[99]

The message revealed that Lincoln liked <u>in rem</u> proceedings no better than the conservative opposition in Congress. But his major objection was to the forfeiture of real estate beyond the life of anyone attainted for treason and that was obviated by the joint resolution Congress had just passed. As for emancipation, he found it "...startling to say that Congress can free a slave within a state." He would rather have had the title to the slaves transferred to the nation prior to freeing them.[100] But Lincoln himself was moving towards emancipation as a military necessity. A correspondent of the <u>Liberator</u> noted that the country's antislavery sentiment rose and fell in inverse proportion to its military success. He wrote sarcastically:

> The disaster at Bull Run brought out the Confiscation Act of 6th of August, 1861 - a specimen of human folly which would disgrace an assembly of Hottentots...A series of successes on the Mississippi, and we forgot our bondsmen ... And Congress labored three months, and labored in vain, to pass a more stringent confiscation act. Next comes McClellan's <u>strategic</u> movement <u>from</u> Richmond, a new fangled name for defeat, and the late confiscation act is born in a day.[101]

The writer accurately forecast that it would never be effective. Lincoln used it only as a lever to persuade the states to return to their allegiance. On July 22nd, he presented his first emancipation proclamation to the Cabinet. On the 25th he issued a warning to the rebels, based on the first section of that proclamation, that unless they returned to their allegiances they would be subject to property forfeiture under the Confiscation Act. Lincoln made a similar use of the act when he issued his preliminary emancipation proclamation on September 22nd, which contained an order to the armed forces to enforce the emancipation clauses of the July 17th act. On January 1st 1863, he issued the Emancipation Proclamation which trumped the Confiscation Act.[102] Its force depended equally on military success to free slaves beyond Union control. As an executive proclamation it lacked even the uncertain judicial sanctions of the Confiscation Act. Addressing a delegation of Chicago Christians on September 13th, Lincoln said of the advisability of his issuing an emancipation proclamation:

> Is there a single court, or magistrate, or individual, that would be influenced by it there? (in the South). And, what reason is there to think it would have any greater effect upon the slaves than the late law of Congress, which I approved, and which offers protection and freedom to the slaves of rebel masters who come within our lines? Yet I cannot learn that the law has caused a single slave to come over to us.[103]

But it is unlikely that Lincoln issued his proclamation because he feared for the legal defects of the Confiscation Act. On the contrary, Republicans had more confidence in law than edicts - if only the President and his Attorney-General would enforce it! During the confiscation debate, and before the issue of the Executive Proclamation, Representative Samuel Blair said that the Supreme Court might sustain the President's power to emancipate by military edict, but he thought it safer to "remove all doubts by needful legislation[104]." Taken together, however, the act and the Proclamation marked the turning point of the war. Thereafter, Congress would become committed to finding the legal guarantees for permanent emancipation which they had reached for in the various Confiscation bills and which had remained undefined.

The treason and confiscation sections of the act were not enforced with vigor or regularity.[105] Confederate leaders, far less the led, did not hang. Although long lists of indictments for treason, and "aid and comfort" reached the Attorney-General's office and the newspapers, they were destined to be entered as "nolle prosequi" i.e. dismissed. The Government could afford neither the embarrassment nor the expense of prosecuting all these cases in areas where loyal juries were difficult to find. Politically, there were times when justice had to be tempered with mercy. Lincoln issued the first Proclamation of Amnesty in December 1863, which exempted those who took it from hanging for treason. Even where successful prosecutions could have been made, the "success" of winning the legal battle had to be weighed against the dangers of making martyrs in troubled areas. Attorney-General Bates wrote:

> It is far better policy, I think, when you have the option to prosecute offenders for vulgar felonies and misdemeanours, than for romantic and genteel treason. The penitentiary will be far more effectual than the gallows.[106]

Yet political wisdom also demanded that while order was difficult to maintain in areas coming under Union Control and while federal officials trying to execute the laws were being harassed in State courts, at least a few cases be kept on hand against leading rebels. The authority as well as the generosity of the federal government had to be demonstrated. The trial of Jefferson Davis - under the 1790 law of treason, not the July 17th 1862 Act - was surrounded by such political considerations. But the amnesty proclamation of Christmas 1868 included all former rebels and brought an end to indictments and trials for treason.

The implementation of confiscation was subject to many of the same political considerations as well as a lot of confusion arising from the complex legal questions which the acts involved. Attorney-General Bates himself, whose duty it was to supervise confiscation proceedings, seemed a little unsure about the *in rem* procedures to be drawn from admiralty and revenue cases. He wrote, requesting information, to four district attorneys with special knowledge of the subject.[107] But although unfamiliarity with the procedures caused practical problems the Supreme Court sustained the constitutionality of the Confiscation Acts, when the war ended.

In the leading cases of *Miller v United States* and the *Confiscation Cases* Justice Strong was faithful to the intentions of the Act's framers.[108] He carefully distinguished the treason from the confiscation sections of the

1862 Act and upheld the latter as a proper exercise of the war power. As such, the constitutional safeguards applicable to criminal trials did not govern proceedings against property. The dissents of Field and Clifford reflected the doubts which conservative Republicans had voiced in the Congressional debate that the line between guilty people and property was not so easy to draw.

Although the Confiscation Acts prescribed procedures which should conform as nearly as possible to admiralty, it left discretion with the courts to work out details. Counsel for defendants in confiscation cases frequently argued that procedures had been defective. The Supreme Court took a sympathetic view of the act and would not allow cavils about technicalities and minor errors of form to blunt it.[109] "Technical niceties are not required in admiralty and revenue cases" wrote Strong in the Confiscation Cases. On the other hand the Court took care to ensure that defendants were not deprived of common law rights where it was possible to reconcile these with confiscation proceedings. When facts about loyalty were in dispute the Court, per Chief Justice Chase, directed that new trials conform to common law procedures regarding trial by jury.[110] But juries were not an essential part of in rem proceedings either. Where a defendant defaulted and property was condemned under the acts, it was held that there were no facts in dispute for a jury to decide.[111] In these cases the Court was satisfied that the substance of the common law had been preserved. Since loyalty was an attribute of people rather than property it was to be expected that courts would find a place for a hearing of these claims. When a defendant actually turned up to assert his loyalty in McVeigh v United States in 1870, Justice Swayne held that the question of his guilt was material to the case and that the district court of Virginia had erred in denying him a personal appearance.[112] Considering how confused Congressmen were about the relationship between traditional common law safeguards to persons and property and the little known in rem proceedings the Supreme Court succeeded in striking a balance. If anything the Court in practice tilted towards the common law, curiously more so in cases arising under the 1861 than the 1862 act.[113] Despite judicial sanction for the act very little property was actually confiscated, though some successful suits were brought in the North and the areas first brought under Union control where the courts had re-opened. The business of enforcing the act was left to district attorneys on the spot, as the Attorney-General constantly reminded those who wrote for his advice! Confused by the complex legal questions, the cost of proceedings, and the unpopularity of the task, local officers often declined to commence suits on their own initiative. Where they did, any advice they received from the Attorney-General was to go cautiously, to be sure of not embarrassing the Government by failure, and often, just to dismiss proceedings altogether. The Administration, both Lincoln's and Johnson's, did not seek wholesale confiscation at a time when they sought to inspire loyalty rather than hatred.[114]

The army showed more zeal for confiscation than the legal departments did. Of the mere $129,680 deposited in the Treasury from confiscation proceeds over half was drawn from confiscations in Louisiana.[115] This can be attributed to Louisiana's being one of the first states to be brought within Union Control, but also to General Banks' efficiency in drawing up lists of property to be used for confiscation proceedings.[116] Conflicts between civil and military jurisdiction were frequent and arose in Louisiana, the District of Columbia, and Virginia. Attorney-General Bates advised "mutual forbearance and comity," but stressed the need for civil rather than military jurisdiction.[117]

He suggested that Secretary of War Stanton order military commanders to deliver confiscable land over to the civil authorities.[118] In 1864, he objected to General Lew Wallace's confiscation orders in Maryland, since they went beyond the recognised right of the army to make temporary seizures, and assumed jurisdiction over titles to property. Bates drew the General's attention to the Confiscation Acts, advising him against any actions which would give rise to accusations that the President was above the law, or provoke painful conflicts of jurisdiction, and a crop of suits against army officers for illegal actions. In reply, General Wallace offered to put his own books, detectives and so on at the service of the Attorney-General, so that he could enforce the Confiscation Acts.[119]

Bates complained to Stanton about similar conflicts of jurisdiction with the army in East Virginia. There was, he said, no excuse for such conduct, since the United States district court was fully organized and holding sessions in Norfolk.[120] But Judge John C. Underwood of the United States district court of Virginia was no happier than the army about the government's lack of vigour. On April 28th 1865, he wrote of these matters to Chief Justice Chase:

> Our great need is a vigorous administration of the laws punishing treason. It seems to me that a <u>little</u> vigor now would be worth more than <u>much</u> hereafter and I confess to considerable surprise and dissatisfaction, on reading what seems to me to be the gingerly and over cautious

> letter of the Attorney-General I send herewith - I cannot believe it reflects the views of the President, and taken in connexion with what the Attorney-General told me the day before the assassination of Mr. Lincoln - that he thought of sending a circular to the District Attorneys, forbidding the further seizure of real rebel property for purposes of confiscation, I really fear the judiciary may not be properly sustained or permitted to exert its due influence in the re-establishment of order and in suppressing the spirit of rebellion.[121]

Shortly afterwards the government did encourage the enforcement of confiscation in Virginia. Advising the district attorney of Norfolk to go ahead with one of these prosecutions against the editors of the Richmond Whig and Lynchburg Virginian, Attorney-General James Speed wrote an unusually strong letter saying that though he had hoped Virginians had suffered enough, it appeared some had not. "Now," he added, "they must be taught that the Government and law are stronger than they are[122]."

Apart from the times when the government admitted the necessity for "teaching the rebels a lesson," there were no mass confiscations. Presidents Lincoln and Johnson, and their Attorney-Generals did not want it. It was expensive, and an embarrassment to their policy of a generous peace. The various proclamations of pardon and amnesty between 1863 and Christmas of 1868, did not necessarily exempt those who took them from confiscation proceedings, in the way that it did with respect to treason charges. In the Supreme Court case of Armstrong's Foundry, in 1867,[123] Attorney-General Henry Stanbery, appearing as special counsel for the United States, put the argument that a pardon had no effect on the proceedings since no criminal offence was involved - simply the guilty predicament of property. Chief Justice Chase, however, rejected the argument in giving the opinion of the Court and held that the effect of pardon was a question for judicial construction. That was the Court's view of the 1861 Act. Inconsistently it took a different view of the 1862 act. In the Confiscation Cases Strong argued that the 1868 Amnesty did not save property from *in rem* confiscations, not dependent on the criminality of the owner, for "No power was ever vested in the President to repeal an act of Congress[124]."

The Attorney-General was, as usual, cautious. He advised his attorneys that where the courts held that a pardon relieved the defendent's property from confiscation they should not make an appeal.[125] Finally, after the granting of amnesty to all rebels on December 25th 1868, Attorney-General William Evarts notified the district attorneys to dismiss all confiscation proceedings.[126]

The burden of failing to enforce the Confiscation Acts cannot be wholly shifted to the Executive. Congress must share the blame. They neither provided clear legislation or money to enforce it. Nor did they ever repeal the joint resolution against working forfeitures for life even when they realised later in the war that it was a millstone around an effective confiscation policy. Insecurity of title remained a problem which would plague any attempts to settle freedmen on confiscated lands. John D. Syrett concludes that "Congress bears an even greater responsibility for the ineffectiveness of Confiscation than Bates because of the deficiencies of the act they had written and their failure to audit the implementation[127]."

Frustrating as these efforts were they were not quite in vain. The debate created a forum for defining the aims of both war and peace. More than that the various Congressional committees became laboratories for considering important constitutional choices and designing tools to implement them. Significantly the first steps were taken towards extending federal court jurisdiction. The fate of enemy property was too important to leave to juries in disloyal districts when hostilities ended. For some Republicans so too was freedom. Although the final Confiscation Act of July 17th lacked clear pathways for the judicial guarantee of personal liberty the debate had called forth a variety of possible procedures which offered freedmen a writ of <u>habeas corpus</u> in a federal court.

Henry Winter Davis worried about the lack of legal guarantees for personal liberty in early emancipation moves. "I suppose no body thought of any legal process," he wrote, "<u>all</u> was concentrated in the authority of the President to <u>use</u> all the negro population at his pleasure against the rebels![128]" The thought would stay with him along with the lessons learned when he offered the Wade-Davis bill to the House in 1864.

CHAPTER 3

Clearing a federal pathway into the States: The Habeas Corpus Act of 1863

The Confiscation debates confronted Republican Congressmen with a question which in one form or another would remain on the agenda throughout Reconstruction. How could they reach across state boundaries to protect citizens in the exercise of a federal right denied by the states? Clearly they would have to find an alternative to state judicial processes, to judges and juries too close to local sentiment. In the Confiscation Act Trumbull and his colleagues instinctively utilised the federal courts, refusing to confuse the memory of the Taney Court's tragically ill-decided *Dred Scott* decision with the clear and continuing relevance of federal courts to federal law. In the absence of a vastly expanded and fully staffed bureaucracy it was all they had and all that would remain when the war was over. The Union would never be anything but vulnerable while it could not provide citizens with ordinary processes to hear and enforce claims under its authority even when that authority was challenged or denied.

Already in 1862 some Republican Congressmen were alive to the potential difficulties of freedmen and women maintaining their freedom in hostile state environments and looked at the possibilities of using federal courts to guarantee their personal liberty. Emancipation continued to school Republicans to the need to offer legal remedies and alternatives to state laws and courts. Meanwhile that very same point was driven home when Congress had to deal with an apparently unrelated issue, that of indemnifying federal army officers for acts done under orders in the course of their duty. Out of their experience with this different problem, Republican legislators began to see a pattern develop and to understand that protecting officers against harassing state prosecutions and maintaining black freedom were variations on a theme. In 1866 when they framed the Civil Rights Act they borrowed extensively and deliberately from the Habeas Corpus Act of 1863. By then they also understood the national dimensions of the problems and the need to clear a path to all the states, not just those recently in rebellion.

Army officers, like all servants of the federal government up to the President, were liable in civilian courts for official acts leading to private injuries. The ethical soundness of the principle needs no restatement. In relatively recent times the Nuremburg and My Lai trials affirm the need to subject a defence of "orders" to other standards than the mere fact of their having been given. Nevertheless within the peculiar context of federalism, suits against federal officers in state civil courts had the potential to become a judicial extension of the battlefield. James G. Randall's estimate that there were 3,000 suits pending against federal officers in state courts suggests that there was more to civilian responses than honest concern for the rule of law.[1] The geography of litigation confirms this suspicion. Typically the cases came from three regions - from Copperhead areas in the Midwest; from Kentucky, where disloyalty and proslavery sentiment abounded; and from states which were loyal but under Democratic administrations, notably New York. The state courts in these areas entertained an endless stream of mostly minor complaints against federal officers for alleged false imprisonments, illegal seizures and trespasses. In addition they challenged federal conscription policies by issuing *habeas corpus* writs for the release of enlisted soldiers, usually minors.

For guidance, the past history of the federal system threw only a little light on the subject. Federalism was a delicate instrument of government. The French observer Alexis de Tocqueville observed how its conflicts resolved themselves into judicial questions. Questions of relative jurisdiction between the courts of state and nation were as important to the outcome as weapons were to armies though success sometimes rested on not using them. James Landis and Felix Frankfurter appreciated the importance of jurisdiction to federalism:

> The happy relation of State to Nation - constituting as it does our central political problem - is to no small extent dependent upon the wisdom with which the scope and limits of the federal courts are determined.[2]

In theory the scope of federal jurisdiction was broad. The Constitution provided that, "The judicial power of the Unites States shall be vested in one Supreme Court, and in such inferior courts as Congress may from time to time ordain and establish" and that this power "shall be extended to all cases, in law and equity, arising under this Constitution and the laws of the United States." In the past, however, less emphasis had been placed on the "scope" of this power and more on its "limits." Although the framers of the 1789 Judiciary Act could have chosen to make the jurisdiction of all federal questions exclusive of the state judiciaries, they did not do so.[3] In practice Congress chose to limit the jurisdiction of the federal courts to cases arising under treaties, cases affecting Ambassadors, other public Ministers and Consuls, admiralty and maritime jurisdiction, controversies to which the United States was a party, and controversies between two or more states, or between citizens of different states.

In most matters the jurisdiction of federal and state courts touched and overlapped to become a dual and compound system of judicature whose boundary lines were neither clear nor settled. Congress deliberately opted to give state courts concurrent jurisdiction of many federal questions.[4] Between the two, the 1789 Judiciary Act built a bridge. Section 25 of that Act provided for appeals from the highest state court to the United States Supreme Court in cases involving disputes about constitutional construction. Also, for the sake of uniformity, and so that a citizen of Massachusetts should have impartial justice in New York, Section 12 of the Judiciary Act provided for the removal of a suit by a citizen of one state against a citizen of another, from the state court in which it was commenced to the federal circuit court. In the one case, federal court jurisdiction depended on the subject matter involved in the suit; in the other it depended on the parties. But in both, it brought state and national law, and the courts of each jurisdiction into contact and possible conflict.

To avoid collisions in day to day business where jurisdiction was shared, the courts applied the rules of courtesy.[5] They developed rules of judicial comity. No court should interpose its process to take out of the hands of another court a cause in which it had taken prior jurisdiction. The federal courts for their part applied the early prohibition which Congress made in a law of 1793 against interfering with state court processes by issuing injunctions.[6] They were also bound to respect the laws of the forum state in diversity cases. The framers of the Judiciary Act responded to fears that federal courts might impose their own rules by providing that state laws were to be regarded as rules of decision in the courts of the United States. Prior to the Civil War the federal courts had made some exceptions to following state judicial decisions on the grounds either that there was no settled law on the subject or that state court constructions were in conflict with the Constitution.[7] Ambiguities abounded as to how far the federal courts were bound to follow state court constructions of common law under Clause 34. In Swift v Tyson, before the Supreme Court in 1842, the question was whether a New York federal court had to follow state common law on a commercial matter. Justice Story held that even if New York court precedents had been settled, it was not necessary for the federal courts to follow them since Section 34 of the Judiciary Act applied only to positive state statutes and their construction, and to common law cases involving title to things having a permanent locality, like real estate. It did not restrict the federal courts to follow state court constructions of mercantile common law. Story's opinion laid the foundations for the creation of a uniform federal commercial law derived from general principles. Recognition that there was a need for such a rationalisation probably muted reactions to it at the time, although much later the decision became a focus for resentment about federal encroachment until it was **reversed** in 1938.[8]

A much more important source of concern was the extent to which state courts could put a spoke in the wheels of federal justice. This may be illustrated by reference to the history of the writ of habeas corpus. There is reason to doubt the daily importance of the writ to civil liberties. The federal writ to release federal prisoners from custody was unusual in the light of the paucity of federal criminal law. Nor does the state writ seem to have been commonly issued to release impoverished state defendants. But the states held dear their right to issue it to inquire into the imprisonment of anyone held under federal authority within their jurisdiction. William F. Duker argues that when the Constitution commanded that "The Privilege of the Writ of Habeas Corpus shall not be suspended" it is likely that the framers intended to restrict Congress from suspending state habeas corpus for the release of federal prisoners.[9] Nevertheless, however jealously guarded, it was not frequently exercised. When Wisconsin's courts invoked the writ to release prisoners held under authority of the Fugitive Slave Law, however, their right to do so was challenged by Chief Justice Taney in Ableman v Booth. If such a power did belong to the states, said Taney, "no offence against the laws of the United States could be punished by their courts without the assent of the courts of the state where the party is held." While the opinion in its day served proslavery interests it would later be used to underwrite the power of federal courts to secure their processes under civil rights laws from state interference. In the words of Harold Hyman and William Wiecek, "purged of its slavery contamination, the Ableman opinion vindicated the tradition of Marshall and Story over localist obstruction[10]."

Localist obstruction had been a problem on other occasions when the political temperature ran high during nation-state conflict. Federal courts had been faced with a situation where they could not rescue people who acted under colour of national law from defiant state processes. Federal habeas corpus could not do for state prisoners what state habeas claimed for federal prisoners. Congress had reacted to these crises by expanding federal judicial power to remove cases from state to federal courts. During the 1812 war New Englanders' opposition took the form of obstructing revenue collection by prosecuting federal revenue officers. Congress reacted by passing a law in 1815 which allowed defendants in such cases to remove suits against them to federal district courts. In 1833 the Force Act countered the crop of harassing suits against revenue officers in South Carolina in the wake of the Nullification controversy by a further removal law. It began to reverse the one-way traffic of habeas corpus between state and nation by setting out a procedure for federal defendants to petition the United States circuit court for a habeas writ to initiate removal proceedings before their trial began in the state court. But the removal power had barely begun to be tapped.[11]

There had beenenough evidence of jurisdictional conflict and federal-state court interference before the war to forearm Congress to some of the difficulties, and the Republican drafters of the 1863 Habeas Corpus Act quickly found their way to these precedents. Nevertheless the precedents were thin both in numbers and in substance. Charles Warren estimated that only about ten cases came up under the 1833 act. There was also very little guidance on what to do about state courts which refused to comply with the law's instruction to remove the cause and proceed no further. As Mitchell Wendell writes:

> In the final analysis, whether federal law would be obeyed in the states depended on the extent of national power. This fact becomes plain when we remember that it was force that overcame the Whiskey Rebellion of 1794, the Nullification Movement in South Carolina, and the attempt at secession of 1861-1865.[12]

Though force might remain the ultimate sanction of law over rebellion in any government structure, the Civil War Congresses sought to make federalism less susceptible to such confrontations by strengthening the machinery of the nation's laws within the states - the nation's courts. Twelve acts were passed between 1863 and 1875 increasing the range of federal questions which could be removed from state to federal courts.[13] As the nation's legislative power extended to matters once beyond its jurisdiction, to civil rights and conditions of citizenship, federal court jurisdiction increased in tandem. The first of these acts was the Habeas Corpus Act of March 3rd, 1863.

The first three sections of the act concerned the question, much debated by pamphleteers at the time and historians ever since, as to when, and by whom the privilege of the writ of habeas corpus might be suspended. Magna Carta was invoked eloquently by both sides in the dispute as to whether the power belonged to Congress or the President.[14] The first section of the Act resolved the matter by ambiguously granting Congressional "authority" to the President to suspend the privilege of the writ. It went on to map out a procedure to safeguard against lengthy detainments of prisoners without cause shown. The Secretaries of State and War were to supply the judges of the federal district and circuit courts with a list of those held as prisoners under federal authority. When a grand jury sat in such an area and terminated the session without finding an indictment against such a person on the list, the prisoner was to be discharged after taking an oath of allegiance. The rest of the act dealt with removal procedures which allowed federal officers prosecuted in state courts to take their cases into federal courts. In the long run these provisions would have as much to do with liberty as those safeguarding the citizen from prolonged arrest without cause shown.

It is no coincidence that it drew heavily on the procedures contained in the 1815 and 1833 removal acts. Senator Jacob Collamer of Vermont, who was closely concerned with the drafting of the act, revealed in the course of debate that his committee had studied that legislation closely.[15] The Habeas Corpus Act provided that any order of the President or "under his authority" should be a defence against prosecution for seizures, false arrests and imprisonments allegedly committed under such order or under any law of Congress. It went on to detail procedures for removing suits where such a defence was pleaded from state courts to federal circuit courts. The defendant began by filing a petition for removal, setting out the facts of his defence. That done, the state court must proceed no further in the case and it would be tried in the federal circuit court "as if it had been brought in said court by original process." Removals could be made, not just while the case was pending, but also after final judgment had been entered, except in criminal cases where judgment went in the defendant's favour. An appeal could be made from the decision of the federal court to the Supreme Court on a writ of error. The act concluded with a two-year statute of limitation. Suits had to be commenced within two years of the wrong complained of.

Democratic critics complained bitterly that here was an act designed to immunise rather than indemnify federal officers for their actions in the course of suppressing the rebellion; that it was railroaded through Congress before members realised what it contained or could articulate their opposition; that in application it afforded no remedy to the injured party; and that it impinged on the judicial power of the states.[16]

Even the bare terms of the act answer some of these objections. It did not deprive the plaintiff of a hearing - only changed the forum to one not charged with ill will against the defendant. A defence of acting under lawful orders was to be established there, and it did not foreclose the possibility of judgement against an officer guilty of gross misconduct. Also, the right of removal was not confined to military defendants. Either party could remove the suit after final judgment and either could appeal the federal court decision to the Supreme Court.

Nor is there any grounds for the assertion that the bill was railroaded through Congress, leaving members ignorant of its contents. There was, it is true, a relatively short, but informed discussion of the bill's contents in both houses. Certainly the subject matter had been before them for three months before they passed it. There was no reason for Congressmen to be any more or less in the dark about its contents than any other bill they voted for that session.

By the winter of 1862 frequent requests came to the Attorney-General's office from the War Department to furnish counsel in suits against officers. The War Department itself augmented its legal resources. On July 17th, 1862 Congress established a new post of Judge Advocate General, filled by Joseph Holt. Holt provided the Department with a "brains trust," the Bureau of Military Justice, whose remit was to research and prepare opinions, supply counsel and keep in touch with what was happening in the field. In January 1863 Attorney-General Edward Bates wrote to Lyman Trumbull of the Senate Judiciary Committee enclosing a copy of a bill which he had drawn up himself on the subject, apparently at the request of several members of Congress. He wrote "Some such bill is, I think, absolutely necessary for the judicial peace of the country, and for the reasonable safety of the officers of the Government[17]."

The House of Representatives took the initiative, however. On December 8th, 1862 Thaddeus Stevens introduced a very brief indemnification bill. It acknowledged that there had been occasions when the privilege of the writ of *habeas corpus* had been suspended. Since there was some doubt as to which branch of the government might lawfully do this, all arrests made during that time were retrospectively confirmed and validated. The President, Secretaries, and all persons concerned in making the arrests were indemnified and discharged from suits and prosecutions. The bill concluded with an authorisation to the President to make future suspensions.[18] Stevens' bill was a limited undertaking, indemnifying against the consequences of arrests made while *habeas corpus* had been suspended. But it was, more fittingly than the final act of March, an 'immunisation' rather than an indemnification, since it contained no court procedure. What chance such a bald immunisation would have had in a state court, however, is open to serious question. Of this bill, a charge of railroading might also be made more justly since it was passed by 90 votes to 45 on the day of its introduction, with virtually no debate.[19] Stevens himself insisted that it was not a bill to indemnify everybody who had committed a trespass in the name of the Government, but simply those who had made arrests at a time when the suspension of the habeas corpus privilege had possibly been illegal. His explanations did not allay the misgivings of Thirty-seven Democrats, led by Clement Vallandigham, who signed a protest at the passage of a bill which "proposes to deprive the courts of the power to afford ....protection[20]."

On January 16th, 1863, Senator Trumbull reported a substitute by way of an amendment to the House bill - one which brought the courts back into the picture, though not in a way which would bring Vallandigham and the Democrats much comfort.[21] The Senate version contained the essence of the final bill - the procedure for removing suits from state to federal courts under a defence of Presidential authority, (or authority under an act of Congress as it was quickly amended to). Where Stevens' bill had provided an extra-judicial procedure only for arrests made while the habeas corpus privilege was suspended this bill extended judicial protection to federal officers for a wider range of alleged offences in the course of their duties, irrespective of whether the writ was suspended at the time.

During the debate considerable attention was paid to the technicalities of removal procedures which must have been unfamiliar to most Congressmen. Conservatives were quickly alerted to the danger of "judicial centralisation." Their alarm was sparked off on January 27th when Senator Harris proposed an amendment to include criminal as well as civil cases in removal procedures.[22] In fact this was not an innovation. The 1833 revenue act had explicitly included criminal cases. It had rarely been used, however, and the political storm which produced it passed over without an extensive debate on its implications for the future of state criminal law jurisdiction.

What worried the bill's opponents was that cases removed to federal courts were to proceed as though brought there by original jurisdiction, to be tried both as to law and facts. The case would thus be tried _de novo_. But what law would the federal courts follow? There was so little federal criminal law, and none at all to cover the cases of robbery and assault or even murder which might well come up to federal courts under the act. While federal courts were obliged to follow the laws of the forum state there was always the fear that they could make room for the imposition of "general principles," as in commerce. It was after all a new thing they were doing. There had been many occasions when Congress had passed penal statutes which enlisted state courts to enforce them. State courts were accustomed to applying federal criminal law, but the federal courts were unused to the business of applying state criminal law.[23] According to the bill's opponents it was a monstrous intrusion on states' criminal jurisdiction to say that federal courts might adjudicate a criminal matter arising between citizens of the same state and treat it as though it was a matter of original jurisdiction. Next to slavery it seemed that criminal law touched the deepest sensitivities.

In 1855, the Democrats had taken a quite different position when Congress considered a proposal to enforce the Fugitive Slave Act by removing cases against its enforcers from state to federal courts. Their proposed removal procedure included criminal cases and brought forth this interesting protest from Republican Salmon P. Chase, to become Chief Justice in 1864:

> It is a bill for the overthrow of State-Rights, to establish a great consolidated Federal Government, a step, or rather a stride, towards despotism.. There is scope enough for your experiment without usurping the criminal jurisdiction of the States. Do not undertake to arrest the sovereignty of the States when employed in its highest duty of investigating and punishing wrongs to life or property within its jurisdiction.. This bill is the monstrous birth of a bad time. The clearest and widest separation possible under the Constitution of the sphere of the National from that of the State judiciary is the true means of peace and harmony. But this bill expresses the very wantonness of contempt for this principle. It is framed as if its express design was to bring on a desperate conflict between the Courts of the States and those of the United States .. What if the State Courts refuse to grant a removal? The end of the road is ruin.[24]

But bad precedents on behalf of slavery made good ones on behalf of democracy, bad Democratic ideas, good Republican. Lyman Trumbull was one of the few who refrained from joining the 'about turn' of the parties. In 1855 he opposed such inroads into the state judicial power. In 1863, he continued to do so, on the grounds that there was no federal law on murder, assault and so on or provision for administering state criminal law in United States courts.[25] In defence of the amendment Senator Harris quoted from Chief Justice Marshall and Story's Commentaries, to the effect that federal court jurisdiction extended to both civil and criminal cases. His colleague Collamer agreed, resting his case on the revenue acts on which this bill was modelled.[26]

Precedents, however, hardly satisfied opponents who were fearful for the consequences to the state judiciary. Democratic Senator Powell argued:

> It has been decided by the Supreme Court that no jurisdiction over crimes against the United States has been delegated to the State courts; and, by parity of reasoning, it would certainly be held by any enlightened court that crimes against the States cannot be transferred to the jurisdiction of the United States courts.[27]

Time would prove him wrong on that point of law. In 1879, the case of Tennessee v Davis came to the Supreme Court under the removal provisions of the 1833 revenue act.[28] Justice Strong held that in this case, where a revenue officer was indicted for murder in the course of enforcing the revenue law, the removal power applied equally to criminal and civil cases, and that "it is in the power of Congress to give the circuit courts of the United States jurisdiction of such a case, although it may involve other questions of fact or of law."

For the present, however, what compounded the sin for the bill's opponents was not only the inclusion of criminal cases but that removal of cases could be made both before and after final judgment had been rendered in a state court - to be tried again as to both law and fact after a state jury had appraised the facts in a state court. Senator Bayard objected that this "must lead necessarily to the entire destruction of the States as regards their own criminal jurisprudence[29]."

Republican Orville Browning added his protest:

> I do very much doubt the power in the first place, and very much more strongly the expediency, if the power exists, of going so far as to annul absolutely the final judgments and decisions of the State tribunals, take the case de novo into the Federal courts, and try the whole thing over again there.[30]

On this point at least the Supreme Court was to prove more sympathetic to the bill's opponents. The question at issue in the 1869 case of the Justices v Murray was whether that part of the 1863 act allowing removal after final judgment was constitutional, and whether the Seventh Amendment, (that no fact tried by a jury shall be otherwise re-examined in any court of the United States than according to common law) applied to facts tried by a jury in a cause in a state court. Justice Nelson, for the Court, gave the opinion that it did and that the part of the Habeas Corpus Act which provided for removals after final judgment was unconstitutional. The proper appeal from a final decision of a state court was a writ of error to the Supreme Court.[31] And so at least one branch of government would not ride roughshod over the states criminal jurisdiction! But removals could still be made at any time before final judgment.

At the time of the debate, however, the Republicans were not intent on violating the Seventh Amendment but rather on making provision for the enforcement of the constitutional authority of the United States inside the states. Working in new territory, they were not always sure of authorities and precedent. Despite objections they carried the amendment to include criminal cases by 27 votes to 15 on January 27th.[32]

To determine what exactly the Republican supporters of the bill did want, the whole context of war policy must be considered. The debate spanned the whole range of Republican policy on arbitrary arrests, confiscation and emancipation. In the House debate, when Representative Wadsworth criticised George Julian for speaking generally of the war and causes of the rebellion rather than sticking to the subject at hand, Thaddeus Stevens interpolated that the discussion quite properly was about the whole policy of the Government.[33]

The avowed object of everything the Republicans did was to restore the integrity of the government, to see to it that the law was respected in the states and that the Union should be a viable instrument of government again. To this end, the protection of federal officers was very relevant. Senator Collamer explained the intentions behind the bill:

> We think that a villain ought to be arrested; that a thief should be arrested, and all breakers of the law; and especially that that law in which the vital existence of the Government is involved should be enforced. Obedience must be enforced, or there is an end of Government.

Of federal court jurisdiction he went on,

> If that provision of the Constitution which gives jurisdiction to the courts of the United States to decide those questions has any force in it, they are the proper tribunal; and the bill is drawn with a

> view to carry those questions there ... Gentlemen who really think that this Government should be preserved against violence by the use of governmental force, I take it, will assist us to perfect and carry through this bill.[34]

And so for Collamer a commitment to the rule of law was the only prerequisite for support of the bill. It did not imply consent to every specific policy of the Republican administration nor was it to throw a blanket of legality around every act.

But the Democrats accused the Republicans of a more devious connection between "war policy" and "law." In both Senate and House, they argued that the bill must not be taken in isolation, but should be seen for what it was - part of a wider plot to throw a curtain of legality around emancipation and confiscation. Senator Garret Davis of Kentucky made a connection between the President's September 1862 Proclamation suspending the privilege of the writ of _habeas corpus_ and the Emancipation Proclamation of 1863 describing it as:

> a comprehensive scheme devised ostensibly to aid in suppressing a great insurrection, and reducing the insurgents to obedience to the Constitution and laws, but in reality to abolish negro slavery everywhere.[35]

The Republicans were indemnifying the executors of that policy, and by implication giving these policies a firmer base. The fear of permanence of things done under military orders, or executive proclamations was the corollory. Davis went on:

> It would strike everybody as absurd to say that the military occupation and use of land would extinguish the title and divest the property of the owner. It would be no less false to assume such a position in relation to slaves. To free them ... would not extinguish the title and divest the property of the owner, which the Constitution declares shall not be done in any mode than "by due course of law[36]."

Of course proclamations and acts of Congress could not be put beyond constitutional doubt by indemnifying those who acted upon them. Individually they would have to stand the test of law. But in the eyes of most Republicans enforcing law and protecting its enforcers from those would resist were closely related. In that sense the Democrats were right.

There was no plot, however. Representatives Julian, Stevens, Walker and Van Horn all spoke of what they perceived as related issues, urging emancipation, confiscation and vigorous support for the army. They did not think they were digressing from the subject matter of the bill before them.[37] More conservative colleagues, like Cowan and Collamer held more to the point that the integrity of government rested on being able to adjudicate suits against its own officers in its own courts. Even common sense was enough to attach Representative Francis Thomas of Maryland to the bill, for the practical but persuasive reason that:

> at all events, I think that in times like these State courts and State juries summoned by the sheriffs elected by themselves, ought not to have exclusive power to determine questions involving the discharge of public duty of public officers acting under the authority of the Government of the United States.[38]

The Senate passed this bill from its Judiciary Committee as an amendment to Stevens' original House bill on January 27th, 1863 by 33 votes to 7.[39] On February 19th, the House refused concurrence.[40] It is likely that their objections were to some of the amendments which conservative senators had succeeded in tacking on to the bill. The Senate had accepted Edgar Cowan's amendment that probable cause for arrest must be shown as part of the federal officer's defence, which would have made preventative arrests impossible. Certainly neither the principle of indemnification nor the removal procedure was disapproved by the House for when the Committee of Conference reported the final bill it retained that procedure, and was accepted by 99 votes to 44 on March 2nd.[41] The Senate accepted the conference report on the same day by a <u>viva voce</u> vote.[42] The Habeas Corpus Act became law on March 3rd, 1863.

It had been duly considered if only briefly debated. It was not "Radical" legislation. Jacob Collamer, the Vermont Senator who had a hand in drafting the indemnification clauses of the bill has been variously styled a moderate, or conservative, but never an extremist. "Judicial centralisation" was not their objective, but rather they sought to cut through local anarchy and see that questions vitally affecting the federal government were adjudicated in its courts. Rather than doing anything to deprive state citizens of their right to "due course of law," they were concerned that the men who served the government should also have that right.

Perhaps they were a little naive in thinking that the Habeas Corpus Act secured that right. One subject which was not fully explored in the debate was what possible sanctions could be applied against state courts if they simply refused to hand over jurisdiction to the federal courts. The act simply required the state court to stay proceedings, once a removal petition had been properly filed.

In the next few years, as state and federal courts came to interpret the act, its weaknesses became abundantly clear. Its provisions of course applied equally to all parts of the Union. Laws which Republicans expected to be obeyed in Georgia had to be obeyed in Massachusetts - and even in Kentucky! Suits under the act came mostly from the border states, where courts were open and strong local prejudice was often directed against federal officers in the course of their duties. Conflicts of jurisdiction between state and federal courts were frequent when some state judges, notably in Kentucky, refused federal court jurisdiction and held the Habeas Corpus Act unconstitutional. Indeed the Kentucky legislature made it difficult for the courts there to do anything else but resist. In February 1866, they passed an enactment making it unlawful for a judge to dismiss a suit on the acceptance of a defence that the alleged wrongs were committed under orders during the existence of martial law or the suspension of *habeas corpus*.[43]

One of the most prominent arguments put forward by the state courts which refused federal jurisdiction, was that the Presidential or Congressional authority from which the "orders" flowed was unconstitutional. In *Eifort v Bevins*, an action against an officer for trespass and false imprisonment brought to the Kentucky supreme court in 1866, Judge Robertson held that the defence of orders was unacceptable because it rested on an unconstitutional source of Presidential power:

> The Constitution of the United States being supreme over the President, as well as over every other citizen, every unconstitutional act done by him must necessarily be illegal and void, and consequently, no citizen or soldier can shield himself from responsibility by pleading an unconstitutional order of the President, which being a legal nullity, could confer no authority.[44]

In a sentence, perhaps, the Republican legislative intention is vindicated. If the unconstitutionality of the President's exercise of the war power was to be the issue which a federal officer was to risk imprisonment for, all vigorous action might be paralysed while troops pondered questions of constitutionality best left to the United States Supreme Court. What the judge was doing in this case, was using the court as a political platform from which to attack Republican policy. Judge Perkins did so too in the Indiana case of Griffin v Wilcox, in 1863.[45] In this case the defendant, acting under orders from the Provost Marshal, suspended the sale of liquor to enlisted soldiers. His arrest of the plaintiff, Griffin, for infringements of the suspension, resulted in his being sued for damages. The opinion in the case barely touched upon the specific defence of acting under orders but focussed entirely on the subject of the unconstitutionality of the Habeas Corpus Act itself, and a general attack on the President's use of the war power.

The state courts found support for the idea that those who executed illegal orders were unprotected in the Supreme Court's opinion in Mitchell v Harmony in 1851.[46] The case arose out of property seizures during the Mexican War. The opinion of the Court was that private property could be taken by a military commander in times of such danger that it would not admit of delay, or where action by the civil authority would be too late. The officer making the seizure could not rely on pleading orders because "an order to commit a trespass can afford no justification to the person by whom it was executed." The opinion was widely cited and followed in the state courts, forgetful that the legality of the orders, the constitutionality of Lincoln's war powers, the confiscation laws, or emancipation was not their remit. They had been asked to ensure that the defence of orders was properly made out and transfer the case to the federal court.

On the more specific technicalities of the Habeas Corpus Act itself, some state courts found a loophole in the phrase "order of the President." Choosing to neglect other phrases which gave the act a wider application, for example "or under his authority" or "any law of Congress," they demanded in some cases that the defendant actually produce a specific written order from the President. Thus it was not sufficient to plead, as the plaintiff did in Skeen v Huntington, appealed to the Indiana Supreme court in 1865, that his "authority" for making an arrest derived from his position as deputy provost marshal under authority of the President.[47] Nor did Judge Robertson in the Kentucky case of Short v Wilson in 1866 accept a plea of authority from a captain in the federal army who seized a mare. Orders had to be more specific.[48] A narrow construction of Presidential authority was a severe limitation on the terms of the act. Given the tendency of the courts to hold that authority unconstitutional, even where it was clearly given, the officer couldn't win. The double hazard is illustrated in the case of

Commonwealth v Palmer in the Kentucky Court of Appeals in 1866.[49] General Palmer was indicted for helping a slave to escape under his General Order Number 32. His plea was that he acted under the authority of the War Department. Judge Robertson, for the court, objected that he had only been "authorised," not specifically "ordered," and furthermore,... "had he pleaded a peremptory order, it could not have shielded him from the penal consequences of an illegal act of glaring usurpation." This had the look of a judicial rearguard action against emancipation and confiscation.

The same state courts sometimes appeared more considerate of Confederate army defenders. The Tennessee courts dismissed a number of suits against officers on the grounds that they incurred no civil responsibility for their acts while in the line of duty. In Price v Poynter the Kentucky Court Appeals reversed a judgment against the chaplain in Morgan's army for his part in taking horses from Poynter for the use of that army. It was the lawful exercise of a belligerent right. The same judge Robertson would not unhold every claim of "orders" however, even for a Confederate defender. In Terrill v Rankin he gave the opinion that unless the orders of the superior officer were authorised by the laws of war, they conferred no legal authority. Judgments as to what constituted "lawful" orders, however, remained subjective.[50]

There are some important qualifications to the idea of widespread intransigence on the part of the state courts however, and to the idea that in no state court could a federal officer possibly secure a fair trial because of the prejudice of judge and jury. For one thing, in a number of cases where federal court jurisdiction was resisted, the highest court of the state was reversing a judgment of a lower state court, originally sympathetic to both the defendant and the Habeas Corpus Act. In the case cited above, of Commonwealth v Palmer in the Kentucky Court of Appeals, the state circuit court had originally dismissed the case against General Palmer. Again, in the Kentucky case of Farmer v Lewis, Judge Hardin found that the lower court judge had been in error in instructing the jury to dismiss a case against federal officers on the grounds that they had set up a defence of orders in the terms of the Habeas Corpus Act.[51] The tale is similar in Hogue v Penn in Kentucky, and Griffin v Wilcox in Indiana. The most interesting case of such a reversal, however, is in Short v Wilson in 1866, again in the Kentucky Court of Appeals. That case was prosecuted for the specific purpose of obtaining a reversal of a lower state court decision to transfer a case against federal officers to the federal courts. It came up under authority of a Kentucky Statute of February 16th, 1866 which read:

> Either party to any suit in any court of this Commonwealth .... shall have the right of appeal .... from the order of any such court transferring .... a cause to any court of the United States, or staying proceedings .... with a view of transferring a cause to any court of the United States.[52]

The Kentucky Court of Appeals may have been peculiarly obstructive on account of the strength of feeling in that state, and neighbouring Indiana was not far behind.

There are examples of co-operative state supreme courts which acknowledged federal court jurisdiction after reversing lower court decisions refusing removal. In many cases the judges neither demanded written orders from the President, nor aspired to comment on the constitutionality of his, or Congress's war powers. They correctly confined their interest to ascertaining whether the defendant had set out a proper petition for removal under the terms of the Act.[53] If he had, there was an end to state court jurisdiction and the case was transferred. This was the opinion of Judge Conyngham in the Pennsylvania case of Kulp v Ricketts, one of the earliest to come up under the act.[54] He held that the federal court was the proper place for the adjudication of Ricketts' defence against a charge of wrongfully arresting Kulp. It was not his court's duty to pass upon the President's right to suspend the privilege of the writ of *habeas corpus*. His court need only see that the petition was set out as required by the Habeas Corpus Act. That act, he maintained, created no new jurisdiction, since jurisdiction over federal questions already existed. It only provided arrangements for the particular court and process of implementing that jurisdiction. Indeed a model judge, if not typical within his state!

Judge Leonard took the same approach in the 1863 New York case of Jones v Seward, where the Secretary of State found himself answering charges of false imprisonment:

> We have nothing to do with the validity of the law as a defence to the action. It is sufficient for the state court that the defence involves the construction and effect of a law of Congress. The case has then arisen when the courts of the United States may have jurisdiction, if Congress so directs.

And he concluded co-operatively,

> It is not our duty to assert the independence of our State sovereignty and jurisdiction; for the final construction and effect of all acts of Congress may be brought before the United States courts by the express provision of the Constitution.[55]

Even Kentucky's Court of Appeals was occasionally co-operative. In Edwards v Ward in 1866, Judge Williams employed similar reasoning to sustain a lower court decision to transfer a case against a federal officer to the federal court.[56] In Indiana Judge Ray reversed a lower state court judgment which had awarded 25,000 dollars damages and denied removal. Reversing, he sustained the Habeas Corpus Act in full.[57]

To further confuse the question of relationships between the highest state courts and inferior state courts, some of the most co-operative state court opinions were reversals of lower court decisions originally taking an unfavourable view of federal court jurisdiction under the act. One such case is particularly worth noting, since it involved Ohio's Supreme Court's issuing a writ of mandamus to the county court to stay proceedings in order that the case might be removed! The case was The State v Fairfield Court of Common Pleas in 1864, in which federal officers filed a petition for removal of a case against them for imprisonment and assault from the state to the federal court. When it was refused, one of the officers, Tod, brought an action in the Ohio Supreme Court for a writ of mandamus against the lower court. The appeal court sustained both the constitutionality of the Habeas Corpus Act and the right to stay proceedings in the lower court in this way.[58] The behaviour of the state courts is fascinating because of these variations. We need to know more about the relationship between state lower and appeal courts as well as between state and federal. What is apparent, however, is that there was an irregular pattern of response to the Habeas Corpus Act, which suggests that a lot depended on the composition of the bench and the geography of public opinion even from district to district in the one state.

Regional differences account for some of these irregularities. Kentucky was undoubtedly the worst offender. An assistant U.S. District Attorney wrote to the Attorney-General's office in February 1866, hinting at the kind of judicial blackmailing tactics which he was forced to employ there. He suggested that pardons to Kentucky rebels be dealt out very sparingly in order to keep a sufficient number of treason proceedings hanging over their heads to counteract the prosecutions against Union officers and loyal citizens. Such tactics, he said, were helping to stave off an attempt by the legislature to impeach Judge Goodloe, whose crime was his willingness to hold a fair trial. He concluded that "the Rebels of any Southern State can be trusted sooner than those in Kentucky[59]."

Personal bias accounts for some of the irregularities. Judge Robertson of the Kentucky Court of Appeals delivered opinions consistently opposed to relinquishing jurisdiction to the federal courts. His colleague on that bench, Judge Williams was known to construe the law more sympathetically.[60] In the Pennsylvania Conscription Cases, an original opinion by Judge Lowrie denying federal court jurisdiction under the Habeas Corpus Act, was reversed several months later when Judge Strong, who had given a dissenting opinion in the case, replaced Judge Lowrie.[61]

Regional differences and personal bias could affect the construction of the act in the state courts. But these things were exactly what the act was designed to counter - to remove the possibility of such subjective pressures by having the question adjudicated in the federal courts. And so the act had to stand or fall by the test of the blacksheep.

Even when removal was granted the problems of construction remained. The arrival of a case on the federal court docket did not ensure an end to arguments about unconstitutional authority or to a construction which demanded the production of a specific written order of the President. Indeed plaintiffs sometimes won substantial damages against officers in federal courts.[62] In the 1873 California case of McCall v McDowell, the judge held that a specific order of the President must be presented. The defendant claimed authority to make the arrest of the plaintiff McCall under Lincoln's proclamation of September 24th, 1862, suspending the privilege of the writ in certain circumstances. The judge overruled that as a defence, because, "judicially I know that it was unauthorized and void[63]." In the United States Supreme Court Justice Field ruled in Bean v Beckwith in 1873 that the defendant's plea was defective in not setting forth any specific order of the President directing or approving the acts in question. It was not enough to rely on the mere existence of a chain of command down from the President, especially in Vermont![64]

The important case of the Justices v Murray in the Supreme Court has already been discussed. The judge held that the sections of the act authorising removals after the final judgment had been given in a state court was unconstitutional. Chief Justice Chase rendered a similar opinion the same year in McKee v Rains.[65] These decisions limited removals to the pre-trial and trial stage.

In general, however, the federal courts gave the Act a sympathetic construction. The constitutionality of the act was tested in 1867, in

Mayor v Cooper in the Supreme Court.[66] Cooper sued the mayor and aldermen of Nashville, Tennessee for trespass on real estate. The defendants pleaded that they acted under the authority of the national government, and more specifically on orders from the military governor, General G.H. Thomas. The case had originally been dismissed by the circuit court for the Middle District of Tennessee for want of jurisdiction. That court - a federal court - had argued that the removal sections of the act were unconstitutional. It was brought to the Supreme Court on a writ of error. Mr. Justice Swayne for the Court reversed this decision. In approving the constitutionality of the act his opinion amply reflected the spirit and intentions of the men who framed it. He emphasised the extent of the judicial power under the Constitution. Far from requiring actual orders of the President as grounds for removal he asserted the government's right to have cases which included a federal question even as an ingredient tried in federal courts. He spoke of that right as one which was essential to the vigour and efficiency of government:

> A different principle would lead to the most mischievous consequences. The courts of the several states might determine the same questions in different ways. There would be no uniformity of decisions. For every act of an officer, civil or military, of the United States, including alike the highest and the lowest, done under their authority, he would be liable to harassing litigation in the state courts. However regular his conduct, neither the Constitution nor laws of the United States could avail him, if the views of those tribunals and of the juries which sit in them, should be adverse. The authority which he had served and obeyed would be impotent to protect him. Such a government would be one of pitiable weakness.

Other federal courts followed the lead and extended the reach of the Act to protect civilians whose transactions were effected under military orders. The case of Mitchell v Clark presented a claim for removal into the federal courts when a lessor sued a lessee for rents which the latter had paid to military authorities during the rebellion by order of the commanding general in Missouri. The claim was upheld by the Supreme Court without the necessity to show evidence of an actual order from the commanding general. Justice Miller's interpretation was in keeping with the terms of the act, which extended protection to federal officers "or any other persons[67]."

It was one thing for the federal courts to assert the extent of their jurisdiction, and another to compel state courts to accept it, and stay proceedings.[68] A statute of 1793 forbade injunctions to restrain the state courts, except in bankruptcy cases. Justice Johnson in Martin v Hunter's lessees in 1816, was of the opinion that it was proper for a federal court to issue a mandamus to a lower federal court. But he did not claim such a right for a federal court to a state court. The 1863 Habeas Corpus Act contained no machinery for enforcing federal jurisdiction if it was resisted. In many of the cases which came up under it, courts cited the authority of Gordon v Longest against such state resistance.[69] In this case a Pennsylvania captain was accused of taking a slave from Kentucky to Ohio, contrary to Kentucky law. He was sued in the Kentucky State Court. As a citizen of Pennsylvania he attempted to exercise his right to have the case removed to a federal court, on grounds of diversity of citizenship. The state court refused. When the case came to the United States Supreme Court in 1842 on a writ of error, Justice McLean gave the Court's opinion that when an application to remove the cause had been made in proper form, it was the duty of the state court to proceed no further in the case. Every step taken subsequently in that court or in the state court of appeals was coram non judice. He ordered the state court to deliver the record to the appropriate federal court. In 1842 Justice McLean could refer to this as "the first instance known to us, in which a state court has refused to a party a right to remove his cause to the circuit court of the United States."

But during the war it became a commonplace. Gordon v Longest was declaratory. **There was an absence of process to intervene effectively.** Judge Blatchford in Fisk v Union Pacific in the federal circuit court in 1869 reminded his court that it had no authority to issue mandamus to compel removal. In other cases unsuccessful defendants in state courts sought a writ of error to the federal court which could then order the clerk of the state court to file a return.[70] These exchanges assumed a mutual courtesy which quite demonstrably had broken down in many areas.

The problem was equally evident in the related question of habeas corpus jurisdiction in conscription cases. The suspension of the privilege of the writ by Lincoln's Proclamation of September 1863 extended to men enlisted in the Union army. Under the terms of the first section of the Habeas Corpus Act, when the privilege was suspended no military or other officer need be compelled to make a return to the writ and produce the body of any person detained under authority of the President. On receipt of a certificate under oath that the prisoner was held under Presidential authority, further proceedings under the writ should be suspended by the judge or court issuing the writ. Any further investigation and discharge was to await proceedings in a federal court. This did not stop the state courts from claiming and exercising a right to issue writs of habeas corpus for the release of soldiers, usually minors, from service in the army, despite Section 9 of an Act of July 1866 which provided that only the Secretary of War could release minors. Not only that, but federal officers who obeyed the Habeas Corpus Act, and refused to make a return to the writ, might find themselves imprisoned for so doing, as in the case of _Farrand_ in the Kentucky courts.[71]

Attorney-General Bates recorded a Cabinet discussion in September 1863, on the question of such conflicts of jurisdiction. President Lincoln, he recalls was:

> .... greatly moved - more angry than I ever saw him - declared that it was a formed plan of the democratic copperheads, deliveratetly acted out to defeat the Government, and aid the enemy. That no honest man did or could believe that the State Judges have any such power.[72]

Bates agreed, and suggested that the judge who issued the writ should be informed of the cause of imprisonment and the officer should refuse to deliver the body, by force if need be. In cases of attempt to punish the officer for this course of action, the officer should be protected, "_by force if need be_." Sanctions against the state court judges must have been discussed, for Bates goes on to say, "I resisted the idea, held out by some, of vengeance, or penal justice, by imprisoning the judge who issued the writ[73]." The idea was to be reviewed three years later when Congressmen discussed an amendment to strengthen the Habeas Corpus Act.

The conscription cases, like the indemnification cases offer an irregular pattern of state court responses and some decisions declining jurisdiction should be noted. In the important case of _Spangler_ before the Michigan Supreme Court in 1863 - an action for the release of an enlisted minor - Judge Martin denied an application for a writ of _habeas corpus_.[74] He ruled that the draft proceeded under a law of Congress, that enlisted men were held under the national authority, and that a state court could not issue a writ of _habeas corpus_ to inquire into the legality of the imprisonment. Though the cases _In re Oliver_ in Wisconsin in 1864, and _In re Shirk_ in 1863 were complicated by alleged criminal offences by the enlisted man, the judges there also declined to issue writs of *habeas corpus* for their release.[75] In many more cases, however, state courts claimed a tradition of concurrent jurisdiction in *habeas corpus* cases, a point of view eloquently argued in another Wisconsin case, *In re Tarble* in 1870.[76]

In these matters, however, the federal courts showed little ambivalence. Of the cases which I examined, only one entertained the idea of concurrent jurisdiction.[77] The others strongly resisted the idea that state courts could disrupt the nation's conscription laws. The case of *In re Farrand* in 1867 serves as an example.[78] A Kentucky court had issued a writ of *habeas corpus* for the release of an enlisted soldier. When the federal officer refused to hand him over he was imprisoned in turn by the state authorities. The judge of the federal district court held that the state court had no right to release the enlisted man when the return of the writ showed that he was held under national authority. The validity of that authority was a question for the United States courts and not those of the states. Finally he held that the state court had no authority to imprison the federal officer for contempt and he was entitled to release on a writ of *habeas corpus* to the state court under the terms of the Force Act of 1833. The tide of *habeas corpus* had turned and the federal government had the upper hand now, using it now to pry cases from state courts where so recently it was used to obstruct their process.

Taney's *Ableman v Booth* opinion was relied upon by the courts to deny state courts the power to release federal prisoners. State courts had argued its irrelevance to conscription on the grounds that it only limited their ability to issue the writ to release prisoners held under federal judicial authority. Conscription involved executive or administrative authority, which was different. The Supreme Court put an end to the distinction in the case of *Tarble* in 1871 and effectively ended the ability of states to release anyone held under federal authority at all.[79] The federal courts in general took a sympathetic view of the framers' intentions in passing the act. The state courts did not, although qualifications have to be made to any generalisation about their "intransigence" and "truculence." There were times when state courts took a sympathetic view of the act. Co-operation of course could not be assumed and the act was designed to work without it if need be. But equally it was not designed to discourage co-operation - perhaps one reason why it lacked teeth initially. The idea was rather to demonstrate that there was a viable pathway out of the states when they would not adjudicate federal questions impartially in the first instance. It seems unlikely that the federal courts in Kentucky would seek jurisdiction or be able to cope with the 3,000 cases on the state court dockets. Nevertheless, by 1866 it was clear that a delicate balance between co-operation and the ability to demonstrate the nation's authority through its courts was not being achieved.

A certain amount of trouble had been anticipated. An act of the same date, March 3rd, 1863, appropriated $100,000 for defraying expenses of suits under the act. It was surely needed. The bulky files of correspondence between the War Department and the Attorney-General's office contain increasingly standardised requests for counsel. Endorsements were made on requests for defence counsel for top military men like Philip Sheridan for "acts done in performance of his duties as Commander of the Department of the Missouri," General Grant, sued in the Supreme Court of Georgia, and General McDowell, answering charges in the California state court.[80] But it was not only generals who were fair game. The cases cover the whole range of rank and officers. A fairly typical request came from Jackson, Mississippi in 1870, for a law officer to defend a second lieutenant of the Sixteenth Infantry in "any action that may be brought against him on account of the part taken by him in recovering from Mr. E. Moody, of Jackson, Mississippi, the possession of a mule belonging to the United States[81]."

Sometimes, district attorneys were confident that such cases would be entered as <u>nolle prosequi</u>, or transferred to the federal courts under the Habeas Corpus Act. The United States attorney in North Carolina wrote of his difficulties in travelling miles between state courts to defend federal officers personally, but assured the Attorney-General's office that, "from what I know of the judges I feel assured that if Nolle Prosequis are not entered (which I believe will be the case) that they will all be removed into the Federal Courts[82]." His optimism was the exception rather than the rule, however. In most areas, the patience of a beleaguered army was fraying. They began to look to their own protection, rather than to the Habeas Corpus Act. In Kentucky in 1866 a Deputy Provost Marshall, E.M. Angel was indicted by a Grand Jury in Greene County for providing passes for negroes. General Palmer, in charge of the department, and himself a frequent target of such suits, wrote to the sheriff of the county to the effect that Angel acted under legal orders and was entitled to protection from illegal and oppressive arrests. Palmer concluded:

> You are notified that Mr. Angel must not be arrested by you by virtue or under pretence or color of the writs issued on said Indictments. If he is he will be discharged by me and you yourself placed under arrest.[83]

It was one way of "staying proceedings," but hardly likely to commend itself to the civil authorities. General Palmer had asked the army's Adjutant-General to approve his action in view of the frequency of these harassing suits.[84] The War Department preferred to use more regular channels, however, and requested the Attorney-General's office for counsel to defend Angel, pointing out that in the absence of martial law in Kentucky, General Palmer was not empowered to carry out his threat.[85]

A further illustration came from Tennessee, where the district attorney arrived in court to petition for the removal of a suit against Major H.W. Smith to the federal courts - only to find that the suits had already been dismissed by order of Major-General Thomas to the plaintiff's attorney![86] (The order dismissed one of the suits in favour of the plaintiff). Commanding officers claimed the authority to intervene by reason of General Orders Number 3, issued by General Grant on January 12th, 1866. It charged commanders in rebel states to issue orders to protect all persons under military authority from suits in state and municipal courts and to protect coloured persons charged with offences for which white persons were not prosecuted in the same way.

For all the subtleties of the federal relationship, the question was raised again then - must the laws of nation over state rely on force? In 1866, Congress sought alternatives in law. On March 13th, Representative Cook introduced an amendment to the Habeas Corpus Act, designed to give it teeth.[87] Explaining the need for an amendment to the law, Representative Cook of the House Judiciary Committee spoke of "evidence before the committee that the state courts in some border states have held, under Section 4 of the act of which this is an amendment, that the order of the President of the United States is necessary to justify the party doing the act[88]." The amendment proposed a more liberal construction of orders to read:

> Any order, written or verbal, general or special, issued by the President or Secretary of War, or by any military officer of the United States holding ... command of the ... place within which such seizure ... or imprisonment was made.

Cook went on to draw attention to the difficulties which had been encountered in removing cases from state jurisdiction. The amendment provided that if a state court proceeded with a case after removal, the judges and other officers concerned might face damages and double costs - after almost eighty years of nurturing respect for each other's jurisdictions and avoiding conflict!

The Democrats instantly objected to the amendment. Representative Harding of Kentucky protested that it was retroactive, giving defendants whose cases were now pending a broader defence; the defence itself was too sweeping, putting the orders of a corporal on the same footing as the President; and finally he objected strongly to sanctions against state judges.[89] These charges, however, did not spark off much debate in the House. For the Republicans, McKee reiterated the simple defence that the Government must be able to protect its men in the states, and have questions affecting them - and the existence of the government - adjudicated in its own courts.[90] Clearly the state courts could not be relied upon to see justice done. The amendment passed on March 20th, 1866 with a display of Republican unanimity, by 112 votes to 31.[91]

It was taken up for discussion in the Senate on April 11th, and became the subject of a more spirited debate than it provoked in the House. Opponents raised the question of sanctions against state court judges, resulting in a motion by Senator Saulsbury to strike out the offending clause. Republican Senator Clark didn't mince words when he replied:

> This Government must be obeyed, and it is not worth having if it cannot cause itself to be obeyed. This proceeding, if attempted to be carried out in a State Court, in defiance of the United States authority, should be void and the judges and everybody else who undertakes to set himself up in this way - for it will not be an honest authority - should be punished for so doing. We have had about enough of this State authority to teach it to yield respect and obedience to the laws of the United States.[92]

Strong words - but in 1866, the Republicans certainly had had enough of state defiance. While they debated this amendment the Joint Committee on Reconstruction was sitting in Washington, gathering a formidable array of evidence of State disobedience to United States law and the hazards facing the minorities who relied upon it. To sue a few judges did not seem so unreasonable in these circumstances. When Senator Hendricks of Indiana suggested that impeachment was a more appropriate censure of a judge, Clark referred him to the situation in Kentucky.[93] There a federal officer had recently submitted a resolution to the legislature that, since widespread amnesty had been granted to rebels and would be used in court as a defence to proceedings, federal officers should have similar protection from proceedings in state courts. The legislature turned it down. "Now," said Clark, "talk of an impeachment of a judge in a state like that![94]" His colleague, Trumbull, cited precedents for sanctions against judges. He referred to a provision of a New York State Statute, and to Kent's Commentaries.[95] But Senator Doolittle found himself in disagreement. He distinguished between the judicial and ministerial functions of the judge in these cases and his exemption from liability in the former capacity.[96]

But the Republicans on the whole had no qualms as to the constitutionality, or advisability of this measure. Several Senators spoke of the removal procedures in general, stressing the need to have federal questions adjudicated in federal courts.[97] It passed by 30 votes to 4 on April 20th. Once again, however, conservatives had succeeded in attaching an amendment to which the House could not agree - a provision making the terms of the amendment operative only on future cases and excluding defences of "orders" to acts done with malice, cruelty, or unnecessary severity (which, as Republicans argued would not be shielded by the act in any case, and only provided another loophole for the states.[98]) But both Houses agreed to the report of the Conference Committee, and the amendment was approved on May 11th, 1866.

Passage of the amendment does not appear to have tamed the state courts. The Kentucky cases of Commonwealth v Palmer and Short v Wilson, denying federal jurisdiction, were decided in the summer term of 1866, after the passage of the amendment. Numerous complaints from the army of harassment at the hands of state courts were recorded in correspondence between the War Department and the Attorney-General's office after 1866. I can find no instances of judges sued for damages and costs under the amendment.

The Habeas Corpus Act and its 1866 amendment were links in a general trend of removal legislation. For all the problems of compelling state courts to accept federal court jurisdiction the Republicans made the procedure an integral part of Habeas Corpus, Civil Rights and Freedmen's Bureau legislation throughout the Reconstruction period. They borrowed it from earlier procedures designed to protect federal revenue officers in hostile state environments and adapted it to a range of problems in the 1860's. They learned more as they went on about how to trump states in matters vital to federal law and government. It was not a disinterested exercise in political science, however, but one intimately related to their wartime political objectives.

Confiscation and emancipation measures would be a dead letter if state courts who disagreed with them could insist on jurisdiction and hold the enforcers of that "illegal" policy responsible in their courts. Of course, the state courts would not and did not surrender without a fight. The Habeas Corpus Act ran a none-too-successful gauntlet in the state courts. Some of the difficulties arose out of the novelty of the situation, while others, as in Kentucky, from a determined attempt to embarass the administration. In some areas the state courts did co-operate, and due procedure was followed. On the whole the federal courts fairly reflected the legislative intention of the act. But the problem of co-ercing the states was not solved. The army sometimes had to abandon hope and protect themselves. Congress tried threatening the judges with sanctions in the 1866 amendment. But the power was not used. The question of finding a workable alternative to force remained. It was more than a question of perfecting judicial machinery. The solutions were political and had to rest on the consent of the people to the laws. But the meeting ground of law and politics was in these areas of contested jurisdiction.

CHAPTER 4

Putting emancipation beyond doubt: The Wade Davis Bill

The Wade Davis Bill got caught up in a political wrangle in a Presidential election year, obscuring the reasons why a united if lukewarm Republican party voted for it. Historians once polarised the choices this way; Lincoln offered generous terms for restoration in his Proclamation of Reconstruction and Amnesty of December 8th 1863. It invited a nucleus of ten percent of loyal men to begin generating new state governments before the war's end, and preferred that they find their own way to abolish slavery and adjust race relations rather than impose it. In response, Republican dissidents invoked radical theories to clothe the federal government with the power to alter state laws and suspend their governments in limbo until such time after the war when a minority of proven past loyalists would begin the process of writing new state constitutions. They would have no choices on the matter of guaranteeing permanent freedom. The bill itself abolished slavery as a matter of federal law and required the states to adopt constitutions renouncing slavery forever. Congress was tougher than Lincoln.

In this scheme of things, the Wade Davis Bill was interpreted as a Radical offensive against a moderate President in a critical election year:

> The Jacobin bosses judged that the best way to control the process and machinery of reconstruction was to force the party to ditch Lincoln as its standard-bearer for 1864 and secure the nomination of an inexorable radical.[1]

It was a view that did not lack support among Lincoln's contemporaries. Secretary of the Navy Gideon Welles thought that one of the objects of the bill was to pull down the administration. It was inspired by "earnest zeal on the part of some, and ambition and intense malignity on the part of others[2]." Representative Francis Blair styled it:

> A bill for the permanent dissolution of the Union, to disfranchise the whites and enfranchise the Negroes to prevent any of the states from coming back in time to vote for Mr. Lincoln for President and to promote the ambition of the Secretary of the Treasury.[3]

Neither observer was free from bias. On Reconstruction, Secretary Welles clung to a view of the inviolability of states rights which kept him well at the rear of his party. Francis Blair had his own political vendetta with the

Radicals, and specifically with Henry Winter Davis, the bill's sponsor in the House of Representatives.[4] Of course the Wade Davis bill was preferred by many of those whose doubts about the continuing viability of Lincoln's Reconstruction efforts had led them to support the brief campaign booms of the unlikely "inexorable radicals" Salmon P. Chase and John C. Fremont. But as fuel for anger it did not burn bright until after its passage on July 2nd 1864 had been checkmated by Lincoln's pocket veto and "insulted" by his veto Message. By that time Lincoln had been nominated on the first ballot at Baltimore, on the face of it, with as convincing a demonstration of Republican support as the Wade Davis bill attracted on the day it passed. Headcounts may be deceptive. Certainly support for the bill was not a dependable indicator of enthusiasms, either for alternatives to Lincoln - or indeed even for the plan of Reconstruction it contained!

It was an equally unreliable index of radicalism. Where historians once emphasised the differences between Presidential and Congressional plans they now discover areas of substantial agreement between them. Both aimed to build new state governments on the basis of suffrage restricted to white, loyal males. The possibility of black suffrage in the Congressional bill had been effectively - if vicariously - killed after a battle to include it in a bill to organise a territorial government for Montana had - just - lost on April 15th, 1864.

Lincoln's loyalty oath seems more lenient because it offered the possibility of a fresh start to men who were prepared to put the past behind them and swear future loyalty. New governments would be their work. But he made the offer while the war was still on and Confederate hopes for victory were still high. The idea was that an oath of future loyalty would only be attractive to those who really meant it. The Wade Davis oath requirement seems stiffer, and in a sense it was since it delayed the start of Reconstruction until fifty percent swore future loyalty. Of that fifty percent, only those who took the "ironclad" oath of past loyalty to the Union were eligible to vote for or participate in the constitutional convention. Perhaps it would not amount to such a commitment, however, to swear future loyalty after the war was over and there was no viable alternative focus of loyalty. Both plans restricted actual participation to a loyal minority, identified in different ways. They differed in timing.[5]

Lincoln himself had not expected to be bound for all time by his ten-percent oath, well aware that its relevance would end when the war ended. In the matter of detaching the wavering or merely silent from support of the Confederacy and strengthening the hand of the loyal Unionists, he would put flexibility before formulae. It was an important difference between

Presidential and Congressional plans that Lincoln would start immediately and "learn by doing" rather than wait for peace. Loyalty was not static. It could be earned by example and participation. But the difference was one of political strategy. The underlying political process of regenerating loyal governments envisaged in both plans had much in common.

This, and the fact that Lincoln never claimed to have pre-empted the work of Reconstruction or cornered the market on future wisdom explains, if it does not justify, his provocative admission that the Wade Davis Bill he had just vetoed was "one very proper plan for the loyal people of any state choosing to adopt it[6]." After all, it was not so unlike his own....except that it replaced political choices by hard law.

The clearest statement of what the conflict over the bill was really all about was contained in Lincoln's Veto Message of 8th July and the angry rejoinder of the Wade Davis Manifesto published in the New York Tribune on August 5th.[7] It was about putting emancipation beyond doubt, making it safe from re-vitalised state laws by guaranteeing freedom in federal law. The bill's sponsors made it clear that it was this, rather than the details of its political arrangements, that made it so vital. But while Lincoln agreed heartily on the need to secure emancipation, he was not prepared to "declare a constitutional competence in Congress to abolish slavery in the states."

Short of constitutional amendment - and that was where they were in the summer of 1864 - Congress had laboured long and arduously to reach agreement on excising slavery from state law forever. Far from being simply a reaction, or a counter offensive to Lincoln's plan, the Wade Davis Bill represented the work of two Congresses to get a law on the subject.[8] It had survived where dozens of its predecessors had died in committees, on roll calls and at untimely adjournments, unable to surmount the constitutional doubts of enough Republicans about crossing state lines to do more than exercise the war power to make captures or emancipate the slaves of active rebels. The bill was not another emancipation measure, acting only on those it emancipated. It aspired to abolish slavery's legal roots and guarantee freedom in courts. That was what mattered.

And it mattered that Congress made the law. It was inconceivable that they would vacate matters of regenerating legal and law-making processes to the Executive, whatever the extent of agreement between them. Charles Sumner made the point frequently heard in both houses of Congress:

In short, if a new government is to be supplied, it should be according to established law rather than according to the mere will of any functionary, to the end that ours may be "a government of laws, and not of men[9]."

From the very beginning of the war the Congressional Republicans had held it an item of faith that the Statute book accompanied the army, legitimising its authority and limiting its discretion. The army was not only in the front line of battle but it was also the bridgepoint where federal authority encountered state law and had to decide what to do about enforcing it. Congress began its search to impose law on these military decisions as early as July 1861 and sought to transfer them to civil governments soon after. What began as a debate about discretion in enforcing existing law evolved into larger questions about changing the law. The Wade Davis Bill had a long fuse. To understand it, it is necessary to trace some of the abortive but educative legislative fumblings of the Thirty-seventh Congress which ended without a law and left Lincoln the gap he filled with his own Reconstruction efforts.

On July 22nd 1861 the House passed the Crittenden resolution and all but seventeen Republicans denied a "purpose of overthrowing or interfering with the rights or established institutions" of the states in rebellion.[10] Three days later the Senate passed Johnson's virtually identical resolution. On July 30th Senator Trumbull introduced a bill from the Judiciary Committee, S.33 for the Suppression of Insurrection, which touched upon the duties of the federal government as caretaker of state law.[11] Its limited objective was to follow the army into rebellious districts as they came under its control and equip it with a legal framework for the restoration of order.[12] In its original form the bill was silent about how far the army was bound to follow state law under these emergency conditions, but it was subsequently amended to provide for the enforcement of such rules "conforming as nearly as may be to previously existing laws and regulations." There is no evidence whatsoever that the drafting of the phrase "as nearly as may be" was designed as a loophole to make the laws of slavery an exception, or to contradict the terms of the Crittenden-Johnson resolutions in any way, but it did give notice of how practical problems quickly put a strain on the Republican constitutionalism of 1860. In these very early days of war Congress was concerned with the deceptively simple procedural problems of a federal authority encountering temporarily dis-functional state laws. Quite soon it would be concerned with the substantive content of these laws and the need to find a constitutional justification first for not enforcing slave laws and then for uprooting them. The emergency summer session of Congress ended in August without a decision on the bill. When Congress reconvened in December events put explicit consideration of these points on the new agenda.

November 1861 saw the capture of the Sea Islands and Union victories in North Carolina, Tennessee, Arkansas and Louisiana in the first six months of 1862 brought part of these states under Union control. In the absence of a Congressional prescription for their governance, Lincoln made the practical responses necessary to keep things moving and provide a rallying point for Southern Unionists. He began to appoint military governors - Stanley to North Carolina, Johnson to Tennessee and Phelps to Arkansas. Perfectly compatibly, Congress experimented with a number of plans for supplying civil governments.

To explain why the federal government had to make such a provision in the first place, it was necessary to explain the states' "absence." Territorialisation was the most prominent legal fiction in 1862. The theory was that by seceding the states had ceased to exist and had reverted to the status of territories. It had the merit of specifically endowing Congress with the power to make rules and regulations for governing them until such times as they were re-admitted to full statehood. The government of territories was also a familiar task, with a reserve of practical experience and tested machinery in the model of provisional governors, legislatures, and courts.

What to do about existing state law was no problem. It no longer existed. While Trumbull's S.33 in July 1861 had raised the tricky constitutional question of enforcing existing rules "as nearly as may be," James Ashley's bill from the House Committee on the Territories, the most important of a number of bills to provide civil governments on the territorialisation principle in the Spring of 1862, declared that laws in conflict with the Constitution ceased to exist along with the governments which made them.[13] As finally reported from the Committee on March 12th, it authorised the President to establish temporary civil governments on the territorial model and specifically forbade the passing of any act establishing, protecting or recognising the existence of slavery.

The bill died on March 12th, 1862, tabled by 65 votes to 56 on the day it was introduced. Interestingly, a two-thirds majority of Republicans opposed its tabling, not itself evidence of their support for its provisions but indicative perhaps of an increasingly serious pursuit of a way of undercutting State law on slavery. Ashley's bill carried other liabilities which made it an unlikely focus of Republican unity. Among other things it abolished racial qualifications for juries and confiscated lands for loyal men, including Negroes. Besides, territorialisation as a means to strike slavery was too strong a constitutional medicine for the conservative Republicans who were only just coming round to accept emancipation as a war measure, carefully designed and very limited. They joined the Democrats to defeat it. What is more interesting is that moderates like John Bingham were prepared to consider it, more concerned with ends than enthusiastic about theory. He stressed these constructive goals:

> Is nothing to be done beside sending conquering armies to burn and destroy as they go? That is a needful thing; but I would also send the white-robed ministers of justice. I would put them in the deserted temples of justice, and place in their hands the sacred scales, and bind them by an oath to do equal and exact justice to the poor and the rich, the stranger and the citizen.[14]

His more radical colleague, Fernando Beaman also offered as a justification for territorialisation the need to fulfil "the obligation of protection and a just administration of the laws." When the states failed in this duty, the federal government must not.[15]

Support for territorialisation dwindled after March. If its appeal was an instrument of emancipation, it may have been overtaken by the promise of success on less dangerous and innovative constitutional grounds.[16] Congress and Lincoln were moving in the same direction. Congress passed an emancipation bill for the District of Columbia in April 1862, an additional article of war prohibiting the return of fugitive slaves by the army, and the Confiscation Act of July 1862. Lincoln kept the pace he deemed appropriate to his own political and constitutional role by wooing the border states to gradual, compensated emancipation and keeping the Emancipation Proclamation in a drawer.[17]

Congress continued to seek a legal framework for civilian government in areas returning to Union control, less because it was out of step with Lincoln - though there was mounting criticism of his military governments - but more because they believed it was their job to make laws which were uniform and binding. Interest shifted from territorialisation to the guarantee of republican government clause. In June 1862 Senator Ira Harris of New York introduced the first of many measures utilising the clause as a repository of power to make conditions for Reconstruction. The clause was at once more radical and more conservative than territorialisation; more radical because it was open-ended and might theoretically have invited limitless federal supervision; more conservative because it tacitly acknowledged the continued existence of states. Wartime Republicans pinned the more conservative interpretation to the clause[18].

Harris's bill did not have a specific emancipation clause and interest focussed on the status of existing law. It provided for the execution of laws not inconsistent with the Constitution but "not interfering with the laws and institutions existing in such states at the time its authorities assumed to array the same against the government of the United States further than shall be necessary to carry into effect the provisions of this act." Really it was a step back to S.33's "as nearly as may be" instruction to the military in 1861. It provoked a lively debate in the Senate on July 7th when Sumner raised the awful possibility that the bill committed the civil governments to administer black codes and proposed to exempt such laws.[19] One possible compromise was to accept an alternative amendment, proposed by Sherman, to confine their instructions to the enforcement of United States law. That suggestion revealed the dilemma of Republicans who carried their constitutional scruples into battle. Senator Trumbull rejected the idea because it potentially limited the civil governments to enforcing only a small proportion of the amount of law necessary to restore order. But, like Sumner, he could not suffer the enforcement of black codes. Yet he could see no principled way under the Constitution of selecting some state laws for enforcement and avoiding others - not without leaving the Executive with an undesirable degree of discretion.[20]

While most of the debate hinged on this dilemma some notice was taken of the role of courts - to what extent they would be obliged to follow existing state law. The provisional courts under the bill were vested with the powers of United States district and circuit courts. They were federal courts and yet their business would arise out of cases between citizens of the same state on matters of state law. Senator Carlile suspected that they would claim a power to try these cases _de novo_, without regard for state rules and precedents.[21] Senator Powell stated the suspicion more boldly:

> The object, the scope, and the intention of it is to send judges and a Governor there for the purpose of indirectly abolishing the institution of African slavery, and overthrowing the domestic institutions of those states under the apparent shield and panoply of the law.[22]

That was already a familiar allegation. But the notion that courts had a special, "indirect" role in attacking state laws and institutions by trying cases _de novo_ and hence creating a body of judge-made federal law to replace existing state law, was just emerging as an argument against extending federal judicial power. It was voiced more often and more explicitly in the debate on the Habeas Corpus Act the following Spring, 1863.[23]

By that time Lincoln had issued the Emancipation Proclamation and Congress was beginning to assess the prospects of its taking root in the legal systems of reconstructing states. To argue that the Wade Davis bill was an attempt to put emancipation beyond doubt implies that Lincoln was somehow less committed to that goal. He was not.... not after January 1st, 1863. Before that he wrote to the military authorities in Tennessee, Arkansas and Louisiana urging them to encourage elections there among the loyal before the Proclamation was issued on January 1st.[24] It was still possible to trade loyalty for exemption and some districts took advantage of it and held elections.

After January 1st it is inconceivable that Lincoln ever contemplated abandonning the Proclamation as the bottom line of Reconstruction. He may have had a different perspective from Congress of where the main threat to its finality lay, however. Danger of failure lay in defeat, either on the battlefield or at the polls, where victory for peace Democrats would have undermined emancipation just as surely. Getting a speedy start to regenerating governments in those parts of the country coming back under Union authority made tactical sense militarily and politically, offering a good example to those still in arms, and hopefully building up a Republican strength there which would soon pay off in Congressional representation and electoral college votes for Lincoln.

More than that it offered the possibility of progressing from emancipation to the abolition of slavery, being two different but related things. Lincoln knew that the Emancipation Proclamation affected only those who were emancipated by it and did not root out slavery from its legal bases in state law. Changing state laws was not work for a Commander-in-Chief of the armed forces, however. Indeed Lincoln would not have located such a power anywhere outside the states themselves. In his view the states were out of their proper practical relationship to the Union. It was not a condition which endowed the federal government with the power to change their laws. There is plenty of evidence that Lincoln encouraged the loyal people of the states to remove slavery permanently themselves. With respect to his showpiece of Louisiana he wrote General Banks in August 1863:

> I would be glad for her to make a new Constitution recognising the Emancipation Proclamation and adopting emancipation in those parts of the states to which the proclamation does not apply.[25]

With respect to the freedmen, Lincoln was genuinely concerned with both their immediate welfare and their long term adjustment to a new economic relationship with former masters. Though he offered no radical vision for restructuring postwar society there was at least the assumption of permanence in his suggestion for adopting "some practical system by which the two races could gradually live themselves out of their old relationship to each other, and both come out better prepared for the new[26]." The "new" was to be free. In November he wrote, "My word is out to be for and not against them on the question of their permanent freedom[27]." In Tennessee, Lincoln prodded the Provisional Governor to forge ahead with the election of loyal representatives. In September 1863 he wrote Johnson, "Get emancipation into your new State government Constitution - and there will be no such word as fail in your case[28]." Republicans who could not countenance a Reconstruction on the basis of anything but permanent freedom could take heart from the President's Springfield letter in August 1863 when he said there must be no compromise on emancipation, that "...the promise being made, must be kept[29]."

The Thirty-seventh Congress had passed the Confiscation Act as a contribution to keeping the promise. But it produced no Reconstruction law. While they worked at it and grumbled about the deficiencies of Lincoln's efforts and the potential pitfalls of Executive usurpation, they nevertheless admitted Louisiana's newly elected representatives Flanders and Hahn in February 1863.[30] Bingham doubted whether it was constitutionally correct for Louisiana to send representatives to Congress in the absence of a state government to authorise their election.[31] Porter agreed that elections instigated by a military governor were invalid and expressed doubts as to whether the people were choosing representatives more agreeable to Lincoln than to themselves. Without wishing to be unduly cynical about the loyal foundations Lincoln relied upon, he understood that the South was still a "hot-bed of treason and rebellion," in need of a strong arm.[32] These were representative of the doubts expressed in debate. On February 17th, the forty-four representatives who unsuccessfully opposed it included an unlikely combination of Democrats like Daniel Voorhees and radicals like Thaddeus Stevens who momentarily shared a vocabulary which included "rotten boroughs" and "executive usurpation." Henry Dawes, Chairman of the Committee on Elections, compared the alliance to "that memorable conciliation between the rival houses of Herod and Pilate, which made common cause in their efforts to overthrow the true gospel[33]."

The lack of alternatives had robbed Congress of the initiative. It was not that time spent on abortive plans had been wasted, however. It was now clear that the price of recognising the continued existence of states was that a clearer and more principled method had to be devised to harmonise state law with the desire of a majority in Congress to ensure freedom. Towards the end of the session they had progressed from attempting to write rules for temporary caretakers and begun to think about how to sink emancipation into the political foundations of new state governments. On March 3rd, 1863 Senator Harris introduced yet another bill to establish temporary provisional governments in the South, again based on the guarantee clause. These governments were to administer state laws, but no law recognising slavery was to be enforced. Giving evidence that Republicans already associated positive rights with the condition of freedom, the bill provided that laws for the trial and punishment of white men should be applicable to all. The major difference between this and previous bills, however, was that it located future responsibility for abolishing slavery in a constitutional convention and prescribed procedures for its election. Like Lincoln they would have the states themselves make the appropriate changes in the law. Unlike Lincoln they would leave no room for discretion. The new constitutions were to contain three mandatory clauses. Certain classes of Confederate office-holders were to be disqualified. There was to be no recognition of the rebel debt. The freedom of slaves was to be guaranteed. The bill came too close to the end of session to hold out any hope of hammering out a consensus from a prolonged debate. Though a motion to table it was defeated, Senator Wilkinson successfully moved to set it aside on March 3rd on these timetable grounds.[34] However controversial in terms of specific procedures and fine detail, let alone the serious doubts which still lurked about the scope of federal power vis a vis state law, one thing was clear. Making emancipation safe had moved from the periphery to centre stage when the Thirty-seventh Congress ended.

In December 1863 when Lincoln issued his Proclamation of Amnesty and Reconstruction, making firmer policy out of experimental beginnings, he too made emancipation a priority. It was based on the pardonning power, and acknowledged the existence of the states, although their governments had been "subverted." It offered pardon to those who would swear future loyalty and obedience to all emancipation measures taken by President and Congress in the course of the war. When enough people had taken the oath, and at any rate no less than tenpercent of the number of votes cast in the Presidential election of 1860, they could take the necessary steps to re-establish State governments. In his accompanying Annual Message of December 8th, Lincoln repeated his commitment to emancipation:

> To now abandon them would be not only to relinquish a lever of power, but would also be a cruel and an astonishing breach of faith.[35]

The plan was offered as a guideline, not to be considered exclusive of all other solutions.

And on the whole, the Republican party accepted it on those terms. There was no immediate outcry about the creation of "pocket boroughs" on the flimsy foundations of tenpercent. Indeed the Wade Davis bill itself began its Congressional career with a similar provision and was only amended to a fifty percent figure in May 1864. Most Republicans instead fixed on Lincoln's commitment to emancipation as being of its essence. The President's secretary, John Hay, recorded in his diary:

> Men acted as though the millenium had come. Chandler was delighted, Sumner was joyous, apparently forgetting for the moment his doctrine of State suicide; while at the other political pole Dixon and Reverdy Johnson said the message was highly satisfactory.[36]

Charles Sumner did not "forget" his doctrine of "state suicide." Like most Radicals who invoked apparently extreme justifications for the exercise of federal power to set conditions for the states in terms of "suicide" of "conquered provinces" or even "territorialisation," what mattered was what the power was for. In October 1863 Sumner had written an article in the <u>Atlantic Monthly</u> explaining his famous "state suicide" resolutions of February 11th, 1862. In it he wrote, "I discard all theory," as long as Congress found the power under the Constitution to make freedom a reality whether it be by the rights of war, or territorialisation, or the guarantee clause.[37] It is not so surprising then that he too welcomed Lincoln's Proclamation and described it this way in a letter to the English liberal John Bright on December 15th, 1863:

> The President's proclamation of reconstruction has two essential features, - (1) The irreversibility of emancipation, making it the cornerstone of the new order of things; (2) The reconstruction or revival of the States by preliminary process before they take their place in the Union. I doubt if the detail will be remembered a fortnight from now. Any plan which fastens emancipation beyond recall will suit me.[38]

Fastening emancipation beyond recall was what mattered. Welcoming the President's resolve on the matter did not, in the eyes of the Congressional party, remove Reconstruction from its familiar place on the roster of legislative priorities. Nor did it make them any less vigilant observers of whether events in Louisiana and elsewhere were in reality deserving of confidence. Seeing was believing. And what was happening in Louisiana in the early months of 1864 was not encouraging.

Lincoln gave General Banks full power to press ahead with the creation of a new state government there. He proceeded to jeopardise the work of the Free State General Committee who had been planning a constitutional convention as the first stage towards setting up a government on the basis of freedom. In January Banks ordered an election on the basis of the old proslavery constitution, deferring a constitutional convention until after a government was formed. He seemed to be playing into the hands of the old planter class, while the only safety for freedmen lay in his annulling the proslavery sections of the constitution by military decree. It was a long way short of what Congress meant by law. In practice Banks' policy was not so disastrous. Elections were won by the moderates under Michael Hahn and slavery eradicated from the constitution - but it was not "the right way[39]."

Moreover, as blank books were sent out to Louisiana, Arkansas and Tennessee to record the oaths of loyal men, news drifted back which raised doubts about their sincerity. Harold Hyman's work on Confederate oath-taking substantiates many of the Republicans' suspicions at the time. If it was not an unmitigated tale of cynical evasion and deceit, it was not a re-assuring measurement of loyalty either. At best it was "less a conviction of conscience than a grudging acquiescence in the verdict of battle[40]."

Emancipation was at risk. As early as the debate on confiscation, Congressional Republicans had expressed doubts about possible judicial constructions of any emancipation proclamation resting on executive war powers. They had never pinned hopes of freedom's permanence on its legality. But they had reserved an opinion on whether loyal men, committed to the proclamation, could give it the sure roots it needed in state laws and constitutions. Faith diminished now. Demonstrably these were shaky political foundations upon which to rest a legally doubtful edict. They would last as long as it took an unrepentant majority to dismantle them. It was at this point that Congress decided the only security lay in writing stronger guarantees of freedom into both sides of the federal equation - into state constitutions, secured by more dependable evidence of loyalty, and into federal law, secured by the federal courts.

This was the Wade Davis Bill. Most of its provisions were drawn from previous bills. It was not the first bill to abolish slavery by federal law. James Ashley had offered a bill on December 21st, 1863 which contained a provision to that effect and was for a few weeks the front-runner of Congressional Reconstruction plans. It was not the first bill to require free constitutions as a condition of restoration. That went back to Harris' bill, cut off by timetable demands in March 1863 and was also a feature of Ashley's bill. But the Wade Davis Bill weaved a path through some other troublesome areas, confining suffrage to whites, providing civil rather than military governors, and emphasising the continued existence of States, all of which re-assured conservatives and made it more acceptable than Ashley's bill. It also contained more specific legal machinery for guaranteeing freedom and the stiffer "ironclad" oath of past loyalty which were its main attractions for those who were increasingly worried that decisions of the battlefield were about to be reversed at state polls.[41]

The Wade Davis Bill became a rallying point for the Republican party at a time when it was confused by choices, undecided and hesitant still on many constitutional points, and yet driven by a sense of urgency as events unfolded. The bill was not so much an inspiration as the lowest common denominator. It made provision for temporary civil government, the re-establishment of state government and the permanent abolition of slavery in state and federal law.

As to temporary government, it authorised the President to appoint a civil governor charged with the duty of administering existing state law, and whatever necessary bureaucracy as authorised previously by state law. Even taxes were to be collected according to previous arrangements. But no law which held anyone in slavery was to be recognised or enforced by the Governor or any court or officer in the state. The bill confirmed the correlation Republicans made between freedom and equality before the law by re-casting a provision which was made at least as far back as Harris' March 3rd 1863 proposal, that the laws for the trial and punishment of white persons should extend to all persons.

As to more permanent political arrangements, these were to begin when military resistance ended. All white male citizens were to be enrolled and when fifty percent had taken an oath of loyalty to the United States, elections were to be held for delegates to a constitutional convention. Only those who could subscribe to the "ironclad" oath of past loyalty were eligible to vote for or be delegates - in other words a further selection was to be made from among the fifty percent willing to swear prospective loyalty. This unspecified number was, as surely as Lincoln's tenpercent, a minority. Former Confederate officeholders were excluded, even if they offered to take the oath. These did commend themselves as more effective procedures for weeding out the disloyal than Lincoln's less structured and formal arrangements, accepting that they were not essentially more democratic.

The constitutional conventions were to incorporate three conditions into the new state constitutions. Confederate civil officeholders and those who held the rank of colonel or above in the army were excluded from voting for the legislature or membership of the legislature, or Governor. Slavery was prohibited forever and freedom guaranteed. No State or Confederate debt should be recognised or paid. These had crystallised as the three essential conditions in all the legislative drafts over the past twelve months. The constitution would then be submitted to the people and if accepted, the President, on authority of Congress, would recognise the state government and the state finally proceed to elect representatives and take part in Presidential elections, their Reconstruction completed.

Section 12 was the federal side of the equation cancelling out slavery. Putting freedom into state constitutions was the most they could do stateside to ensure permanence, although even that could not outlive the determination of state majorities to undo it on the day when re-admission removed federal authority from their soil. Section 12 looked beyond Reconstruction and created a permanent federal interest in the states to guarantee personal liberty. It declared all persons held to involuntary servitude in these states forever free. If they or their descendants were subsequently restrained from their liberty, the federal courts had the duty to discharge them on a writ of _habeas corpus_. Any person convicted of an attempt to hold such a person to slavery was liable to a fine and imprisonment. Once again then, the federal courts found themselves in the frontline, the permanent federal presence in the states when the army left. They provided a judicial safety net to complement the changes in state law which would hopefully be the fruit of the political consent envisaged by the bill's Reconstruction plan.

A federal Constitutional amendment would have been better. Lincoln would have preferred it. Congress would have preferred it. It would have put the matter beyond constitutional doubt and applied across the Union, where the Wade Davis bill only applied to the rebel states. But it was the failure in June of the resolution for a Thirteenth Amendment abolishing slavery to pass with the necessary two-thirds majority that made the Wade Davis bill urgent. It was left as the only alternative way to "emancipate all slaves, to give them and their paternity the writ of habeas corpus in the United States courts wherenow if free they could seek protection[42]." It was important not to end the Thirty-eighth Congress and face an uncertain Summer in an election year without achieving that much certainty.

In the debate most Republicans avoided phrasing the bill as an assault on Lincoln's policies. The President's Reconstruction Proclamation, said Fernando Beaman in the House, was a beacon light and "what he has thus happily initiated we must fashion and complete[43]." Others prefaced their remarks in similar vein and went on to highlight what they regarded as specific weaknesses which had to be made good by law.

Their doubts centred on two particular points - the likelihood of building truly loyal governments from Lincoln's plan and the shakieness of the Emancipation Proclamation in law. Henry Winter Davis voiced the fears of colleagues who were suspicious of Southern white promises of future loyalty:

> There is no fact that we have learned from anyone who has been in the South and has come up from the darkness of that bottomless pit which indicates such repentance. There is no fact that any one has stated on authority at all reliable that any respectable proportion of the Southern states now in rebellion are willing to accept any terms that even our opponents on the other side of the House are willing to offer them.[44]

Fernando Beaman argued that many Southerners might take the oath to avoid punishment, save their estates, or take control of the new government for their own purposes. He warned graphically that, "the oaths of men whose hands are dripping with innocent blood should be received with great caution[45]." Nor did Lincoln's plan specifically require that emancipation be secured in new state constitutions.

Shaky political prospects underlined the Emancipation Proclamation's vulnerability in law. Speech after speech questioned its likely fate all the way up the judicial system from state courts to United States Supreme Court. Henry Winter Davis spelled out the hazards of failing to anchor law to politics:

> It is therefore under the scheme of the President merely a judicial question, to be adjudged by judicial rules, and to be determined by the courts. It is a question whether each individual negro be free. It is a question whether the master has the right of seizure, or the negro can control himself. It is to be determined by the writ of _habeas corpus_. It is a question of personal right, not a question of political jurisdiction. Its fate in the State courts is certain. Its fate in the courts of the United States under existing laws is scarcely doubtful.

> I do not desire to argue the legality of the proclamation of freedom. I think it safer to make it law.

He concluded,

> The purpose of the bill is to preclude the judicial question of the validity and effect of the President's proclamation by the decision of the political authority in re-organising the State governments.[46]

Henry Winter Davis did not mean to exclude legal solutions by political ones. In his mind law and politics were inextricably linked. After all, even the passage of the Thirteenth Amendment, which would have put slavery's fate beyond doubt, would not have obviated the need for a law on Reconstruction. Davis made that point:

> If adopted it still leaves the whole field of the civil administration of the States prior to the recognition of State governments, all laws necessary to the ascertainment of the will of the people, and all restrictions on the return to power of the leaders of the rebellion, wholly unprovided for.[47]

The Wade Davis Bill was an attempt to generate political arrangements which would make the laws of the state compatible with the laws of the United States.

While the Wade Davis Bill would have expanded the jurisdiction of the federal courts to enforce Section 12, the question of the validity of a master's claim under state law was not to be a matter for judicial decision. The courts' discretion was limited to ascertaining the facts of any alleged attempt to hold anyone in slavery, and to release them on a writ of *habeas corpus*. It was this which Democrat J.C. Allen, a dissenting member of the Select Committee found most threatening to states rights. He objected:

> The twelfth section abolishes slavery in these states as far as an act of Congress can abolish it. It not only abolishes it, but it takes away from the courts, as far as an act of Congress can take away, the power of passing upon the right of Congress to abolish it.[48]

Here was the echo of the confiscation debate on *in rem* proceedings. It had utilised the federal courts but limited their discretion to ascertaining the facts about the predicament of the property. The Habeas Corpus Act also by-passed state judicial discretion by making simply the facts of orders under which federal officers acted removable to the federal courts. Indeed it occurred to Representative Denison that it might well be part of one grand design to rob the states of their rights. He referred to the Habeas Corpus Act as further evidence and linked it with the present Wade Davis Bill as part of one attempt to legalise the unconstitutional acts and proclamations of the President.[49] Presumably he too was thinking about the Emancipation Proclamation. He was right. Henry Winter Davis had also thought it "safer to make it law."

The bill contained the maximum of conditions which the Republicans were prepared to insist upon. They could not afford to go further without exposing the differences inside the party. And so on May 4th when Representative Rice of Maine proposed to strike out the word "white" wherever it described electoral qualifications, Henry Winter Davis refused to yield the floor for that or any other purpose.[50] Many Republicans were prepared to embrace the issue of black suffrage. In the same session of Congress preliminary votes on Senator Wilkinson's amendment to strike out "white" from the electoral provisions in a bill to provide a temporary government for Montana, found twenty-two senators and fifty-four members of the House in favour. In the end, however, they would not risk passage of the bill for the sake of pressing a divisive issue.[51] And so it was with the Wade Davis bill. Its emancipation provisions were too important to risk it for. The bill was pressed to a vote on the same day, May 4th, having avoided opening the suffrage question. Thaddeus Stevens' preamble to the bill, implying the non-existence of the states and regarded as a test vote on the radicalism of its supporters, was voted down by seventy-six votes to fifty-seven. The Republican majority clung to the safety of the less controversial contents of the bill, which passed by a comfortable seventy-three votes to fifty-nine on the same day. It was too mild for Thaddeus Stevens, who abstained from the vote.[52]

The bill ran into some trouble in the Senate. Senator Wade reported it from the Committee on the Territories on May 27th, with amendments. But it was not taken up for debate until July 1st, dangerously close to the end of the session.[53] Like the House, the Senate resisted the suffrage issue, and on Ben Wade's initiative voted against the committee's amendment to strike out "white" from the electoral qualifications for the constitutional convention, by twenty-four votes to five.[54] Then events took an unexpected turn. B. Gratz Brown proposed a substitute which offered an escape hatch to the doubtful and would have had the effect of postponing all Congressional action on the subject until the next session.[55] It said simply that insurrectionary districts should not be allowed to cast votes for electors for President,

Vice-President, Senators or Representatives until the inhabitants had returned to their allegiance. The passage of this substitute on July 1st, by twenty votes to thirteen was a surprise, representing not a planned revolt against the bill, but a temporary loss of direction from Wade's committee.[56] While the issue hung in the balance, Senator Sumner gave further evidence of the importance which the bill's supporters attached to its emancipation features. Fearing that the bill was lost, he offered a resolution "...to recognise as a statute the Proclamation of Emancipation, putting it under the guaranty and safeguard of an Act of Congress." The Senate, however, would not accept it in this form.[57] Order was restored the following day when Wade re-asserted the authority of his committee. The Senate receded from its amendment and agreed to the House bill. The Wade Davis bill passed on July 2nd.[56]

Everything waited on Lincoln's approval. John Hay records Lincoln's dialogue with Senator Zachariah Chandler, when the President pushed the bill away, without signing it. Lincoln objected that the bill had been placed before him just a few moments before Congress was to adjourn, and that it was too important to deal with so summarily. Chandler expressed again its importance for emancipation, when he said, "If it is vetoed, it will damage us fearfully in the Northwest. The important point is that one prohibiting slavery in the reconstructed States." But it was that very point on which the President expressed doubts as to Congress' authority.[59]

He expressed them again, on July 8th, when he issued a message explaining his reasons for pocket-vetoing the bill. He was not prepared, he said, to commit himself inflexibly to one single plan for reconstruction, or abandon the work which had already been done in Arkansas and Louisiana. Nor was he prepared to "declare a constitutional competence in Congress to abolish slavery in the states" - rather do that by constitutional amendment. But then came the astonishing statement that:

> Nevertheless I am fully satisfied with the system for restoration contained in the bill as one very proper plan for the loyal people of any State choosing to adopt it, and that I am and at all times shall be prepared to give the Executive aid and assistance to any such people.[60]

To many Congressmen, it was a strange idea of law that the President should offer to execute a bill which, by his refusal to sign it, was not a law - and to execute it, at that, only if the people preferred it to his more flexible edicts! Small wonder that the message was greeted by an outraged response from the bill's sponsors. The Wade Davis Manifesto was published in the New York Tribune on August 5th. The President's refusal to sign the bill had made an election issue out of the differences between the two proposals for reconstruction. For that reason, the Manifesto had the air of a Radical campaign broadside against the President. But in many ways it remains a valuable reflection on the intentions of the framers.

It attacked the governments of Louisiana and Arkansas as "more creatures of his will," their free constitutions resting on the flimsiest of political arrangements, and on the will of the military. They preferred their sterner arrangements, and they preferred the rule of law. As the Manifesto said, "the bill governs the states _by law_, equalizing all before it, the proclamation commits them to the lawless discretion of military governors and Provost Marshals." Lincoln's Reconstruction Proclamation, they went on, contained no guarantee of freedom, "leaving slavery exactly where it was by law at the outbreak of the rebellion." It exacted an oath in support of the emancipation proclamation. But even if that proclamation would stand up to a Supreme Court test, it exacted no guarantee of state laws, or constitutions, and "the right of a slave to freedom is an open question before the State courts on the relative authority of the State law and the proclamation." There was no doubt which authority the state courts would find the more binding. An oath to such a proclamation was meaningless. It might bind the one-tenth who took it, but not the nine-tenths who would succeed to the control of the State government. When that happened, the federal government would be left without any means to protect the freedman in the states, for, by defeating the bill, the President had defeated the freedman's legal remedy of a _habeas corpus_ writ from a federal court.

They expressed shock and anger that Lincoln should then offer to execute the bill as "one very proper plan for the loyal people of any state choosing to adopt it!" How? The Manifesto thundered, "A more studied outrage on the legislative authority of the people has never been perpetrated."

The outrage was felt by many more who would not break ranks and express it openly while their party's fortunes hung in the balance in the months preceding a crucial election. Thus Republican Albert G. Riddle later recalled that, although the masses were strongly in support of Lincoln's re-election, "at the Capital, thinking Union men were quite unanimous in sustaining Mr. Wade and Mr. Davis, as was the majority of both Houses of Congress[61]." Frederick Douglass lamented Lincoln's veto as yet another example of his policy, "Do evil by choice, right from necessity[62]." Secretary of the Treasury

Salmon Chase recorded his disappointment in his diary, as well as his fears that the President and his chief advisers had not rejected the possibility of a reconstruction with slavery. He also recorded that Senator Pomeroy intended to go buffalo hunting and then to Europe![63]

Such action would have been, in the long run, regretted. For in the cold light of day Republicans had time to think more clearly about the failure of the Wade Davis bill, and to stop regretting it in the light of later events. George Julian afterwards wrote that, "the passage of the somewhat incongruous bill vetoed by the President, would probably have proved a stumbling block in the way of the more radical measures which afterwards prevailed[64]." Perhaps the only people who might later have regretted it were the more conservative Republicans. Indeed Senator John Sherman alleged many years after the events that, in conversation with Charles Sumner, President Lincoln had expressed his regret that he had not approved the bill.[65]

The shortcomings of the bill were discovered by Republicans in the second session of the Thirty-eighth Congress which met in December. Many of them had voted for the original bill. But circumstances had changed. Lincoln had won in November, and some of the tensions had gone out of Congress's relationship with the Executive. In January when the House successfully passed the resolution calling for a thirteenth amendment to the Constitution, abolishing slavery, some of the old urgency attaching to the Wade Davis bill as an anti-slavery measure had gone. These were the circumstances in which James Ashley re-introduced the Wade Davis bill in January, with two important amendments.[66] One required Louisiana and Arkansas to go through the enrolling phases of the bill, that is, to obtain an oath of loyalty from fifty percent of the electorate. It thus challenged the existence of 'loyal' governments already there. The second amendment cast some light on the weakness of the original bill. It required the states to accept not only the abolition of slavery, but also the corollory of freedom - a guarantee of civil rights. It provided that in the new state constitutions:

> Involuntary servitude is forever prohibited, and freedom and equality of civil rights before the law are guaranteed to all persons in said State.

The objection to the original bill which Congressmen now raised most frequently was that it failed as a guarantee of freedom. It is difficult to determine how much of this criticism sprang from an honest attempt to make a better bill. The criticisms came both from those for whom the bill as a whole was now too tame, and from those who wished to drop it in favour of a more conservative solution. Representative Kelley thought that the bill did not go far enough to guarantee freedom until it extended the suffrage to the freedman. He proposed an amendment to that effect on January 16th.[67] On the other side, there were Republicans like Dawes and Eliot who criticised the bill's failure to guarantee freedom and equality under the law but did not propose firmer guarantees.[68] Eliot proposed a substitute bill requiring states to establish republican governments, prohibiting slavery and guaranteeing freedom and equality of rights before the law. But it contained no machinery for doing so.[69] Dawes wanted a plan which would leave more discretion to the loyal men in the states.[70] Not radical enough for some, too radical for others, the bill had lost its attraction as a rallying point for Republican unity. On January 17th, the House decided to postpone further discussion on it by 103 votes to 34. Henry Winter Davis was right when he observed that "A vote to postpone is equivalent to a vote to kill the bill." Re-introduced on February 20th, it was tabled the following day.[71] The Thirty-eighth Congress, like its predecessor, was to end without a reconstruction measure on the statute book.

One disappointed man was the bill's original House sponsor, Henry Winter Davis. He marvelled that representatives who voted for the bill in the previous session should suddenly discover that it sanctioned the enormities of the laws of slavery. Cynically he suggested that the discovery was prompted by the intervening election. Patronage considerations caused some of his colleagues to jump on to the successful President's bandwagon. He could not see how the bill failed as a guarantee of freedom, since:

> I took some credit to myself for putting in a brief space the shortest possible declaration that all men should be equal before the law .... and that I had come, in these words, as near annihilating the black laws of the South as gentlemen could have done if they had spent tomes in writing out the provision for that purpose.[72]

But, whatever their motivation, the bill's critics were right. It was less than a positive guarantee of freedom and equal rights under law. Its importance in 1864 was that it contained more of a guarantee than Lincoln's plan - but it was less than Davis claimed. The section of the bill which made the link between freedom and the positive protection of rights in law, was that which set out conditions for the <u>provisional</u> governments. Section ten authorised the provisional governor not only to refrain from enforcing laws by which slaves were held to service, but also to see that "the laws for the trial and punishment of white persons shall extend to all persons." To that extent it implied a standard of conduct for state justice under a free constitution. The sections which set out conditions for the restoration of loyal state governments contained the vague requirement that the freedom of all persons in the state was to be "guaranteed." Though Republicans did associate freedom with equal protection under the laws, they had a habit of assuming that when slavery was abolished, black codes would fall too. This was a mistake. Henry Winter Davis perhaps took a false pride in "guaranteeing" freedom in the "shortest possible declaration." Perhaps it needed some "tomes" of definition - on such matters as testimony, contractual powers, property and family law. The provision of the bill which extended the jurisdiction of the federal courts to the issuing of a <u>habeas corpus</u> writ against enslavement suffered the same limitation. It was some protection against bodily re-enslavement but no guarantee against subtler forms of slavery at the hands of discriminatory and unequal laws.

The Wade Davis bill was a half-way stage between the Confiscation Act of 1862 and the Civil Rights Act of 1866. It picked up one of the procedures discarded in 1862 - the writ of <u>habeas corpus</u> as a guarantee of personal liberty. It wrote freedom into federal law and made the federal courts its guarantor. It attempted to fasten freedom on the states by organising loyal minorities to change their constitutions. It seemed more reliable than Presidential Reconstruction. But it had limitations. It applied only to the states which had been in rebellion. If Lincoln doubted the constitutional competence to free the slaves this way, so might the courts. The Thirteenth Amendment offered safety and a further opportunity to clarify the relationship between freedom and equal laws, touched on in the Wade Davis bill. Though the Republicans never quite aspired to write Henry Winter Davis' "tomes" of definition, events would prompt them to at least a few lines of it in the Civil Rights Act of 1866.

CHAPTER 5

Free at Last: The Thirteenth Amendment

On June 15th, 1864 the Thirteenth Amendment resolution failed to pass through Congress with the necessary two-thirds majority, leaving the Wade Davis Bill the only great antislavery measure of the session. In turn, its veto in July robbed the freedman and his posterity of the right to a writ of *habeas corpus* from a federal court ..... but not for long. In January Congress did muster a two-thirds majority in favour of the resolution and three-fourths of the states ratified the Thirteenth Amendment by December 1865. Whatever else it did, the amendment was a sure and certain guarantee for all time that any person held to involuntary servitude would be entitled to release on a *habeas* writ from a federal court.

Resisting the idea that it did more, that it invited the federal government to guarantee and maintain civil rights, Senator Edgar Cowan spoke in 1866 about what he believed the amendment meant when it passed:

> The breaking of the bond by which the Negro slave was held to his master; that is all. It was not intended to overturn this Government and to revolutionize all the laws of the various States everywhere. It was intended, in other words, and a lawyer would have so construed it, to give the Negro the privilege of the *habeas corpus*; that is, if anyone persisted in the face of the constitutional amendment in holding him as a slave, that he should have an appropriate remedy to be delivered.[1]

In contrast, Lyman Trumbull, who played such a prominent part in the drafting of the Civil Rights and Freedmen's Bureau Acts defended these measures as appropriate sequels to the Thirteenth amendment. His expectations of "breaking the bond" amounted to more than the absence of physical bondage, as this extract shows:

> With the destruction of slavery necessarily follows the destruction of the incidents of slavery ..... those laws that prevented the coloured man going from home, that did not allow him to enforce rights; that did not allow him to be educated, were all badges of servitude made in the interests of slavery. They never would have been thought of or enacted anywhere but for slavery and when slavery falls, they fall also.[2]

It was the demonstrated failure of freedom to fill the space left by slavery that prompted Republicans to activate the enforcement clause and provide "appropriate legislation," that is, remedies for rights they believed inherent in the Thirteenth amendment's capacity to keep pace with what it meant to be free.

While the Supreme Court has even yet to construe what "badges and incidents" of slavery are abolished by the force of the amendment on its own, without ancillary legislation, the courts of both state and nation have had many occasions to reflect on the framers' intentions when they have passed upon the "appropriateness" of the civil rights laws which it parented. Judicial opinions echoed the choice between substance and form implicit in the dialogue between Cowan and Trumbull. Federal circuit Judge Emmons charged the grant jury in Tennessee thus:

> The thirteenth amendment abolished slavery only; it did no more ..... The rights of legislation secured to Congress in the amendment was that only of creating penalties for a violation of its provisions, and providing securities against the re-establishment of slavery either generally or in particular instances.[3]

Compare these and other post-Slaughterhouse federal court opinions - or the majority of state court opinions at any time after the war! - with the generous language of Justice Swayne on circuit less than a year after the amendment was ratified. He believed it incumbent on the courts to "carry out the wise and benificent purpose of Congress in passing the Civil Rights Act of 1866 to effect an 'act of great national grace'". The Thirteenth amendment, he concluded in U.S. v Rhodes, did more than abolish slavery. It established freedom. Its commands trenched directly upon the power of the states and the people of the states.[4]

Scholars have not exhausted the debate. Jacobus tenBrock's "neoabolitionist" argument that the Republican framers intended a revolution in federalism to bring about a "consummation of abolitionism broadly conceived" has met with little enthusiasm and a lot of criticism.[5] If such far-reaching changes were their intention, then why did they choose language borrowed from the Northwest Ordinance which had never been interpreted as meaning anything more than the prohibition of forced labour? Why did they reject Charles Sumner's alternative language which was much more pregnant with possibilities - "All persons are equal before the law, so that no person can hold another as a slave?"

Charles Fairman offers what seems a plausible explanation:

> To supporters of the amendment, there was glory enough in abolishing the institution which had long poisoned the nation's entire life. They rejoiced in the expectation that once the cause was eradicated, the baneful consequences would disappear. With a poor comprehension of social behavior, they did not perceive how enduring would be the mores that were entwined about it.
>
> The debates seem not to support a conclusion that the men of the 38th Congress had a clear view of the ultimate results of the amendment. Indeed it would have been surprising if, when the war had not yet ended, and when efforts were bent upon abolishing its cause, the participants had taken thought for the problems of another day. Planning was not a Congressional practice. Had the question been brought into focus, there could not have been agreement among two-thirds of the House.[6]

Circumstancial evidence also seems to lend support to a more limited view of the undertaking. To earn a two-thirds majority it was necessary to persuade not only a handful of Democrats, but also to assure Conservative Republicans who had a healthy respect for states rights that no revolution was at hand. The amendment applied to every state, some like Delaware and Maryland now painfully parting with slavery voluntarily but not ready to accept equality. Mindful of these circumstances, any war of quotations about original intent would have to include a selection denying a purpose to revolutionise the federal system to put the Negro at the white man's table, in his daughter's bedroom, or even at the polls.[7] Political reality, longstanding constitutional convictions, and simply "not knowing" what the future would bring seem to argue caution in describing what Republicans had on a sometimes far from collective mind in 1865. It seems safer to emphasise the endless affirmations during the debate that the amendment was a conclusion, a crowning, a fitting end to wartime emancipation, removing all constitutional doubt, rather than to suggest that it unabashedly looked to the guarantee of substantial freedoms.

But when it is appreciated that the Republicans had for some time associated positive rights with freedom and made a start towards protecting them in hostile state environments in their wartime Reconstruction plans, then "starting places" and "fitting ends" lose their significance. While it is true that many Republicans indulged in wishful thinking that logic would compel the transition from emancipation to meaningful freedom they did not count upon it. An absence of specific suggestions in the debate about how the enforcement power might be used in the future - and even disavowals that it would bring about radical change - does not betoken naivity, unless they had forgotten everything else they were learning about "enforcement" to protect federal officers in State courts and restore loyal governments. It seems unlikely.

The debates "were conducted on a level of hyperbole befitting the fervor which had attached itself to the issue after thirty years of agitation[8]." The reader might well sympathise with Fernando Beaman, who remarked during an earlier debate on the Wade Davis Bill that any man who could originate one new idea in relation to slavery should have it patented and be ranked as one of the greatest discoveries of any age.[9] When the resolution finally passed in January 1865, the artist Clark Miller was to make plaster casts of the crania of those who supported the measure.[10] Many of those who spoke for it had the air of men whose crania were about to be immortalised, rather than persuaders upon whose skills crucial votes depended.

After considering a number of proposals the Senate Judiciary Committee reported the following resolution for a Thirteenth Amendment on February 10th, 1864:

1. Neither slavery nor involuntary servitude, except as a punishment for crime, whereof the party shall have been duly convicted, shall exist within the United States, or any place subject to its jurisdiction.
2. Congress shall have power to enforce this article by appropriate legislation.

When the debate began in the Senate on March 28th, the ground was already well worn. Republican speeches on the whole were concerned with familiar themes; that the preservation and future peace of the Union depended on the removal of the source of the rebellion; that the institution itself was a great wrong which had condemned the slave to every conceivable injustice, and threatened to lose the liberty of both races in a rebellion against democracy. Predictably they were concerned to end it forever. Echoing the debate on the Wade Davis Bill, many Republicans made it clear that they doubted the legality of the President's Emancipation Proclamation. For the present, it depended on the army. If it became a judicial question in the future there were few doubts as to its fate in the state courts. It might fare little better in the Supreme Court. All in all it was too precarious a gauntlet to run. The courts could hold it for nothing. An incoming administration could reverse it. It applied only to a limited area in the South, and it did nothing to uproot slavery from state law. That would take more than Executive action.[11]

It would also take more than Congressional action according to Lincoln. Republicans had been aware of the problems of finding guarantees for permanent emancipation since 1862, when they experimented in the Confiscation Act of July 17th with the remedy of giving the freedman the right to a writ of habeas corpus from a federal court. The idea was dropped then, but revived in the Wade Davis Bill, which of course never became law. But it would not have resolved all constitutional doubts. In the Veto Message which Lincoln prepared but did not serve on the Confiscation Act, and then again in the veto message which he did issue on the Wade Davis Bill, the President expressed doubts as to the constitutional power of Congress to abolish slavery in the states.[12] The courts might well have shared his doubts. There was too, another loophole to the permanent extinction of the institution. The Congressional measures applied only to areas in rebellion. Residents of Alabama might still purchase slaves in Kentucky or Delaware. There was only one way to put the matter beyond constitutional doubts, one way to extinguish its roots in state law, one way to ensure against the whims of a court, or the passing political complexion of a President or Congress - a constitutional amendment.

The Thirteenth Amendment was complementary to the Emancipation Proclamation. Lincoln himself had no doubts about that. "The original proclamation has no constitution or legal justification, except as a military measure," he wrote to Salmon Chase in September 1863, when Chase suggested extending it to parts of Virginia and Louisiana under Union control.[13] Constitutional amendment was the only way to achieve lasting change. Lincoln suggested an amendment for gradual, compensated emancipation as early as 1862. In his veto message on the Wade Davis bill, doubting the powers of Congress to emancipate, he expressed his firm support for the proposed Thirteenth Amendment. When the resolution finally passed Congress, the New York Tribune reported the following account of Lincoln's remarks on the relationship between the Proclamation and the amendment:

> He thought all would bear him witness that he had never shrunk from doing all that he could to eradicate Slavery by issuing an emancipation proclamation. But that proclamation falls far short of what the amendment will be when fully consummated. A question might be raised whether the proclamation was valid. It might be added that it only aided those who came into our lines and that it was inoperative as to

> those who did not give themselves up, or that it would have no effect upon the children of the slaves born hereafter. In fact it would be urged that it did not meet the evil. But this amendment is a King's cure for all the evils. It winds the whole thing up.[14]

Years later, in 1882, the debate on the necessity for a constitutional amendment was re-opened, when an article by James C. Welling in the North American Review, denying the legal validity of the Emancipation Proclamation, sparked off a reply from one, Aaron Ferris, who disagreed.[15] The Thirteenth Amendment, he said, was unnecessary. Though the Supreme Court had never actually tested the Proclamation, there was every reason to believe that they would have sustained it, as they sustained "almost without exception," the other Presidential acts exercised under the war powers. He cited precedents for the abolition of slavery by proclamation. During the Revolution, the British commanders Sir Henry Clinton and Lord Dunsmore made use of proclamations to liberate slaves belonging to colonists. Mr. Ferris did not consider the freedom of the British commanders from the limitations of federalism, and the U.S. Constitution! He did, however, lose his own case for the superfluity of the Thirteenth Amendment, when he argued that the Proclamation was valid, "unless subsequently reversed, vacated, or modified by a superior tribunal" - which, he said, it hasn't been!

The Republicans wanted to remove the "ifs" and "maybes," and they were agreed that the only way to do it was by a constitutional amendment. As Trumbull argued, it would be difficult to show that this was unconstitutional, since the Constitution provided quite clearly for its own amendment. No such doubts were raised on the Republican side, except as to whether three-fourths of the states <u>then</u> represented in Congress should ratify it, as James Ashley argued, or three-fourths of <u>all</u> the states, which was Trumbull's argument, and the one which prevailed.[16] Clinging to straws, some Democrats argued that, as a State institution, slavery like marriage was not subject to amendment. Senator Hendricks of Indiana argued that slavery was especially immune from such interference, since it was a domestic institution existing prior to the adoption of the Constitution, and over which the states had delegated no power to the federal government. Only a unanimous vote of the states could abolish it. On the whole, however, arguments on the amendment had to be about whether it was morally right, or politically expedient, rather than about the correctness of the method.

Republicans were agreed on all three counts - its justice, expediency, and correctness. They were agreed that slavery must go. If they did not define what they meant by freedom they inferred it by their diagnosis of what other things slavery had deprived men of apart from locomotion. Senator Clark categorised the affront of slavery to liberty in familiar terms:

> She has bound men, women and children, robbed them, beat them, bruised and mangled them, burned and otherwise murdered them. To their cries she has turned a deaf ear, to their complaints shut the courts, and taken from them the powers to testify against their oppressor. She has compelled them to submit in silence and labor in tears. She has forbidden their instruction, and mocked them with the pretence she was christianizing them through suffering.[18]

When slavery was abolished, so too, in Clark's eyes, were these deprivations, giving way to the right to work for a living, to marry, to speak their minds, to testify, and maintain rights in a court of law. Senator Johnson spoke of the inalienable rights of <u>all</u> men, regardless of colour,[19] Representative Ingersoll of the free man's right to the fruits of his own labour and the enjoyment of his family ties, rights of which he could be robbed by no white man.[20]

The most explicit statement of a positive connection between freedom and rights, came from Charles Sumner in the Senate. On April 8th, 1864, he proposed an alternative form of the amendment, to read:

> All persons are equal before the law, so that no person can hold another as a slave; and the Congress shall have power to make all laws necessary and proper to carry this declaration into effect everywhere within the United States and the jurisdiction thereof.[21]

In a speech explaining his preference for this form, Sumner outlined his plan for the permanent abolition of slavery.[22] First, he said, it must be attacked through the courts. Though the prestige of the courts had sunk under the influence of slavery, now he thought, in this regenerated republic, they could be expected to interpret the Constitution on behalf of liberty. But action by the courts was not enough. Secondly, it was the duty of Congress to strike at slavery wherever they could, by abolishing the slave trade for example, or setting the nation's own house in order for equality before the law by passing the laws which he was at that very time proposing in the Senate, to establish the rights of coloured witnesses to testify in the federal courts.[23] Yet all this was not enough. Finally, it must be done by the people, in the form of an amendment to the Constitution. Anxious that this amendment should be expressed in its most effective and perfect form, he suggested the language of equality before the law, sketching its origins in the Greek language, and its present currency in European constitutions. It was, he said, not a phrase common in America, but:

> It will be felt at once that this expression, "equality before the law," gives precision to that idea of human rights which is enunciated in our Declaration of Independence.[24]

Sumner, then, quite explicitly brought to the meaning of freedom the concept of equality before the law, and an obligation on the part of the national government to extend its protection to all men in the service of that concept. Faced with the opposition of Senator Trumbull and his colleagues, however, Sumner withdrew his proposal the same day.

Three years later, this episode in the debate was alluded to in a Kentucky court case. The question at issue in Bowlin v Commonwealth was a Negro's right, under the 1866 Civil Rights Act, to give testimony against a white defendant.[25] The judge held that the Thirteenth Amendment was no basis for such legislation, since its framers intended only the abolition of slavery, not the guarantee of positive rights. Freedom did not make a former slave a competent witness, in violation of state laws on the subject. As evidence of this, he cited the hostile reception which Sumner's "equality before the law" substitute received in the Senate.

Certainly, Trumbull did express some scepticism about borrowing the phrase from foreign constitutions, particularly the French, which he said was a notably precarious instrument of government. It was unnecessary, when they had a perfectly clear American precedent at hand in the Northwest Ordinance of 1787, on which the Judiciary Committee had modelled the amendment.[26] Senator Howard's reaction is more instructive. His objections to Sumner's alternative wording was that it was meaningless in a legal and technical sense, a phrase unknown to a common law court. Why, he said, it might even be understood to mean that a woman would be the equal of her husband before the law! In conclusion, he remarked that the Northwest Ordinance was already well understood by the people, and "no court of justice, no magistrate, no person old or young, can misapprehend the meaning and effect of that clear, brief, and comprehensive clause[27]."

It is true that the language of the Ordinance had not been construed to associate civil rights with freedom. Many of the states to which it applied did not extend the equal protection of the laws to free Negroes. But

Senator Howard did not extol the virtues of "the good old Anglo-Saxon language employed by our fathers in the ordinance of 1787" as a device to restrict the amendment to abolishing only the physical trappings of slavery. In retrospect, when speaking on the Civil Rights Bill in 1866, which embodied Sumner's concept of equality before the law, he said that as a member of the Judiciary Committee which framed the Thirteenth Amendment, he knew that its "friends and advocates" had contemplated the possible use of the enacting clause which was now being made.[28] Perhaps it was the awful prospect of accidentally benefitting women rather than extending rights to blacks that persuaded Howard to stick to familiar phrases![29]

Further evidence of the unfamiliarity of some contemporaries with the phrase "equality before the law," comes from Attorney-General Bates' diary. On February 10th, 1864, he wrote of a previous attempt by Sumner to introduce the phrase into the amendment:

> 1. What is <u>equality before the law</u>?
> 2. Does <u>that equality</u> necessarily prevent the one from becoming the slave of the other? The ordinance of '87 and all the constitutions made in pursuance thereof, provide that persons may be sold in slavery <u>for crime</u> - is that repealed?[30]

A few months later, he was still confused, writing:

> Yet some zealous persons (and good withal) in order to intensify (and Frenchify) the thought, will have it (adding unwarrantably, to the words of the declaration) that men are created equal "before the law." Now, it is precisely <u>before the law</u>, that men are not equal; because, independent of their intrinsic qualities, the law takes pains to make them unequal. The son of 24, though, possibly, a wiser and better man than his father of fifty, is not eligible, as his father is, to either house of Congress or to the Presidency. And why not? Simply because the law says <u>no</u>. Whatever he may be, by nature, nurture, and virtue <u>before the law</u>, he is not his father's equal.[31]

But this was to confuse political with civil rights, and to confuse restrictions universally applied with those applied on grounds of race.

Republicans did not support the Thirteenth Amendment with a view to interfering with the electoral laws of the states. But in the debate on this resolution, and on the related subject of reconstruction, they did connect freedom with the rights of man, the inalienable rights of life, liberty and the pursuit of happiness. All men must be equal before the law in their right to these. If the phrase was unfamiliar, the idea was not. And Sumner was quick to drop it, yielding to the opposition of his colleagues, saying that the most homely text containing the rule would be more beautiful than any words of eloquence. He apparently did not consider that the Judiciary Committee's version excluded the rule or restricted Congressional action in making it good.

The extension of the idea that a free man had rights, and that he was equal in them with others before the law, was the Lockean principle that governments were instituted among men to maintain their natural and inalienable rights. By the Thirteenth Amendment, Congress had power to enforce its guarantee of freedom by "appropriate legislation." Democrats had no doubts as to what that meant. Representative Mallory charged the Republicans with the intention of using the enacting clause to invade the reserved rights of the states, and protect the Negro against state laws and actions which infringed his "rights[32]." Beyond that, Democratic opponents of the measure were very much alive to the political consequences of the amendment. With the vestiges of slavery removed from the Constitution, the rule that a slave was three-fifths of a man for the purposes of representation would also be abolished, and southern representation subsequently increased. So, said Democrat Edgerton, no man who knew the motives of the party in power would doubt that their policy in passing the resolution was first, to make the negro a citizen, second to protect him everywhere in defiance of existing state laws and constitutions, and finally, make him a voting citizen.[33] Complaints and prophecies of this kind were standard Democratic fare.

The lack of stout denials from the Republicans has been interpretated by Jacobus TenBroek as signifying agreement. He writes that the debate reveals:

> that the proponents of the measure intended thereby a revolution in federalism; that the opponents of the amendment understood that intended purpose and made it virtually the sole basis of their opposition to the amendment; that the amendment was passed by Congress in the face of the well-articulated fear that it would revolutionize the federal system .... that is, with complete agreement between proponents and opponents as to its effect.[34]

Undoubtedly the Republican majority could not conceive of a free man's life being anything other than one in which he enjoyed fundamental, natural rights. They did not define precisely what these were - even if they could have - because to do so would have limited freedom to what it meant in 1865. Instead they believed that freedom grew in lives rather than lists and that "inalienable" rights could only be secured by reference to what threatened to make then alienable in practice. If people remained unfree after slavery was abolished, that would be the time to identify precisely what stood between them and freedom, and to provide remedies.[35]

That was why the Thirteenth amendment had an enforcement clause. The debate did not focus on its possible uses in circumstances where Southern legislatures might attempt to hold freedmen in new forms of servitude short of bondage. It is unlikely that Republicans would spend much time talking about how states could not be trusted to respect a constitutional amendment when they had expended so much energy on getting such an amendment because the states could not be trusted to respect anything else! But it hardly betokens "a poor comprehension of social behaviour." Even Democrats were aware of the Negro's uncertain future. "Dispose of the slavery question and the negro question remains" was Democrat Yeaman's warning to the House during discussion of the Wade Davis Bill.[36] Reconstruction debates make it quite plain that the Republicans had very real reservations about white Southern intentions and would not be satisfied until political arrangements were achieved which assured both loyalty and a commitment to equality under law. The Thirteenth Amendment debate should not be treated in a vacuum as though it had nothing to do with what they were trying to achieve in the states. Republican Orth argued, like many of his colleagues,for an expansive Congressional power to provide proper guards and checks for the protection of individual rights in these communities, to keep a guardianship over them as long as necessary, and to see that both the name and spirit of slavery was erased from every state constitution. To both slaveholder and slave, he concluded, the government's duty was "giving to each equal protection under law.[37]"

The Democrats thus sang an old song about the invasion of state rights and the hazards of 'enforcement' .... at least so far as the South was concerned. What seems to suggest that this was anything about their arguments with respect to Section 2 of the amendment which compelled Republicans to take more notice was that their votes counted on this occasion, and the amendment applied to every state. Unlike territorialisation or the guarantee clause it was a permanent grant of power.

In all probability the Democrats who voted "Yea" in January 1865 were convinced that slavery's final hour had come and, like Senator John Henderson of Missouri were simply not "deterred from doing an act of simple justice from fear of the consequences[38]." Whatever pressures were brought to bear to win or buy their votes, a promise not to use the enforcement clause was not one of them. Nor is there reason to suppose that those who voted "Nay" hovered on the brink of "Yea" and would have done so had clause 2 been omitted.

It mattered that the amendment applied to the whole Union. So did the Habeas Corpus Act which conservatives had also dubbed a harbinger of federal revolution. During the debate Republicans avoided reference to racially discriminatory laws in states like Ohio, Indiana, Delaware and Maryland, though in 1866 much more was to be said about the potential incompatibility of some of these laws with the Civil Rights Act. By way of assurance Trumbull and others pointed out then that no state had anything to fear unless it fell short of compliance with federal law.[39] It was not until 1866 that laws which prevented Negroes giving testimony, or restricted their property and contract rights were explicitly put into this category. The space between the passage of the Thirteenth amendment and the Civil Rights Act of 1866 was where understandings of what tools a man needed to be free grew in response to circumstances. Many Northern states did not wait for Congress to fill that space with legislation but began, albeit patchily, to set their own houses in order as part of a wider reform process which has been called "self-reconstruction. Although racism was by no means confined south of the Mason-Dixon line, there was a growing sense in the North that time had caught up with overtly unequal laws which deprived "free" Negroes of basic civil rights, just as surely as it had caught up with slavery. While suffrage battles were lost in most of these states between 1865 and 1869 there were other advances in their allocation of citizenship rights. Illinois, despite a long record of discrimination was the first to ratify the amendment and promptly began to erase black laws from the statute book. Massachusetts Republicans passed the nation's first public accommodation law in 1865. Philadelphia desegregated the street cars after an unsuccessful legal battle to achieve the same had been thwarted by the state Supreme Court. Iowa's Supreme Court led the way to desegregate schools and public accommodation.[40] Much remained to be done, of course, but self-righteous or not the feeling in these states was that they had nothing to fear from a constitutional amendment that abolished slavery and empowered Congress to pass "appropriate legislation."

Of course Trumbull and his colleagues on the Senate Judiciary Committee were deeply imbued with States rights constitutionalism. There was never an occasion when they crossed state boundaries without agonising over the constitutional proprieties governing interactions between federal and state law. But not crossing them was far more dangerous. Preferring that the states themselves do the work of giving freedom content, restoring loyal governments, or respecting the indemnification of Union officers, they would nevertheless "take on" those who did not. They would do it by bridgeheads rather than invasions, by providing rights and remedies triggered by state shortfalls and failures rather than by occupying the whole ground of states rights in everyday law. There ought to be a better word than "federal revolution" to describe it, one that would take account of this conservatism but still acknowledge how far they were prepared to redefine federal responsibilities for freedom. Perhaps it is reform.

Whatever use of the enforcement clause they had in mind with respect to freedom, however, the charge of some Democrats that they intended to make Negroes "voting citizens" was wide of the mark. Surprisingly little was said on the Republican side about the effects of emancipation on Southern representation in Congress. In his Introduction to the Constitutional Law of the United States John Norton Pomeroy took this as evidence that the problem was probably overlooked at the time the amendment was adopted.[41] Yet, if the Democrats were so aware of the effects of the abolition of the three-fifths rule on the distribution of power, it is unlikely that the Republicans were not equally so. Shortly after the passage of the resolution in the House on January 31st, 1865, Senator Sumner introduced a proposal for a reapportionment amendment.[42] The subject, however, was not taken up until the Thirty-Ninth Congress. The Republicans would not risk passage of the amendment by drawing attention to the touchy subject of black suffrage, an objective to which neither the party nor the Northern people were as yet committed. In a negative way, they were not prepared to say that freedom might bring the Negro no political rights. Kentucky Senator Garret Davis' outrageous proposal to add a proviso to the amendment that no person whose mother or grandmother was a Negro could be a citizen of the United States or eligible for office was, not surprisingly, voted down by 28 votes to 6.[43] But as yet, they were not prepared to make a positive assertion that political rights were a condition of freedom. In the same Congress they had deliberately omitted a proposal for open suffrage in the Wade Davis bill, to avoid risking its passage, and refrained from pressing the issue in the bill to provide a temporary government for Montana for the same reason. In 1865, it was not expected that the Thirteenth Amendment would do the work of the Fifteenth. Time and, once again, events separated the two.

On April 8th, 1864, the resolution passed in the Senate with a comfortable margin of 38 votes to 6. In the House vote on June 15th, the vote was 93 in favour, 65 against - short of the necessary two-thirds. But when the resolution was called up again on January 31st, 1865, it passed by 119 votes to 56. A full Republican turnout, the vote of the Speaker, and the 'Yeas' of seventeen Democrats and Unionists, with eight useful Democratic abstentions, gave it the necessary two-thirds majority. A number of events had occurred between the first vote and the second, to explain this change of heart.

As Sherman marched across the South, it was clear that victory was at hand. It could no longer be argued that passage of the amendment would prevent the South from laying down their arms and offering to return to the Union. It was too late to save their slaves. Already, in the abortive peace negotiations in the autumn of 1864, it was clear both that the Confederacy was unwilling to make terms of any kind, and that Lincoln did not propose to offer any that did not include emancipation.[44] Military success decided the issue. The Democrat, Samuel Sullivan Cox did claim, however, that he came to the House that morning prepared to vote for the resolution and changed his mind when he heard that peace messengers from the South were on their way to see General Grant.[45] A likely story! But, for the Republicans, it was much too late to be sensitive to Southern wishes.

Signs of change from the border states, too, in the autumn of 1864, made Republicans less uneasy about the effect of the amendment on opinion there. In October, Maryland opted for voluntary emancipation. If the example was followed by the rest of the border states, as it seemed likely that it would, the amendment would not damage their electoral prospects there.

President Lincoln's support for the measure may have been useful in persuading some Democrats to vote for it or abstain. The President's Annual Message of December 6th, 1864 strongly recommended its passage.[46] But he had already declared his support for it on June 9th, 1864 at the Baltimore Convention, a few days before Congress failed to approve it by the necessary two-thirds. The difference in December, and the most important factor was that he then spoke from a position of strength, after a successful election. The people had endorsed a President and a party who both supported the amendment. Lincoln was able to point out that it was only a matter of time before the increased majority of Republicans in the Thirty-Ninth Congress would pass it.

The vote itself was exciting. Samuel Cox recorded, "Every Republican is in his seat, and for the amendment[47]." There was a feat for party organisation! James G. Blaine attributed it to the behind-the-scenes efforts of the skilful parliamentarian James Ashley, who had charge of the resolution in the House.[48]

The behaviour of the Democratic party is the subject of some speculation. Six Democrats who voted "Nay" in June, absented themselves from the vote in January. Several observers agree that it was deliberate, and represented a tacit approval of the amendment.[49] Three Democrats who abstained on the first vote, voted 'Yea' on the second. More strikingly, eleven Democrats and Unionists changed their votes from Nay to Yea. Eighty-two percent of those who changed their vote were "lameduck" Congressmen. One possible explanation is that, with no constituency pressures to fear, these men might be more likely to exercise independent judgment on the vote. The significance of this statistic however, pales when a similar analysis is made of the whole Democratic party. Over two-thirds of them were "lameducks" and did not change their votes. The intervening election probably was significant, to the extent that it did demonstrate the will of the nation, to which Representatives must have been sensitive.

Several other contemporary sources suggest a different common factor among those who changed their votes, or abstained. Charles Dana recalls his part in persuading three Democrats, two from New York, and one from New Jersey, to vote for the amendment resolution.[50] He was told, he said, to give them what they wanted. Two wanted internal revenue collection appointments at their disposal, the other an important appointment to the New York custom house on behalf of a Republican. Samuel Cox alleged that Republican party funds were behind Democratic votes.[51] Certainly they made use of patronage and "influence." Republican Representative Albert G. Riddle, from Ohio recollected some of these manoeuvres:

> A New Yorker greatly desired a federal place in New York; he had a brother, a Democrat, in the House, who was assured that his vote for the abolishing amendment would largely augment his brother's chances. There was also a contest for a seat in the next House - a Democrat in the present House was a party to that contest; he came to see that the result would depend entirely upon his vote on the impending 13th Amendment. It was found necessary to secure the absence of one Democrat from the House on the day of the vote. A railroad in Pennsylvania was threatened with the passage of a bill by Congress greatly adverse to its interests - the bill was in Mr. Sumner's hands, ready to be reported; the road had struggled to have action

on the bill <u>deferred till the next Congress</u> – thus far without avail. The lawyer for the railroad was a Democratic member of the present House.[52]

Secretary of State William Seward had a lobby working for the amendment. It included W.N. Bilbo of Nashville, George O. Jones, and Richard Schell, hard at work to get the support of New York Democrats. That there was a price, perhaps even of a political rather than material nature, is suggested by John and La Wanda Cox. Seward was never negligent of his own political interests, and they suggest that he used the shifting alliances at the time of the amendment, to build up a conservative coalition. They conclude:

> In plain words, Seward in pursuing Democratic votes for the Amendment had let it be understood that there would follow a generous policy of peace and reconstruction, and that there would be a secure political berth for moderate Democrats in a new Conservative coalition.[53]

Seward's correspondence with Governor Perry of South Carolina, over the meaning of the enacting clause, lends further weight to this view. The Governor wired the President that he feared the clause would give the federal government control over the race question. Seward replied on November 6th, 1865, assuring him that his fears were groundless, that "... the clause is really restraining in its effect, instead of enlarging the powers of Congress." The President, he said, considered South Carolina's ratification as indispensable to her restoration to the Union. Nevertheless, South Carolina, Florida, Alabama and Georgia tacked on provisos to their ratifications, to the effect that any attempt by Congress to legislate on the political status or civil relations of the former slaves would be contrary to the Constitution, even as amended.[54] These conditions were rejected. Seward's statement that the powers of Congress were restrained, however, must be explained in the context of his political ambitions. It was not the meaning of the Thirteenth Amendment which most of his Republican colleagues in Congress would have given.

Georgia's ratification of the amendment on December 6th, 1865, gave it the necessary three-fourths vote of the states, and Seward proclaimed the amendment ratified on December 18th. Johnson's insistence that acceptance of the amendment was a condition of restoration, assured the votes of the Southern States. Even if their assent was half-hearted, it was better to accept Johnson's terms than be left to the mercies of the Congressional Republicans. Most of the Southern states ratified it by the time of Seward's proclamation, though Mississippi rejected it on December 2nd, 1865 and Texas delayed ratification until February 1870. The admission of Nevada to the Union was seen as a device to secure an extra vote for ratification. Charles Dana quotes Lincoln as saying, "It is easier to admit Nevada than to raise another million of soldiers[55]." In the end, Nevada's vote did not prove so crucial, though it might have done.

It was now up to the courts to interpret the meaning of the amendment. By that time, however, formal freedom was a fait accompli. Slaves did not seek a writ of habeas corpus. Masters did not sue to recover the body of the former slave. But they did sue to recover his price. The dockets of the state courts were full of cases where promissory notes for slaves had been given by purchasers while slavery was legal under state law. Now they pleaded emancipation as a defence against paying the original owner. The issue was complicated by the fact that almost all the new Southern state constitutions, approved by Congress, contained clauses prohibiting state courts from taking jurisdiction of contracts involving notes on slaves since abolition had rendered such contracts void. Pressures to maintain continuity and respect the sanctity of contracts, however, competed with a natural desire to wash hands of slavery. The war could not cut through legitimate contractual relationship without incurring risks to social and economic order and trust. No state could impair the obligation of contracts. The case for making an exception of promissory notes on slaves had to rest on something more than moral disdain. Although these cases have little relevance to the relationship between freedom and civil rights they nevertheless give some insight into judicial attachments to traditional state roles in private law matters.

The Supreme Courts of Georgia, Florida, Alabama, Arkansas, South Carolina and Kentucky structured arguments for the validity of slave contracts entered into prior to emancipation, and in one case even after the Emancipation Proclamation had been issued! That was in McElvain v Mudd in 1870, when Judge Peck spoke for Alabama's Supreme Court to the effect that a promissory note made in February 1864 in a state of admitted "uncertainty" was valid under state law at the time and the purchaser must honour it.[56] Small wonder that Republicans had doubted the legal effects of Lincoln's Proclamation!

The Arkansas Supreme Court's ruling in Jacoway v Denton was representative of many cases in which contracts were upheld, State constitutions notwithstanding.[57] Judge Gregg held that the provision in Arkansas' 1868 constitution which nullified slave contracts was unconstitutional in that it impaired the obligation of contracts. The note was binding under the laws in existence at the time it was made and there was no legal distinction between contracts for the sale of slaves and any other contracts. Though the contract stated that the slave was a slave for life, the purchaser and not the seller must bear the risk of any change in the status of the slave due to accident, death, an act of God, or emancipation. Such an argument even persuaded the Supreme Court of the free state of Illinois on one occasion. In _Roundtree v Baker_ the court held a promissory note on a slave valid in the face of the Thirteenth Amendment on the grounds that it had a duty to respect the laws of the state at the time and place it was entered into (i.e. Kentucky) rather than where it was enforced.[58]

Not all state courts followed this line of argument. Louisiana's Supreme Court was a notable exception. Judge Taliaferro argued in two 1867 cases, _Austin v Sandel_ and _Wainwright v Bridges_ that emancipation had not only put an end to slavery but also all contracts based on it.[59] The prohibition against impairing contracts had no application to the sovereign power which prohibited slavery.

The United States Supreme Court chose continuity, and affirmed that promissory notes on slaves made under _ante bellum_ laws had to be honoured by purchasers. In _White v Hart_ and _Osborn v Nicholson_ in 1871 the Court reversed decisions from Georgia and Arkansas respectively which had denied the validity of promissory notes.[60] Justice Swayne argued that by the time the Thirteenth Amendment was adopted the rights of the purchaser had become vested, and "Right acquired by a deed, will, or contract of marriage, or other contract according to statutes subsequently repealed subsist afterwards as they were before, in all respects as if the statutes were still in full force." To do otherwise would be to take away a man's property without due process. Nor could state constitutions invalidate the contracts. Though approved by Congress, these constitutions violated the contract clause of the U.S. Constitution. Chief Justice Chase, finding his long-held belief that slaves could never have been the subject of property contracts in conflict with his enthusiasm for continuity and legitimacy in private law, was the lone dissenter in both cases. In his view these contracts were against sound morals and natural justice, and the laws which once supported them were annulled by the Thirteenth Amendment. But, for his colleagues, where the price and not the body of the slave was the issue, the Thirteenth Amendment and the new state constitutions had altered nothing.[61] The courts on the whole preferred to ignore abstract morality in favour of contractual stability and continuity.

In some cases the principle was extended to give freedmen the benefit of welfare provisions in wills which had been drawn up under the assumption that slave laws would continue in perpetuity. The Supreme Court of Kentucky magnanimously decreed that slaves freed "prematurely" by the Thirteenth Amendment were nonetheless entitled to the legacy of two hundred dollars each which was to have been theirs when they were manumitted by a man's will on his wife's death. What's more, they no longer had to leave the country in order to enjoy it.[62] On at least one occasion, however, the Thirteenth Amendment worked a positive harm to freedmen. In 1868 the same Kentucky court held that the amendment destroyed the obligation of the master towards the slave as well as his right to his labour. It negated the provisions of a will for the care and burial of former slaves "and placed them where all other free paupers belong, as a charge on the public charity[63]."

But the courts also had plenty of opportunity to pass upon the substantive meaning of the amendment when they came to adjudicate cases under the various civil rights laws which Congress passed in pursuance of its declaration of freedom. What rights were inherent in freedom? What kind of legislation was "appropriate" to protect it? Could the federal government protect the individual, black or white, under it, only against discriminatory state action, or could they reach the individual violator?

John Jay wrote enthusiastically to Chief Justice Chase, of his high expectations of the Court in answering these questions:

> The decision which I most wish to see pronounced by your Court is that the adoption of the Amendment abolishing slavery has destroyed the only exception recognized by the Constitution to the great principle of the Declaration of Independence and that from the date of the adoption of the amendment all persons black and white stand upon an equal footing, that all State legislation establishing or recognizing distinction of race or colour are void.[64]

But the courts were not to live up to these expectations. At first it looked as if they might. Two decisions in the lower federal courts in 1866 took a broad view of freedom under the amendment, and Congress' power to guarantee it by the Civil Rights Act of 1866. The issue in U.S. v Rhodes was the right of a coloured witness to testify against a white defendant in a criminal case, a right secured under the provisions of the 1866 Civil Rights Act but contrary to Kentucky state law.[65] Justice Swayne was sympathetic to the accord between the amendment and the act, pointing to the continuity between the membership of the two Congresses which passed them. Unlike other amendments to the Constitution he said, this one trenched on the power of the states and the people of the states. It made the former slave free and gave him rights. The same year, on circuit in Maryland, Chief Justice Chase held, in the case of Turner, that the terms of certain indentures holding Elizabeth Turner in apprenticeship to her former master violated the Thirteenth amendment and the Civil Rights Act.[66] They would have kept her in virtual slavery. Thus a private contract, sanctioned by Maryland's racially discriminatory apprenticeship laws, was invalid.

These two cases in 1866 set the compass for judicial interpretation. They confirmed that the Thirteenth Amendment enlarged the power of Congress to eradicate slavery and its "incidents" and that in doing so it reached the conduct of individuals as well as states. Although the federal courts continued to acknowledge these two features what happened was that the "incidents" of slavery came to be severely restricted and "state action" spilled over from the Fourteenth amendment to dull the effect of the Thirteenth on private wrongs. Aside from a handful of maverick cases it was not until 1968 that the Supreme Court put a broad understanding of its meaning back into harness with an equally broad understanding of its reach, and rediscovered the Thirteenth amendment.[67]

As to content, the warmest affirmations of the inherent correlation between freedom and rights in the 1870's came from dissenting opinions and the arguments of Counsel on the losing side. When the thorny issue of black testimony in Kentucky reached the Supreme Court in the test case of Blyew v U.S. in 1871, it was federal attorney Benjamin Bristow who argued that the Thirteenth amendment had "worked a radical change in the condition of the United States[68]." It was, he said, unreasonable to suppose that its framers meant to give freedmen only the small share of freedom enjoyed by free blacks, for:

> In this age no man can be called free who is denied the right to make contracts, sue and be sued, and to give evidence in courts. No man is really free who is not protected by law, from injury. So long as he is denied the right to testify against those who violate his person or his property he has no protection, and is denied the power to defend his own freedom.

But when Justice Strong gave the court's opinion that it had no jurisdiction because the black woman, Lucy, was dead and beyond being affected by the denial of black testimony against her murderers, it was dissenters

Bradley and Swayne who kept faith with original intent and argued a broader purpose. In Bradley's words, "The power to enforce the amendment by appropriate legislation must be a power to do away with the incidents and consequences of slavery, and to instate the freedmen in the full enjoyment of that civil liberty and equality which the abolition of slavery meant."

In the Slaughterhouse Cases, it was dissenter Field who approvingly quoted Senator Trumbull on the relationship between freedom and rights, and described the Fourteenth amendment as a proper supplement to the Thirteenth.[69] But it was Miller for the Court who inferred that the Thirteenth Amendment only abolished slavery. It reduced the significance of his acknowledgment that the amendment tapped "the great source of power in this country, the people of the states, for additional guarantees of human rights; additional power to the Federal government; additional restraints upon those of the states." What a power to have no use for!

If there was any heroism in dissent it was short-lived. In 1879 Justice Field dissented in ex Parte Virginia to one of the few broad interpretations of the Thirteenth Amendment after Slaughterhouse. Countering Strong's assertion that the amendments were intended to bring freedmen "into perfect equality of civil rights with all other persons" he reminded the Court of the immediate circumstances of its adoption, and that its purpose was to end slavery and allow the Negro to earn the fruits of his labour. "The people in adopting them did not suppose they were altering the fundamental theory of their dual system of government," he objected.[70]

Other federal judges suffered from contracting vision during these years. William Woods initially upheld the government's power under the civil war amendments to reach both state and individual deprivations of rights. The case was United States v Hall, in the Alabama federal circuit court in 1871, and the issue was the state's failure to protect citizens in their right to free speech and association in face of a conspiracy to deny them.[71] Just three years later he would deny the power of Congress to reach private violations of civil rights under the Enforcement Act of May 31st, 1870.[72] His argument, that where an act of Congress was directed against the action of individuals and not of the states, the law was broader than the amendment on which it purported to rest, was the one which ultimately triumphed on the Supreme Court, at least with respect to the Enforcement Acts. Woods joined the Court in 1880 and two years later had the pleasure of transplanting his own arguments from the lower courts to strike down Section 2 of the 1871 Enforcement Act, which like the 1870 act was parented by the Thirteenth Amendment and punished private violations of federally guaranteed rights. That was in U.S. v Harris where an armed mob had been indicted for murdering a black and beating others whom they had taken out of the sheriff's custody in Tennessee.[73]

Justice Bradley evolved a different view of the potential reach of the Thirteenth Amendment, beginning with the 1866 Civil Rights Act. Already in the early seventies state court opinions on the act had begun to infer a "state action" limitation. Judge Temple argued in dicta in the California case of The People v Brady that "the apparent purpose of the amendment was not to prevent the illegal duress of individuals. It was aimed exclusively at the institution of slavery as established by the laws of the States[74]." On circuit in Texas, Bradley turned his mind to the point. In Texas v Gaines in 1874 he denied a right of removal under the Civil Rights Act to a defendant indicted for bigamy in the Lafayette County Court, who claimed he couldn't get a fair trial on account of local prejudice. "We think," said Bradley, " [the act] is intended to protect against local disabilities and legal impediments to the free exercise of the rights secured, and not by private infringement of those rights by prejudice or otherwise when the laws themselves are impartial and sufficient[75]." The passage was cited approvingly by other federal courts and Bradley himself confirmed it in Ex parte Wells on the grounds that the language of the Civil Rights Act embraced "law, statute, ordinance, regulation or custom" and limited its reach to private individuals acting under hostile state legislation.[76]

That Bradley had not intended to infer a "state action" limitation on the Thirteenth amendment itself may be deduced from his opinions on the Enforcement Acts and the Civil Rights Act of 1875, all of which directly operated on individuals, whether acting under state laws or not. It was his disagreement with Judge Woods over whether racially motivated violence by lawless combinations was punishable under the Force Act of 1870 that had taken the issue to the Supreme Court in U.S. v Cruikshank. Although Bradley concurred in dismissing the indictments for lack of a showing of racial motivation, he did not argue that private conspiracies were beyond the reach of the Thirteenth Amendment. His most classic statement of the enforcement potential of the amendment was in The Civil Rights Cases:

> Under the Thirteenth Amendment, the legislation, so far as necessary or proper to eradicate all forms and incidents of slavery and involuntary servitude, may be direct and primary, operating upon the acts of individuals, whether sanctioned by State legislation or not.[77]

The price of this insight was a narrow reading of freedom. In his opinion the Civil Rights Act of 1875, which provided that all persons were entitled to equal access to inns, public conveyances and places of amusement was not "appropriate" to the eradication of slavery's "badges and incidents," since the purpose of the amendment was to vindicate "those fundamental rights which appertain to the essence of citizenship." They did not include social rights. It was left to Justice Harlan in dissent to defend the organic concept of freedom which Republicans began with in 1865.

Thereafter, outside Harlan's brilliant dissents, few lights shone. The case of U.S. v Morris in the district court of Arkansas in 1903 was not typical.[78] The defendants, who were charged with conspiring to injure and oppress black citizens in their right to lease and cultivate lands, challenged the constitutionality of the Civil Rights Act. The Court sustained the Act and argued that it was quite appropriately based on the Thirteenth Amendment rather than the Fourteenth since it extended protection against individual infringements. The right to lease and cultivate land was fundamental to freedom. "Shall the courts," asked the judge, "be less liberal in construing constitutional provisions in favour of freedom than those in favour of slavery?" The answer was Yes. Two years later the Supreme Court appeared to pronounce a death sentence on the amendment's fragile hold on life. The case was Hodges v United States, the issue a conspiracy to deprive black workers of their right to perform work they had contracted to do.[79] Justice Brewer denied that the case presented a violation of a federal right under the Civil Rights Act. He agreed that the Thirteenth Amendment acted upon individuals but only to effect this limited "freedom:"

> The meaning [of the Thirteenth amendment] is as clear as language can make it. The things denounced are slavery and involuntary servitude and Congress is given power to enforce that denunciation. All understand by these terms a condition of enforced compulsory service of one to another.

This was even further away from freedom than Bradley in the Civil Rights Cases. It completed the work begun in Slaughterhouse of relegating the Thirteenth amendment to the sidelines of constitutional history.

In the sidelines it had its victories against peonage and against tribal slavery. When an Indian defendant in In re Sah Quah claimed that both he and his "slave" belonged to a tribal culture whose customs permitted slavery, the District Court of Alaska held they were subject to the Thirteenth amendment and released the man on a writ of *habeas corpus*.[80] There was no escaping "services" which were owed to the state, however, such as services to the army, the militia, on the jury, or even working on public roads near one's home if the state so ordered.[81] But the state could not compel a man to labour for another to pay off a debt.[82]

Congress had wider horizons, higher hopes in 1865. It was not that they aspired to design a Utopia in which there were no distinctions among men. But they did intend to remove from the real world all obstacles to being free. In time, if new obstacles appeared, they would clear them. But time was not on their side. By the 1870's the courts had begun to place a few obstacles on the course themselves. They stood one step further away from Congress in contemplating federal revolution. The Supreme Court recognised the validity of slave contracts made under *ante bellum* laws - for the sake of stability and continuity. They shrank from using the amendment to strike down discriminatory and unequal laws, or to reach individual violations of civil rights. There was, of course, a time lag between the adoption of the legislation and litigation in the courts. By the 1870's, most Northerners were as anxious to return to peace and quiet as the "old men" of the bench were. The possibilities of profound change had been within reach, but they were prepared to go only so far and no further.

CHAPTER 6

Standing on the Threshold of Citizenship - but what is it?

All men were to be free. Free - few words in any language could be so elusive of definition or description. But if philosophers could take a lifetime to speculate on its meaning, events set a more urgent timetable for the Thirty-Ninth Congress. Clarity was a luxury enjoyed only by those who believed that the Thirteenth Amendment meant nothing more than the absence of chattel slavery and the right of a man to a writ of *habeas corpus* if anyone tried to hold him in that condition. But the majority of Republicans who believed that it encompassed a dynamic condition of freedom were explorers in their own land. It was only in using their own freedom as a compass for those who enjoyed it for the first time that they discovered what ill-charted and changing terrain they were in. White Americans were accustomed to living under two governments, nation and state, as citizens of both. They believed that as citizens twice over they enjoyed rights. But beyond pious affirmations there had not been a great deal of systematic thought given either to the content of citizenship or to the relative responsibilities of state and nation for its maintenance.

When Attorney-General Bates was asked for an opinion in 1862 as to whether or not free Negroes were United States citizens, he wrote of a

> fruitless search in our law books and the records of our courts for a clear and satisfactory definition of the phrase *citizen of the United States*..... For ought that I see to the contrary, the subject is now as little understood in its details and elements, and the question as open to argument and speculative criticism as it was at the beginning of the Government. Eighty years of practical enjoyment of citizenship, under the Constitution, have not sufficed to teach us either the exact meaning of the word, or the constituent elements of the thing we prize so highly.[1]

Even with respect to who were United States citizens, Bates was right. The simple and clear declaration later made in the Fourteenth Amendment that "all persons born or naturalized in the United States and subject to the jurisdiction thereof, are citizens of the United States and of the State wherein they reside" was eighty years in the making. It put to rest a difference of opinion among Bates' predecessors in the Attorney-General's office on the point, as well as alternatives which had flourished in ante-bellum Southern state courts and borne poisonous fruit in the U.S. Supreme Court's Dred Scott opinion.[2] Chief Justice Taney denied that free Negroes could be citizens of the United States, even if their home states had made them state citizens. He had not always taken such a bifurcated view of citizenship. Dissenting in the Passenger Cases in 1849 he had argued that "every citizen of a State is also a citizen of the United States[3]." The imperative of distinguishing between white and black Americans, however, led him to abandon any automatic correlation and turn to history instead to freeze United States citizenship in the alleged white preferences of the framers. Thus, he wrote, when the Constitution was framed, those who were citizens of states became citizens of the nation. But that result could not have been intended to include blacks who "were at that time considered as a subordinate and inferior class of beings, who had been subjugated by the dominant race, and, whether emancipated or not, yet remained subject to their authority, and had no rights or privileges but such as those who held the power and the government might choose to grant them." It was not true. Free blacks had enjoyed civil and in some cases political rights. Not only did this "most egregious mis-statement of his long opinion" deny Negroes original citizenship of the nation, but it shut the door against promotion to that status.[4] Even if a State conferred citizenship on its black inhabitants thereafter, it would not elevate them to national citizenship since the States could not introduce new members to the nation. Congress possessed the sole power of naturalisation. History has heaped enough hot coals on Taney's logic as well as the racism which perverted it. It is cited here only as confirmation of Bates' point about how muddied the concept of citizenship was. It was not just neglect, however, but the agility of legal minds in seeking alternatives to simpler concepts like universal, birthright citizenship in order to exclude blacks which put the first obstacle to clarity in the way. And so it was with the matter of what rights attached to being an American citizen.

Prior to the Civil War it was in 1787 that white Americans last thought so intensively about the ingredients of freedom and at that time they looked to secure it more by wise political arrangements than by lists. The colonists' struggle for independence from the British led them to believe that great danger lay in clothing any government, or any part of government with power enough to deprive a man of his liberty. The genius of the Constitution was thought to be its great institutional checks and balances which released enough power at all levels to govern effectively, but not enough to do so in an arbitrary or tyrannical way. All power was limited by the ultimate sovereignty of the people, expressed in the fundamental law of the Constitution. Nowhere in that document did the people lodge a power to infringe their natural rights to the enjoyment of life, liberty and property. It was an institutional way of looking at rights. If the body politic was safe from despotism, then by reference, in the best of all possible worlds, so too was the body of the individual.[5]

It followed that since governments lacked the power to infringe fundamental rights, there was no real reason to spell them out. Individual liberty was well enough taken care of in the working parts of the Constitution, in the stated purposes of its Preamble and in its specific prohibitions on titles of nobility, _ex post facto laws_ and bills of attainder, as well as its guarantee of the _habeas corpus_ writ in normal times. That was the argument of Alexander Hamilton and the Federalists who had no use for a Bill of Rights. The addition of the first ten amendments in 1791 was a concession to those who had doubts as to whether an as yet untried and untested battery of checks and balances was sufficient security for individual rights against the tendency of governments in the real world to seek rather than deny themselves power. But the Bill of Rights was an additional safeguard, never offered as a definitive description of the rights of American citizens. Even if such a perfect statement had been within the linguistic reach of its framers they would not have considered it either necessary or wise. The classic statement that rights were not so reducible and that the Bill of Rights were a selection, rather than the whole, was the Ninth Amendment's reservation, "The enumeration in the Constitution of certain rights, shall not be construed to deny or disparage others retained by the people."

While rights remained "out there," their fate and that of the ones they chose to mention, would continue to depend to a large extent on whether Hamilton was right that the living and growing space for Americans' freedom inhered in the Constitution's political arrangements. It was only when legislatures, courts, and executives of both nation and state took their part in making a living instrument out of a collection of words that its adequacy for the protection of rights would be put to the test. As that happened, political conditions changed. The progressive extension of the franchise to all white American men altered the way they thought about their rights from a "representative" democracy in which all citizens enjoyed rights but only some voted, to a "participatory" democracy in which the hallmark of being a "full citizen" was the right of suffrage. The exercise of the vote came to be seen as the key instrument which made the checks and balances work, and which made governments careful of the rights of their citizens.

The second major change in the political dynamics of the new nation was that although the Bill of Rights had been attached to the Constitution primarily out of a fear that the nation was the likeliest threat to individual rights, in practice this turned out not to be so. The way power and responsibilities were distributed between state and nation in the first seventy years, the Bill of Rights was never called to the frontline to correct the balance within the federal system of an overmighty national government outgrowing its checks and balances. The nation was given so little to do and the states so much. And yet the situation where it might be the states and not the nation which posed the more significant threat to fundamental rights had been anticipated by so few.[6]

The idea that local environments provided the ripest conditions for the nurturing of freedom through participation triumphed in the politics of states rights. The nation was assigned a vitually non-existent role in the daily incidents of citizenship most likely to test the Bill of Rights. Guarantees of a speedy and fair public trial, immunity from double jeopardy, self-incrimination and so on had little relevance as a limitation on the nation because there was so little federal criminal law. Even where Congress did make some crimes federal, such as the murder of a United States marshal, robbing the mails, or counterfeiting, it enlisted the aid of state courts for enforcement.[7] What was true of the rights surrounding trial and punishment was also true of search and seizure. As Jacob Landynski found in tracing the history of the Fourth Amendment, "Like some other Bill of Rights provisions [it] remained for almost a century a largely unexplored territory. One does not have to seek far to find the reason. Until the latter part of the nineteenth century, the criminal jurisdiction of the federal government was seldom exercised by Congress[8]."

For all its sparseness of contact with individuals, Congress did sometimes reach Bill of Rights matters. The First Amendment's restraints on the nation, however, did not protect eighteenth century Americans from seditious libel laws which punished political criticism. The Sedition Act of 1798 made it a crime to publish "any false, scandalous and malicious writing" intended to bring the government into contempt or disrepute or to excite hatred. The law was vigorously pursued by a Federalist administration which denied that it was the intentions of the First Amendment's framers to do anything more than proscribe prior restraint. It was never tested before the Supreme Court, but the strength of reaction against it may have advanced the case of its opponents and heightened expectations of free speech and political discussion well beyond original understandings.[9]

Slavery had its national victories over First Amendment freedoms. Under the "gag rule" of May 1836 Congress was obliged to table petitions and resolutions relating to slavery without discussing them. Southerners countered the argument that it was a violation of the First Amendment's right to petition Congress by insisting that the Amendment's coverage was limited to matters within Congress' constitutional competence. Slavery was not. The anger engendered by the rule and so ably articulated by John Quincy Adams helped to fuse anti-slavery and free speech causes, awakening some white citizens to the potential alienability of rights which they had assumed to be adequately protected by the Bill of Rights.[10] As a limitation on the nation the Bill of Rights was either interpreted narrowly in the face of countervailing interests or relegated to the sidelines for want of government contact with individuals.

As a limitation on the states, which had a great deal more to do with the rights and responsibilities of their inhabitants, the Bill of Rights was even less a measure of the rights of an American. When Barron sued the Mayor and City Council of Baltimore for ruining his wharf in Baltimore harbour by diverting streams in the course of roadworks and leaving a huge heap of sand near the wharf, his counsel argued that it was a violation of the Fifth Amendment's guarantee against taking property for public use without just compensation. For the Court, John Marshall ruled that the amendment did not apply to the states:

> In almost every convention by which the constitution was adopted, amendments to guard against the abuse of power were recommended. These amendments demanded security against the apprehended encroachments of the general government - not against those of the local governments. In compliance with a sentiment thus generally expressed, to quiet fears thus extensively entertained, amendments were proposed by the required majority in Congress, and adopted by the states. These amendments contain no expression indicating an intention to apply them to the state governments. This court cannot so apply them.[11]

As the late nineteenth century constitutionalist John Norton Pomeroy commented on Marshall's decision in <u>Barron v Baltimore</u>, while the United States were forbidden to deprive a person of any of the rights contained in the first ten amendments to the Constitution, the States could infringe on them all with respect to their own inhabitants, at least in so far as it was consistent with their own organic laws.[12] For some antislavery thinkers, however, the rights of Americans could not be so casually buried in Baltimore's roadworks. For Alvan Stewart, Joel Tiffany, William Goodell and other radical antislavery minds the Bill of Rights was not only a limitation on all governments but also a source of national power. It was the nation's responsibility to ensure that all Americans of whatever race or class or creed enjoyed their fundamental, natural rights. They were no more impressed by Barron v Baltimore's limitations on the applicability of the Bill of Rights than they were by Dred Scott's denial of citizenship to black Americans.[13] Granted that they flew in the face of orthodoxy as constitutional lawyers would have defined it, they may well have articulated the belief of ordinary Americans that the Bill of Rights should count for something anywhere in the land, in the same way that Englishmen's faith in Magna Carta was founded on essence rather than technicality. It was unlikely that Barron v Baltimore was as well known as the Bill of Rights.

John Marshall's opinion that the Bill of Rights was not a limitation on the states did not exhaust the nation's interest in the rights of her citizens in the states however. Article IV Section 2 provided that, "The Citizens of each State shall be entitled to all Privileges and Immunities of Citizens in the several States." The clause was about the rights which a migrant citizen might expect to enjoy while temporarily resident in another state. It was not an invitation to the nation to adjust the relationship between the state and its own citizens. As to content, there was little case law for guidance and of that there was more than one possible approach to interpretation. It could mean that an out-of-state resident was entitled to a full measure of whatever rights were enjoyed by the citizens of his host state; or that he was entitled to some but not others, depending either on the special nature of the rights or on his own "place" in the spectrum of citizenship rights; or that in common with all other citizens of states he was clothed with a general, national citizenship embodying fundamental rights, which was portable anywhere in the Union; or combining these concepts it could mean that migrants were entitled to a general content of citizenship, with the expectation that states would fill in the details and perhaps add to them from a range of 'privileges' enjoyed by their own citizens, but certainly not subtract from fundamental rights.[14]

Very few states were prepared to offer migrants the full package of citizenship rights in perfect equality with their own citizens. Special economic privileges and voting rights were the most commonly cited reservations which awaited evidence of the migrants commitment to taking a full share in the life of the community. These reservations were shared both by courts which chose to read the comity clause as offering migrants a package of state citizenship rights and those which interpreted it as a suitcase of portable national rights. Thus, although Justice Bushrod Washington's opinion in the

1823 case of Corfield v Coryell stands for the idea that the comity clause entitled state citizens to a body of common, fundamental rights rather than merely what the host state chose to offer, it did not include the rights of non-residents of New Jersey to fish oysters out of New Jersey waters.[15] More controversially, Justice Washington did include the right to vote among the privileges and immunities of citizenship but only "as regulated and established by the laws or constitutions of the state in which it is to be exercised." Only the women's movement, however, arguing their own case for suffrage under the Fourteenth Amendment in the 1870's ever took the sentence seriously.[16] Senator Lyman Trumbull carefully disentangled the sentence from the rest of the paragraph when he made use of Corfield as an analogue to the rights protected by the Civil Rights bill in 1866.[17]

Scholars who interpret the Civil Rights Act as a list of limited, enumerated, rights find support in Justice Washington's prefatory remarks that he had "no hesitation in confining" privileges and immunities to those which were by nature fundamental.[18] But if he confined the rights to those which were fundamental he did not confine what he meant by fundamental:

> protection by the government; the enjoyment of life and liberty, with the right to acquire and possess property of every kind, and to pursue happiness and safety; subject nevertheless to such restraints as the government may justly prescribe for the good of the whole. The right of a citizen of one state to pass through, or to reside in any other state, for the purposes of trade, agriculture, professional pursuits, or otherwise; to claim the benefit of the writ of habeas corpus; to institute and maintain actions of any kind in the courts of the state; to take, hold and dispose of property, either real or personal; and on exemption from higher taxes or impositions than are paid by the other citizens of the state; may be mentioned as some of the particular privileges and immunities of citizens, which are clearly embraced by the general description of privileges deemed to be fundamental; to which may be added the elective franchise, as regulated and established by the laws or constitution of the state in which it is to be exercised.

Accepting the risk that Justices like politicians may make free play with language, unaware of the significance which others will later seek in their words, it may nevertheless be advanced as a hypothesis that his opinion would not have raised many eyebrows at the time, since he expressly purported to be describing what he believed citizens the Union over were already safely enjoying ...... and then only some of the rights; since it was too "tedious" to enumerate them all.[19] Whatever the relationship between Corfield and the Civil Rights Act it was not that they both represented limited enumerations of rights.

Interpretations which favoured state - selected rather than general formulations of privileges and immunities also distinguished between some privileges which were exclusive to state citizens, and fundamental rights which were to be enjoyed by all. Among fundamental rights which state courts attached to the comity clause were the right to hold, acquire and transfer property and enjoy its protection in the same way and under the same laws as other citizens, freedom from special taxes and liabilities on account of their status as migrants, the right to sue and be sued, access to courts and the right to security and protection of personal rights.[20] Thus, whether an out-of-state citizen brought his own rights with him from a general stock, or shared in those which his host state gave its own citizens, he would be assured of enjoying fundamental rights - in theory at least.

Taney's Dred Scott opinion, however muddled and confused on the matter of free blacks' citizenship was one of the strongest statements that the comity clause was a national guarantee of reciprocity in a very substantial area of state-held civil rights. These rights must have been strong medecine for he argued that slaveholding states would have refused to ratify the Constitution if they had believed the clause included Negro citizens. As migrants it would have exempted them from police regulations which applied to other blacks in the state, entitled them to go where they pleased, to hold meetings on political affairs, speak their minds, and carry arms, all things which would have been subversive of slavery. After Taney had cleared the problem out of the way to his own satisfaction by excluding Negroes from citizenship within the meaning of the Constitution, it was clear that white citizens temporarily out-of-state could count on full equality with other citizens in respect of personal and property rights and the strong hand of the nation to secure it:

> for they would hold these privileges and immunities, under the paramount authority of the Federal Government, and its courts would be bound to maintain and enforce them, the Constitution and laws of the State to the contrary notwithstanding. And if the State could limit or restrict them, or place the party in an inferior grade, this clause of the Constitution would be unmeaning and could have no operation; and would give no rights to the citizen when in another State. He would have none but what the State itself chose to allow him. This is evidently not the

> construction or meaning of the clause in question. It guarantees rights to the citizen, and the State cannot withold them.

He could have been talking about the Fourteenth Amendment, rather than transient rights, restricted to whites only, and to be overtaken by the State's power to allocate whatever status and incidents it liked after residence was established.

With respect to white citizens' rights no State would have publicly proclaimed that in these matters it was anything other than the very crucible of liberty compared with its neighbour. Even with respect to white rights, however, some citizens found that there were gaps between what host states offered them and what fundamental rights they expected to enjoy either by reference to general principles of citizenship or by comparison with other citizens in the state. When Massachusetts citizen Samuel Hoar was excluded from South Carolina in 1844 in an attempt to abort his efforts to test that state's discriminatory black seamen's laws, his case became something of a cause celebre among those who believed that the rights of speech and movement were protected by the comity clause.

More commonly the distance between what states offered and what out-of-state citizens expected was measured by free Negroes. When a black citizen of Massachusetts or Pennsylvania moved to a state which did not accord its own free blacks that status, it raised the question whether in effect one state could make another observe a higher standard for its citizens than it did for its own by drawing from the idea of a general, or national entitlement to rights guaranteed by the comity clause. Taney's ingenious answer was to make enjoyment of the comity clause depend on being a United States citizen as well as a State citizen, despite the plain words of the text. Many state courts had already applied different but equally muddled reasoning to exclude free blacks from state citizenship on the grounds that you could tell a citizen by the fact that he had rights and since blacks did not exercise rights they could not be citizens - all this before "Catch 22[21]."

Apart from outright exclusion from citizenship, another method of diluting comity clause rights was to make the privileges and immunities of citizenship a variable feast, expanding and contracting according to what states offered people of "the same class or condition" or "under like circumstances" or "similarly situated." This was the argument of the

Minnesota Supreme Court in Davis v Pierse in 1862, that the clause meant:

> not absolute equality of rights and privileges with every citizen of each State of the Union, but all such privileges and immunities in any State as are, by the constitution and laws thereof, secured or extended, to her own people of the same class, and otherwise similarly situated.[22]

Antislavery theorists rejected the idea that rights were relative to what states chose to allow similarly situated inhabitants. While a sliding scale of 'special' privileges or additions to fundamental rights was to be expected in a federal system, a sliding scale with respect to fundamental citizenship rights was not to be tolerated. Abolitionists began to argue towards a concept of national citizenship. Their case was that the federal government had both the duty and the power to secure its citizens fundamental rights. Defence counsel William Ellsworth argued Prudence Crandall's right to educate out-of-state black children on the grounds that it was the intention of the comity clause "to declare a citizen of one state to be a citizen of every state, and as such, to clothe him with the same fundamental rights, to be where he might which he acquired by birth in a particular state[23]." Although abolitionists "swam upstream" when it came to arguing that federally-secured rights also limited state governments in their relationship with their own citizens, they draw from some ideas about the scope of "privileges and immunities" and national primacy in comity clause matters which had wider circulation. Chief Justice Taney's opinion in Dred Scott, just as much as Corfield gave broad content to "privileges and immunities" - once blacks were excluded from its benefits. In the same opinion Taney argued a strong case for national primacy over state defaulters, albeit only until residence was established.

It should not have mattered whether fundamental rights were enjoyed by migrants as a consequence of states including them in whatever arrangements they made for their own citizens, or whether they drew from an independent source of rights understood as a "common denominator" among American citizens. Both roads should have led to the same result, the full protection of the rights to life, liberty and property. The failure of states to offer that much either to all migrants from sister states, or indeed even to all their own inhabitants persuaded antislavery constitutionalists of the need to secure these rights nationally. Of course the comity clause was an unsuitable vehicle for nationalising civil rights. It was about the rights of state citizens in the special circumstances of residing in another state as non-citizens. It did not invite the federal government to interfere in the way that Kentucky or California allocated privileges and immunities among their own citizens. It was little wonder that Attorney-General Bates found the concept of national citizenship so elusive. The Constitution contained much evidence that citizens had rights but no way of securing them in the States.

The safety of leaving so much to the states was an item of faith rather than constitutional inquiry. The guiding star in the states rights constellation of values was to be left alone, free from the unwanted intrusions of national government. In the local community, free enfranchised men could assert and maintain their rights and shape their own destiny in an environment of their own making. Southern constitutionalist John Randolph Tucker expressed his exaggerated faith in these conditions which nurtured a man's freedom "to accomplish all which by nature he is fitted to accomplish, without hindrance from his fellows and without help or interference from his government. The world the arena, man the athlete, government the mere police, God the arbiter, and the reward the laurel he can gather and the crown he can win[24]." In this jungle some men's rights were bound to be held for nothing by the superior claims of the strong, as the slave's were. But even with respect to the lives of the strong, Tucker's description fell short of accuracy. The states did not stand by and watch life's race. They intervened to make different rules for different classes of citizen, and to distribute benefits and burdens in ways which ensured that the "laurels" and "crowns" were not prizes in an open contest.

There was not a complete void, however, between the United States Constitution and the local jungle. States also had constitutions. They varied in quality and durability. Some were skeletal instruments of governments while others approached statutory proportions of great detail and were regularly altered to find room for new detail. Like the United States Constitution the powers which they described and distributed among executive, legislative and judicial departments were not unlimited. They all contained bills of rights, some less inclusive and some more inclusive than the federal Bill of Rights. Some were much longer, like Kentucky's in 1792, which contained twenty-eight sections.[25] Comprehensiveness or even clarity was not always proportionate to length, however. Benjamin F. Wright's studies of early constitutional conventions reveal loose draftsmanship, the casual borrowing and transplanting of natural rights formulae among neighbours and a more mechanical than thoughtful choice of rights.[26] Sharing these observations Leonard Levy writes:

> These documents, which we uncritically exalt, were imitative, deficient and irrationally selective. In the glorious act of framing a social compact expressive of the supreme law, Americans tended to draw up a random catalogue of rights that seemed to satisfy their urge for a statement of first principles - or for some of them. That task was executed in a disordered fashion that verged on ineptness.[27]

No more than the U.S Constitution's Bill of Rights did these documents aspire to offer a definitive description of the rights of Marylanders or Hoosiers or Texans. What mattered was politics and local prejudice; whether state governments had the political will to observe these rights themselves or secure them against a man's neighbours intent on depriving him of them. The lack of discussion about the vulnerability of state citizenship, outside of the antislavery and women's movements, has been all too readily taken as evidence that most citizens were happy that their rights were adequately protected, and if they were not they would vote the offenders out at the next election. The Century Edition of the American Digest of cases up to 1896 contains only nineteen pages of cases on "Personal, Civil and Political Rights" out of fifty volumes. Bills of rights rusted, it seemed, for want of being breached and except for property rights, most Americans lived rather than litigated free lives. Constitutional limitations on States were not pursued or even studied with the same vigour and intensity as restraints on the nation. It was 1868 before there was a widely known scholarly work on the subject. Its author, Thomas McIntyre Cooley, made the distinction between the powers of state and national government, that "The government of the United States is one of enumerated powers; the government of the States are possessed of all the general powers of legislation." Therefore:

> We look to the Constitution of the United States for grants of legislative power, but in the constitutions of the States to ascertain if any limitations have been imposed upon the complete power with which the legislative department of the State was vested in its creation.[28]

When Cooley wrote after the war, both national powers and state limitations were pursued more earnestly. But even before the war there had been some occasion to think about restraints on the plenary powers of the states. State governments may not have been "Leviathans" - they did not have the money - but Jacksonian legislatures discovered the public good and the police power, and prompted some of their citizens to seek constitutional limitations. State governments responded to the insatiable demands of a growing economy for internal improvements and infrastructure.[29] "Dynamic capital" - new private enterprises and corporations - competed for the help which it was within the power of states to give in the form of franchises and charters, or the use of eminent domain powers to release private property to public purposes of railroad and canal building. The power to promote, however, carried with it the potential to regulate, and the power to favour some economic interests carried with it the power to disfavour others. It brought states into sensitive areas where "static capital," like the owners of private property taken under eminent domain power or those with long-vested economic interests sought limitations on state benefits to "dynamic capital".

To protect vested interests State courts occasionally dipped into the Pandora's box of "higher law" constitutionalism which Justice Chase had opened in Calder v Bull in the United States Supreme Court in 1798.[30] In that opinion he articulated the idea that legislatures were limited by "natural law" or "the social compact" or "general principles of law and reason," even in the absence of express limitations:

> I cannot subscribe to the omnipotence of the state legislature, or that it is absolute and without control, although its authority should not be expressly restrained by the constitution or fundamental law of the state.

He went on to give examples of the kind of conduct which lay beyond state legislative competence:

> A law that punishes an innocent action...... a law that destroys, or impairs the lawful contracts of citizens; a law that makes a man a judge in his own case; or a law that takes property from A and gives it to B; it is against all reason and justice for a people to entrust a legislature with such powers; and therefore it cannot be presumed that they have done it. The genius, the nature, and the spirit of our state governments amount to a prohibition of such acts of legislation; and the general principles of law and reason forbid them.

It was too dangerous a concept to float free but too useful to be discarded. For a while Chief Justice Marshall usefully anchored it to the contracts clause to serve vested interests in Fletcher v Peck and Dartmouth College v Woodward but in the federal courts at least, the doctrine went out of fashion in the 1820's and its revival in the form of substantive due process followed the Civil War.[31] Although the intervening years were dominated by positivism in the sense that federal judges, qua judges declined to find a place for "higher law" in the disposition of slavery matters, the idea never went away.[32] Though strictly tailored to serve vested property rather than antislavery interests state courts continued to find a use for it as a limitation on state powers. In the 1830's and 1840's some state court judges attached the language of higher law to the due process or law of the land clauses of their own state constitutions in order to defeat the purposes of married womens property acts and temperance laws.[33] It was a small tributary of judicial activism in a tide of constitutionalism which emphasised the release rather than the restraint of state powers. It emerged again in the 1850's, notably in Wynehamer v New York and even lurked in the shadows of two Supreme Court cases, Murray v Hoboken and Dred Scott at a time when dynamic capital had made enough gains to prompt rediscovery of higher law doctrines in order to consolidate them.[34]

On the whole, however, state court judges were unlikely explorers of constitutional limitations. Some of the greatest of them, like John B. Gibson of Pennsylvania's Supreme Court were apostles of judicial self-restraint. The less distinguished, increasingly elected by popular majorities, were likely to feel the same tensions as the legislatures, moved to co-operate with progress and create conditions for the release of economic energy but tempered occasionally by the ingrained respect of their class for vested property rights. Of course the release of economic energy could be hampered as well as helped by a state power which effectively regulated corporations or fashioned the power of eminent domain to hold their activities to publicly beneficial purposes. But the instrumentalism of the 1820's and 1830's had served dynamic capital well as a means of fashioning the common law to maximise conditions of freedom for business without giving state regulatory power room to grow.

A more powerful current in favour of state limitations was the growing feeling in the 1830's among those who had not benefitted from the redistribution of economic power in the 1820's and 1830's that state legislatures had not acted responsibly in chartering corporations and banks, lending money and so on. Jacksonians demanded that their legislatives cease granting special privileges to corporations and instead pass general incorporation laws imposing standard conditions and some controls on corporations. From the 1840's new constitutions increased executive powers and restrained that of legislatures, specifically in the matter of granting charters to corporations and lending money. Louisiana's constitution of 1845 became a model for others. Among other things it restricted the state's power to pledge its credit or lend money, and forbade special corporate charters.[36] It was an attempt to impose some order on the economic jungle by organic law rather than legislation. State legislatures had subsidised and abetted the redistribution of wealth but they had not won the battle for control and responsibility. Imposing constitutional limitations on their powers was an attempt to accomplish this by another route. It was another dent, though like the state courts use of "higher law" doctrines to protect vested interests, not a deathblow to the prevailing notions of plenary powers.

Different economic interests had different reasons for seeking limitations on state powers, some to avoid regulation, others to achieve it. Their contest was for a share of power and prizes. It proceeded upon the assumption that fundamental civil rights were safely theirs. The vast potential reaches of the police power could easily have undermined that assumption, however. The police power was the least understood and most ill-defined of all state powers, the likeliest to shake the dust from bill of rights.[37] According to Chief Justice Redfield in Thorpe v Rutland and Burlington R.R. Co. "This police power of the State extends to the protection of the lives, limbs, health, comfort, and quiet of all persons, and the protection of all property within the State." Under it, "persons and property are subjected to all kinds of restraints and burdens[38]." It embraced everything from ordinary police functions, to quarantine and poor laws, as well as dangerously vague responsibilities for moral welfare, including regulatory powers over "houses and women of prostitution, gambling, drinking-shops and foundlings[39]." In addition to the police power, states also had autonomy over their own criminal laws and procedures, so close to Bill of Rights concerns for fairness. They also decided who voted, when a minor reached majority, what constituted marriage and what rights and responsibilities flowed from that status. Although white, self-reliant, self-supporting male citizens may have believed they had little to fear from this conglomerie of powers so long as they remained honest and sober, there were others for whom it was not so, some of them citizens, some of them not.

If women's freedom and citizenship had been the model for black men's rights in 1866 they would not have got far from the plantation. Any catalogue of married women's disabilities at common law would predispose its reader to imagine that state bills of rights did not apply to them. They had no rights to choose their domicile, no right to the fruits of their own earnings, or to enter into contracts, hold and transfer property, make a will or testify against their husbands. It was small wonder that feminists in the 1830's and 1840's drew comparisons between coverture and slavery. Damage to a wife, like damage to a slave was an injury to the husband or owner, whichever the case may be. Even with the consent of a kind master marriage was almost as difficult to terminate in divorce as slavery was in manumission. Mrs. Elizabeth Stanton capitalised on the image of the runaway slave when she wrote that liberal divorce states were to women what Canada had been to fugitive slaves.[40] Of course the comparison with slavery could be stretched to make an eloquent point. Frederick Douglass, campaigner for the rights of blacks and women offered a different perspective:

> Other women suffer certain wrongs, but the wrongs peculiar to women out of slavery, great and terrible as they are, are endured as well by the slave woman, who also has to bear the ten thousand wrongs of slavery in addition to those common wrongs of woman. It is hard to be underpaid for labor faithfully performed. It is harder still not to be paid for labor at all ..... It is hard for the widow only to receive the third part of the property of her deceased husband; it is harder still to be a chattel person to all intents and purposes. It is hard to enjoy a qualified right to one's children; but it is harder still for a woman to have no rights which white men are bound to respect.[41]

Besides, the common law as interpreted by Blackstone was on its way to becoming a dinosaur with respect to the rights of married women. In America, as in England, some women enjoyed property rights by resort to trusts and equitable remedies designed partly at the behest of fathers to protect property from profligate sons-in-law and their creditors. The sheer necessities of economic life in a young and expanding nation also helped change old legal ways. Women ran businesses in their husband's absence and acted as executors in eighteenth century America.[42] Although trusts and equity arrangements favoured only better off women, the benefits were extended to all in the nineteenth century when state legislatures passed Married Womens Property Acts. Mississippi was the first in 1839, though New York and Pennsylvania's laws in 1848 offered more substantial property rights. Lawrence Friedman's estimate, however, that seventeen states had followed their example by the mid 1850's does not take account of how partial and gradual the changes were at first. Full contractual capacity, equal guardianship rights and the right to her own earnings were won in most areas outside New York, after the Civil War and not before.[43] Lacking these essential rights women's citizenship was different from their husbands. They could well have stood to gain from a definition of freedom which included the right to the fruits of one's labour, to make contracts, and to sue and be sued.

Yet they were citizens. The fact that they did not vote or enjoy "full" citizenship rights was often cited as proof that black citizens need not vote as a consequence of that status. In that respect women's citizenship was a useful model for newly freed Negroes, at least in the eyes of those white Americans who were unprepared to make their own rights the appropriate measure. But Republicans encountered a different problem. If they phrased definitions of civil rights for freedmen too broadly they might accidentally benefit women. Charles Sumner provoked such a reaction in 1864 when he proposed a Thirteenth Amendment to read "All persons are equal before the law." In 1866 John Bingham's original proposal for a Fourteenth Amendment which would clothe Congress with the primary power to make laws for the equal protection of life, liberty and property ran into similar objections when former New York judge Robert Hale alerted Congress to the awful possibility that it might affect married women's property rights.[44] While women's citizenship was an unpromising blueprint for black freedom, black citizenship was too promising a model for women's!

Free Negroes, North and South were another category of Americans whose citizenship rights, where they were acknowledged, were less than the full measure. Like women their situation varied greatly according to where they lived and generalisations are treacherous.[45] North of slavery black citizens were excluded from voting in all but five states and even where they voted, as in Massachusetts it had not freed them from legal and extralegal discrimination. Their free movement between states was restricted by immigration laws which stopped them at the borders, or required them to post bonds or give evidence of employment. Some states, like Massachusetts appreciated the inconsistency of these laws with the position espoused by many Northerners in opposing Missouri's admission to the Union with a constitution barring free Negroes, and either repealed or stopped enforcing them. The west and midwest were particularly inhospitable to free Negroes, however. Five states prohibited Negro testimony in cases where whites were a party, severely restricting the likelihood of justice. They were barred from the juryroom in most states and the bedroom in all, though anti-miscegenation laws were hardly a measurement of citizenship since they also punished whites. The law was only the tip of the iceberg of discrimination, most of which was extralegal and touched every aspect of their lives. Evidence of pervasive prejudice and discrimination did not alter the fact that they were citizens, however, and did enjoy some meaningful fundamental personal and property rights which distinguished them not only from slaves but also from free blacks in the South.

In the South black freedom was the more dangerous because it lived side by side with slavery and threatened subversion. Just after the Revolution Southern States were not as insecure about their peculiar institution as they became later and their constitutions offered all free persons protection of natural rights. The free Negro population flourished and multiplied and became "the fastest growing element in the Southern population," but the tide was turning even by the 1790's and the law became an instrument of social control and repression.[46] Free blacks were forced to register in most states and were subjected to harsh police regulations which restricted their freedom to associate, to carry arms or to entertain slaves. Their testimony was banned in cases involving whites. Under Draconian penal codes they suffered harsher penalties than whites. They were excluded from some jobs by law and served apprenticeships in others under laws which were cousins to slavery. Manumission became more and more difficult, and states made it a condition that freed slaves be removed beyond their borders. It was a condition which was almost impossible to fulfil since sister states forbade free blacks entry to avoid becoming a dumping ground for their neighbours unwanted population. The logic reached north of Mason-Dixon, but the intensity of fear was uniquely Southern. The law's restrictions were a barometer of that fear and escalated in response to the growing attacks on slavery from outside, reaching a peak in the 1850's. It was not that the volume of law necessarily reflected the lives free Negroes led, since policing never kept pace with the desired degree of social control and law sometimes indicated a loss of control. There was more law in the Upper South than the Lower, though not necessarily less freedom. Nor did the law blot out every right. Ira Berlin found that "the free Negro's only right that escaped unscathed was his ability to hold property - a striking commentary on the American idea of liberty." Fragile differences preserved distinctions between "Slaves without masters" and slaves with. It was enough to make free blacks an elite after emancipation. Some, especially in the cities had made themselves just enough room to survive with some sense of freedom. But it was not what Republicans meant by the word in 1865.

In a society where citizenship was held to be the corollary of freedom it was hard to explain why free Negroes enjoyed a very different kind of citizenship from free whites.[48] The status of women and children as citizens without "full citizenship" rights could be explained away by reference to the responsibilities of men for their protection. But a different rationale had to be found to explain the "half-way" house of citizenship which free Negroes "enjoyed." Not all states acknowledged that they were citizens. Some Southern courts had fashioned their own arguments for excluding them from that status on different but just as implausible grounds as Dred Scott. Kentucky's learned appeal court dug into Roman history for evidence that no one could be a citizen of a state who was not entitled to the privileges and immunities of the highest class. Since free Negroes demonstrably did not have these privileges, they could not be citizens.[49] The case, Amy v Smith was cited and the logic followed in neighbouring Tennessee in the 1838 case of The State v Claiborne.[50] Ingeniously the court found an argument not only for denying that Claiborne was a citizen but also for excluding him from the state's bill of rights which spoke of "persons" rather than citizens. The judge found that Tennessee's restriction on free blacks entering the state was not a violation of either the comity clause or the bill of rights because a free black man was not a free man in the sense of Magna Carta! Thus, said Judge Green:

> An emancipated slave is called a freeman in common parlance, and in reference to his former status he is, having acquired privileges and immunities which he did not enjoy before. But in reference to the condition of white citizens his condition is still that of a degraded man, aspiring to no equality of right with white men and possessing a very few only of the privileges pertaining to a "freeman" or "citizen."

It was not convincing but it was attractive to Southern courts, or some of them. In North Carolina the same year as Claiborne Judge William Gaston took the bolder step of including free blacks as citizens, after a scholarly analysis of the meaning of the term in British and American history.[51] It may be doubted how valuable a passport this was to the enjoyment of privileges and immunities, however, since he found no constitutional objection to a law which singled out Negroes to be hired out to labour if they failed to pay a fine, since legislatures "may rightfully so apportion punishment according to the condition, temptation to crime and ability to suffer, of those who are likely to offend."

Two ideas about citizenship warred within all these opinions. One was that citizenship rights were divisible in one way or another according either to the substance of these rights, or who claimed them, or from which government they claimed their protection. Thus it was possible to be a citizen without being a "full citizen" entitled to vote, serve on juries and hold office; "equal" enjoyment of citizenship rights meant only the right to be treated in the same way and to the same measure as other "similarly situated" people;

state and national citizenship were two separate things as in Dred Scott. Arguments favouring the divisibility of citizenship rights in these three ways were to a large extent invented as rationales for treating blacks and women as second class citizens, though it could also rebound on "the highest class of citizens."

The other emerging idea of universal, birthright citizenship, and the entitlement of all to rights and equality under law, nationally guaranteed, was not free from some of the same notions of divisibility. Most Republicans began in 1865 with the conviction that civil rights were the essential corollory of freedom but took longer to move towards the idea that political rights were a corollory of citizenship. At that they would still have drawn a dividing line, at women for example.

But in 1865 the Republicans picked up another theme from past understandings of the nature of citizenship and stressed its common elements, those which were common to all citizens and all jurisdictions. While they declined to define them in language other than "such as" or "including," some rights cropped up so regularly that they formed a shared kernel of expectations. It was hardly surprising that common denominators were to be discovered in speeches and judicial opinions. States had borrowed so much from each other and from the United States Constitution when they wrote their own bills of rights. Of course there were variations and exceptions.

Every state had some provision guaranteeing free expression though some, like Massachusetts and Rhode Island specified press freedom but not speech. Freedom of religion was subject to greater variations. New Hampshire's 1793 Constitution encouraged the "public worship of the Deity" and only Protestants were eligible to be governor or legislator. Many Southern states, including Tennessee, Louisiana, North Carolina and Virginia excluded clergymen from civil office and a few also barred unbelievers. In Arkansas "No person who denies the being of a God shall hold any office in the civil department of this State, nor be allowed his oath in any court[52]." Criminal procedure was even less uniform. Some states preferred to bring charges by indictment rather than grand jury even in capital cases and at least one had no guarantee against double jeopardy.[53]

Variations among the states amounted in some cases to shortfalls from the national Bill of Rights. This is advanced by Charles Fairman as one reason why the Fourteenth Amendment could not have been understood as applying the Bill of Rights in its entirety to the states.[54] They would either have raised objections during the ratifying process - which they did not - or changed their own laws to bring them into alignment with the Bill of Rights.

Yet surely New Hampshire did not lurk guiltily in the shadows of the Fourteenth Amendment for fear that because her constitution did not specifically guarantee free speech it was not one of the privileges and immunities which she offered her citizens? So too with the merits of grand juries over indictments, or modifications of jury trials in civil cases. What was "incorporated" was a standard rather than a method. In that sense the Fourteenth Amendment included more rather than less than the Bill of Rights, for it reached for the conditions of freedom which had been on the minds of the framers in 1787 and which had not worked as well as they'd hoped. In 1866, however, it unequivocally included blacks.

The debate is distorted by concentrating on lists. States had always had them and they had never been a measurement of rights. What mattered, as in 1787 was the "dynamics" of freedom - making rights work in the context of the everyday exercise of power.

CHAPTER 7

Citizenship's New Dimension: Rights Enforceable at Home

When Andrew Johnson took office in 1865 times had changed. Slaves were free and it seemed that a commitment to making freedom meaningful was not exclusive to the Republican party. In October the New York *World* carried this:

> A conclusive refutation of the charge falsely made against the Democratic party that they are willing to exclude negro freedmen from that justice and *equality before the law* which is their right ..... We believe that President Johnson, as we know that we do the views of the great mass of the Democratic party of the North, in saying that this *equality before the law* ought not to be and cannot prudently, be denied to negro freedmen.[1]

A few months later it might have read as a news item, but in the autumn of 1865 Republicans still had high hopes of the President. It was true that Radicals had been bitterly disappointed by his failure to make black suffrage anything more than a suggestion for voluntary action in the seven southern conventions scheduled to meet between August 1865 and February 1866. Having watched Lincoln "grow" on the matter, however, and putting the best possible construction on some of the things Johnson said to them, they were slow to give up on him. Centrists who had just begun to move leftwards on the suffrage issue, lacked the certainty to go on moving in the face of Johnson's lack of commitment and the rebuffs which black suffrage had suffered that summer in Northern intraparty wrangles and at the polls in Connecticut. Becalmed, the party lacked the necessary cohesion and direction to approach Reconstruction boldly. Meanwhile, between President and Congress there seemed to be enough safe, common ground to build upon. Johnson was believed to be sound on such matters as securing black civil rights and acknowledging Congress's right to legislate on Reconstruction and decide whether or not to seat Representatives. The Republicans, especially its cautious centre was disposed to co-operate.[2]

The extent of common ground between Johnson and the Republicans was deceptive. Unbeknown to either of them in full measure, they were separated by a chasm of misunderstanding. Behind Johnson's use of words like "guarantees," "freedom" and "equality of civil rights" lay a world of different assumptions from those of Republicans. Quite apart from the President's political ineptness and the well-documented racism which hardly made him unique even among Republicans, it is clear that his background and political assumptions were such that even if he shared a vocabulary with the Republicans in Congress, he was talking a different language. Added to this, his talent for studied ambiguity and implied agreement with whoever he was talking to lulled moderates into false security and kept Radicals on a low heat. By the spring of 1866 all would be clear. As far as Johnson was concerned, the responsibility for equality before the law ended where it had always done, in the states - which meant that it never began. In the face of a mountain of evidence that his Reconstruction plans were simply not working he was unable to contemplate the extension of federal power into what he regarded as the exclusively State business of governing relations among their citizens. Anything Johnson had to say about justice to freedmen was in the realm of a faith which turned out to be misplaced, rather than good works. It was not enough.

When Congress met in December 1865 the Republicans set about the unfinished business of the Thirteenth Amendment. Eight Southern legislatures were in session that month, equally busy in work which threatened to undo it. Mississippi was the first to design black codes, and the others followed with Texas at the tail end. They were a curious amalgam of paternalism and racism but were universally characterised by white control rather than black choice. Vagrancy laws, discriminatory apprenticeship laws and restrictive police legislation governed work and social intercourse. With apparent incongruity the same laws extended "civil rights" on such matters as allowing Negro testimony in cases where only Negroes were a party. Mississippi took no trouble to camouflage the law's purpose.[3] Other States like Virginia and Louisiana explored the subtleties of applying general law in just as effective ways to discriminate against Freedmen's civil rights. Something had to be done. Thus, even while Johnson relinquished control over local affairs to new civil governments in the Carolinas, Alabama and Georgia in December, Trumbull's Senate Judiciary Committee worked on believing that they fought on the same side. The Thirty-ninth Congress, like its predecessors was about to become a schoolhouse.

Trumbull and his colleagues in Senate and House were in no doubt that the enforcement clause of the Thirteenth amendment addressed itself to just the kind of thing that was happening in the South.[4] While Democrats and some conservative Republicans like Edgar Cowan regularly denied any other purpose but that of ending chattel slavery, the majority of Republicans were just as sure that denials of civil rights offended the substance and spirit of the Amendment, triggering the enforcement power. Senator Howard, who had served on the Judiciary Committee which framed it, said:

> I take this occasion to say that it was in contemplation of its friends and advocates to give to Congress precisely the power over the subject of slavery and the freedom which is proposed to be exercised by the bill under our consideration. (The Civil Rights Bill).[5]

Representative Thayer in the House:

> When I voted for the second section of the amendment, I felt in my own mind certain that I had placed in the Constitution and given to Congress ability to protect and guaranty the rights which the first section gave them.[6]

That is not to say that the whole Republican party premeditated specific uses of the enforcement clause. Between 1865 and 1866 lay the gathering evidence that freedom was not self-executing. Perhaps many of them had not known what they meant by freedom until they saw it denied yet slavery gone.

On January 5th 1866 Trumbull introduced two bills from the Judiciary Committee. The Freedmen's Bureau and Civil Rights Bills were designed to extend national protection to freedmen's civil rights in the states without entering the minefield of black suffrage and Reconstruction theory. Trumbull believed he was working well within the perimeter of common ground with the President.[7] Johnson vetoed both.

The Freedmen's Bureau Bill seemed innocuous enough. The Bureau had been established by act of Congress in 1865. As its originally prescribed life span of one year drew to a close, it was clear both that it had by no means outlived its usefulness and that it was in trouble. Understaffed and overworked the Bureau's staff struggled to help freedmen and white refugees cope with the odds against them. Bureau agents supervised labor contracts, settled freedmen where possible on abandoned lands, adjudicated cases in which they were involved, dispensed medical aid and attempted education. The problems were plentiful enough to daunt a bevy of well-funded modern welfare agencies but they were compounded by lack of funds, local hostility, and the magnanimity of President Johnson in dispensing pardons which enabled unrepentant civilians to go on dominating local life. Careless use of the pardonning power and his policy of restoring lands to ex-Confederates on the strength of the May 29th 1865 Amnesty left the Bureau short of both the economic and moral wherewithal to give effective aid. Bureau agents, some of them half-hearted part-timers and army officers awaiting demobilisation, either succumbed and merged with the local scenery, or acted courageously and constructively against the tide. Those who chose the latter - and their numbers were impressive - were as vulnerable as the people they were trying to help. Their sole protection was the army and it was not much less vulnerable. On January 12th, as Congress prepared to debate the bill, the War Department was obliged to issue General Orders No.3, authorising commanders to protect their own men in the course of duty, loyalists and freedmen occupying abandonned lands, and blacks charged with offences for which white persons were not prosecuted or not punished in the same way, from prosecution in state courts. "Protection" consisted of discontinuing all such prosecutions pending in any other than a federal court and forwarding all papers to military headquarters. Taken together, Trumbull's two bills anticipated these problems and were designed as much to protect the helpers as the helped by law rather than self-reliance. Bureau Commissioner General O.O. Howard had gathered evidence from his subordinates at first hand and co-operated closely with Trumbull in the framing of the Bureau Bill. Together they fashioned a bill which would not only extend the Bureau's life but also strengthen it at the points which experience had shown were weakest.[8]

Introduced on January 5th, the bill was reported back from the Judiciary Committee on January 11th with amendments. It needed no other constitutional justification than that it remained necessary under an extended "grasp of war" rationale to make temporary arrangements to help the helpless until they were strong enough to help themselves. It was the bill's opponents, notably Senator Hendricks, who understood that it was based on the Thirteenth Amendment and rejected its appropriateness. Republican arguments were simply on grounds of necessity and war powers, reserving the resources of the Thirteenth Amendment for the debate on its companion Civil Rights Bill.

The bill extended the life of the Bureau indefinitely. Some of the provisions applied to the whole country, others only to states recently in rebellion. Its relief provisions had nationwide application. The Secretary of War was to direct whatever supplies, medical aid and so on as he thought necessary for succour and shelter to the needy, provided they were deserving. Section 4 dealt with available, unoccupied public lands in Florida, Mississippi, Alabama, Louisiana and Arkansas. The President was authorised to set land aside, in parcels not exceeding forty acres, for rental and possible future purchase by refugees and freedmen. Section 5 was about the abandonned lands in the sea islands and around Charleston which had been settled by freedmen and which were shrinking under Johnson's pardonning powers. It sought three years security of tenure for their occupants and the provision of alternative lands thereafter. The Bureau's Commissioner was authorised to build schools and asylums on available land after these were returned to owners. There was fuel enough in all this for opponents of government intervention and "special treatment" of blacks to wax eloquent. Judging from the short debate on the bill, however, its potential for inequality by making blacks and refugees the special favourite of the laws did not worry Democrats half so much as the potential for equality before the law contained in the bill's judicial sections.

In states where the ordinary course of judicial proceedings had been interrupted by rebellion, the civil rights of freedmen or any others deprived of them on account of race were placed under the jurisdiction of the Bureau and its military protector. The bill did not define civil rights but tied standards for black persons to whatever whites enjoyed. They "included" (i.e. were not "limited to") the right to make and enforce contracts, to sue, be parties and give evidence, inherit, purchase, lease, sell, hold and convey property, 'and have full and equal benefit of laws for the security of person and property "including" the constitutional right to bear arms,' and not to be subject to any different punishments than whites. Fines and prison sentences awaited anyone who infringed these rights under colour of law, custom, or prejudice. Jurisdiction would cease when discrimination ceased or when states were restored and their courts functioning. All Bureau personnel were put under military protection and jurisdiction.

Hendricks of Indiana led off the Democratic attack.[9] The features he found most objectionable were its judicial provisions. It was a bill to undermine the states. It gave jurisdiction in cases arising under state law between citizens of the same state to "irresponsible" federal creations, not part of the judicial system but part of the military establishment. He feared that the section placing Bureau employees under military protection and jurisdiction was yet more evidence of a Republican plot to put its policies beyond the reach of (state) law by indemnifying those who executed it. Hendricks wanted to know whether an agent offending state law in the course of his duties could be held to account in the courts of the state. It was not for the sake of Georgia or Alabama that he voiced these concerns, but for his own Indiana too.

Trumbull offered him the reassurance that, unlike the relief provision, the judicial features only applied to those States in which judicial proceedings had been interrupted by the rebellion, and not to those which enjoyed their full constitutional rights. The section putting Bureau employees under military protection did apply to all the States but far from being designed to put them outside the law it made them responsible under military rules and regulations. Hendricks' guess was right, however, if it was that Bureau officers were to be linked into removal procedures to carry their cases into the federal courts. Section 3 of the companion Civil Rights Bill specifically included them. Trumbull was as committed to ideas of law and responsibility as any man in Congress and he was not about to make a virtue out of the strong presence of the army in its judicial arrangements. The bill was, he said, a temorary expedient. When states were fully restored its functions would be replaced by the civil procedures contained in the Civil Rights Bill about to come up for discussion. That was cold comfort for Hendricks and his political allies. It is doubtful if they derived any more from Trumbull's suggested method of avoiding the operation of both bills - Make all equal before the law yourselves:

> If the States will not do it, then it is incumbent on Congress to do it. But if the States will do it then the Freedmen's Bureau will be removed, and the authority proposed to be given by the other bill will have no operation.[10]

If it was hard to do justice it was harder still not to. Trumbull aspired to touch the States at their weakest point - pride. They would have to decide which they wanted more, the freedom to treat blacks unequally, or freedom from federal "interference" to compel equal treatment.

Historically States preferred to do things for themselves. At every turn the bill's opponents betrayed their deepest unease at the idea of a federal agency taking over traditional state functions. Senator Edgar Cowan's thoughts on the relief arrangements echo down through the New Deal:

> I say that the freedmen of Pennsylvania ask no relief from the Freedmen's Bureau. Pennsylvania relieves her own destitute and her own poor. She is not a pensioner upon the United States Government for any favors of that kind. I say too, that if it is to extend beyond relief, and to administer municipal law there for the benefit of the freedmen, Pennsylvania administers her own municipal law.[11]

Two suggested amendments illustrate the point that what really concerned its opponents was its implications for their own states. Edgar Cowan's attempt to amend the bill by confining its operation to states "such as have lately been in rebellion" was defeated by 33 votes to 11.[12] The Senate also rejected Garret Davis' amendment to strike out that section which placed Bureau agents under military jurisdiction.[13] He spoke at length of the dangers of Bureau courts adjudicating cases between citizens of the same state and themselves being unaccountable to the courts of that state. It was a sensitive issue in his home State of Kentucky where there was an estimated 1,500 suits pending in state courts and the Habeas Corpus Act of 1863 had cut a pathway across state lines to allow for their removal into federal courts. His arguments cut no ice with the Republicans. In the Senate the bill passed on January 25th by 37 votes to 10 in a roll call only notable for its demonstration of Republican unity.[14] With Cowan absent they were unanimous.

In the House, Thomas D. Eliot of Massachusetts took charge, arguing sheer necessity as well as justice. Without protection, "much injustice will be done to these freedmen, and there will be no one there to tell the story[15]." Other Republicans spoke enthusiastically of the bill's potential for providing schools and education.[16] Representative Moulton, a Democratic maverick who voted with the Republicans, spoke enthusiastically of its potential to keep blacks in the South and urged colleagues to vote for it:

> Why? The very object of this bill is to protect the freedmen and refugees in their rights; and let me say, whenever the coloured man is completely and fully protected in the Southern States he will never visit Illinois and he will never visit Indiana and every Northern State will be depopulated of colored people as will Canada.[17]

Neither prejudice nor even high moral purpose show on the roll call. The bill passed on February 6th by a resounding 136 votes to 33.[18] There was a slight delay while adjustments were made between House and Senate and agreement was reached on February 9th. Then came the bombshell. Johnson vetoed it on February 19th.

It is curious that Trumbull seems to have been taken by surprise. He must have known from General Howard that part of the Bureau's difficulties were caused by Johnson's policy of returning control over local affairs to civilians and restoring lands to them which the Bureau counted on for freedmen. He must have known that the black codes were not an act of God but of legislators in states Johnson now believed reconstructed. All the moderates had had to go on was his rhetoric.

The veto message demonstrated why that was so treacherous. Johnson still professed to share with Congress the "strongest desire" to protect the freedmen in their property rights and their "independence and equality in making contracts for their labour." In fact the Republicans who voted for the Bureau Bill wanted more. They wanted equality before the law. Johnson baulked at providing machinery to achieve it. He detailed his objections to the judicial features of the bill, echoing many of the points already made by Midwestern Democrats and Cowan in the debate. High among these he criticised the extension of military jurisdiction and protection to Bureau officers in all parts of the country. He shared the view that its procedures appeared to have been designed to avoid accountability. To his mind the civil authorities, especially the courts of nation and state were adequate to the task of protecting freedmen. It was a fanciful thought in February 1866.

Beyond procedural objections the message settled down to the politics of prejudice and the lifelong convictions of states rights. Freedom was guaranteed by constitutional amendment and the law of supply and demand. White folks had never had government money to care for their destitute. To spend it on blacks was insulting, weakening to the moral fibre, and expensive. The message ended on a controversial political note with his objection to the passage of divisive legislation at a time when unity should be their objective, and when the eleven states most affected by it were unrepresented, though in his eyes they should be because their governments had been fully restored.

One sound observation he made was that the bill placed too much power in the Executive - sound that is, if Johnson was going to use his executive power to sabotage the Bureau the way he had in 1865. As William Brock observes, some of Johnson's objections were valid if one assumed that everybody, including the President, was going to act badly.[19] It was certainly not that he took a restrained view of his office. Later in the veto message he argued that his office gave him a more compelling claim than Congress to protect the states, since his was the national voice, theirs the local. On the strength of that he recommended harmony and the recognition of States restored to loyalty. While he "would in no wise interfere with the discretion of Congress with regard to the qualifications of members" his meaning was plain. Reconstruction was primarily Executive business, just as the rights of freedmen were state business.

If Lincoln was reputed to have lagged just a few weeks behind Congress on important issues, Johnson was not even travelling, let alone in the same direction. Trumbull replied to the veto in one of the most eloquent speeches of his career:

> The President believes it unconstitutional: I believe it constitutional. He believes that it will involve great expense; I believe it will save expense. He believes that the freedmen will be protected without it; I believe he will be tyrannized over, abused and virtually re-enslaved without some legislation by the nation for his protection. He believes it unwise; I believe it to be politic. I thought, in advocating it, that I was acting in harmony with the views of the President.[20]

He emphasised the consistency of the legislation with the President's Annual Message in which he had said that "we shall but fulfil our duties as legislators by according equal and exact justice to all men, special privileges to none." It was too late, however, to either shame or reason the President into accord. Whatever allowances could have been offered for his early ambiguities he knew what he was doing now. On February 13th he had told Gideon Welles of his intention to veto it and betrayed to him his paranoia about Radical conspiracies against himself and Tennessee. It was not to be the last time in American history that a President built a wall around himself and incurred the risks of simply not knowing what was going on outside. Seward offered him a draft veto message which would have disappointed but not outraged the Congressional Republican.[21] The preference for outrage was his own and it threatened to become a habit, to judge by his performance on Washington's Birthday when he treated a group of serenaders to unedited comment on some of his Radical opponents. In the Senate the bill failed to pass over the veto by one vote short of the necessary two-thirds. In the House it re-passed with ease. The vote showed that Republican patience was severely frayed. Two months later it would be quite ended.

If fears for the usurpation of state functions in home constituencies had fuelled midwestern opposition in the Freedmen's Bureau debate, it was only a foretaste of what was to come. The Civil Rights Bill, S.61 introduced on the same day, applied nationwide. It was not a makeshift arrangement but the structure which would stand once the military scaffolding of the Bureau bill was removed. Before it came up for debate Senator Saulsbury gave notice of its enormity, that "for the first time in the history of the legislation of this country it is attempted by Congress to invade the States of the Union and undertake to regulate the law applicable to their own citizens[22]." Whether it was such powerful medicine, or simply pursued the "limited objectives" of securing certain enumerated rights - but no more - remains controversial among historians and still more so among lawyers who pick the historical bones of Jones v Alfred Mayer Co.[23]

The Civil Rights Bill began with a definition of who a United States citizen was. Leaving aside untaxed Indians it included everyone born in the country and not subject to any foreign power. It was the definition which enjoyed common currency among abolitionists and Republicans and the debate confirmed their belief in the three points of a triangle - birth/allegiance/the protection of government.[24]

The bill did not then proceed to define what rights attached to the status of being an American citizen. Instead it chose to tie the idea of a common national denominator to the variations which states already made in fleshing out the detail of their white citizens rights and responsibilities. These variations were believed, rightly or wrongly, to already contain common minima. The bill chose the same formula as the Wade-Davis Bill and the Freedmen's Bureau Bill. What was good enough for white citizens in their home states was good enough for black. While it created no new rights, as Trumbull and others frequently insisted, it did create a new dimension - equal protection of them at home, underwritten by the nation.[25]

Citizens were to enjoy "the same right .... to make and enforce contracts, to sue, be parties and give evidence, to inherit, purchase, lease, sell, hold and convey real and personal property, and to full and equal benefit of all laws and proceedings for the security of persons and property." Up to that point in the text it would have revolutionised many state laws relating to married women. But the act went on to indicate that these were not rights to be enjoyed equally by all citizens but the same rights "enjoyed by white citizens." James Wilson explained what was on the minds of the drafters with respect to that phrase. "Unless these qualifying words were incorporated in the bill," he said, "those rights might be extended to all citizens, whether male or female, majors or minors[26]." The bill had to be carefully drafted, not to avoid giving black citizens civil rights but to ensure that equality in these matters was strictly racial. A black woman's citizenship was to be as different from her husband's as a white woman's from hers. Republicans clearly had no intention of trampling willy-nilly on state sensitivities in these matters.

Rights were not nationalised in the sense of being singled out from a sea of state citizenship and defined in a different way. As Herman Belz writes, "the purpose of the civil rights bill was to guarantee intrastate equality before the law[27]." Behind this idea, however, there was an assumption that fundamental rights belonged to people by reason of their being citizens of the nation as well as the state. Entitlement to "the same" personal and property rights assumed not only that these things were already enjoyed by whites, but also that they formed the recognisable basis of expectations in every state. Citizenship was both general and particular, both national and state, dimensions of the one idea. Trumbull borrowed from Justice Washington's opinion in Corfield v Coryell less because it was a definitive enumeration of the "privileges and immunities" of citizenship, more because it expressed the idea of a common pulse, and an expandable but not contractable baseline.[28]

Garret Davis criticised Trumbull for clouding the issue by inappropriately transplanting rights from the comity clause. The clause was about the rights of migrants and had no relevance to the relationship between states and their own citizens.[29] This bill, however, said Representative Kerr, did enlarge the privileges and immunities of blacks, not as citizens of the nation but as citizens of the states. He warned against confusing these things by misleading references to ideas of comity.[30] It was not that Trumbull, for one, was so poor a lawyer that he did not know the comity clause was about migrants. While insisting that the bill invented any new privileges and immunities he said simply, "how much more are the native born citizens of the State itself entitled to these rights[31]."

In the debate, it was opponents rather than supporters who clamoured for definition and enumeration in order to be sure that some rights were not included. As originally drafted Section 1 began "That there shall be no discrimination in civil rights or immunities among the inhabitants of any State or Territory of the United States on account of race, color, or previous condition of slavery." It was only on March 13th that the section was stricken, partly in response to Bingham's constitutional objections and also because the clause had become the focus for the bill's opponents to chew and worry over what "civil rights" might mean. Suffrage, jury service and integrated schools were the common cues for panic and elicited reassurance from Republicans which inevitably drew on the language of "enumerated" and "limited to." Thus Trumbull rejected the charge that civil rights included suffrage. "This bill," he said, "relates to civil rights only[32]." Representative Thayer argued that the bill's enumeration of rights "precludes any possibility that general words which have been used can be extended beyond the particulars which have been enumerated[33]." James Wilson denied that the bill was an instruction to admit black citizens to the polls, the jury or the same school as whites.[34] On March 13th Section 1 of the bill was stricken, accompanied by James Wilson's explanation that "some gentlemen were apprehensive that the words we propose to strike out might give warrant for a latitudinarian construction not intended." He prefaced that, however, by assuring the bill's supporters that it did not materially change it.[35]

Evidence that the Republicans intended to "limit" the bill to civil rights is not evidence that they intended limited civil rights. Undoubtedly many Republicans were coming to see political rights as indispensable to civil rights. Speaking to constituents on November 7th 1866 Radical George Boutwell of Massachusetts made the point that without equal participation in government there could be no equal protection of the laws. The Negro must be the principal, as well as the agent, the maker as well as the subject of law.[36] Although political and civil rights were usually distinguished by Republicans there was also a tradition of overlap. In Corfield Judge Washington had mentioned the elective franchise as one the the privileges and immunities of citizenship "as regulated and established by the laws or constitution of the state in which it is to be exercised." Several law dictionaries and manuals like Webster's Unabridged and Worcester's were well-thumbed by Congressional debaters at the time and linked suffrage to citizenship. Nevertheless the Civil Rights Bill was about civil rights. Republicans left their hands untied for the future, however, by rejecting Senator Saulsbury's proposed amendment to insert "except the right to vote in the States" by a decisive 39 votes to 7. A similar attempt in the House also failed.[37]

Subtracting the vote, jury service and perhaps also an integrated education from "civil rights" left everything else. The Civil Rights Bill was "emumerated" in the same sense as the Freedmen's Bureau and in almost identical terms except that in the Bureau Bill the word "including" was expressly used twice while in its companion bill it was implied. No doubt the original Section 1 had been thought to convey the sense that, with respect to civil rights at any rate, the selection which followed was not intended to be definitive. There is no evidence that it was stricken in order to avoid a "latitudinarian construction" of fundamental civil rights; the key to the scope of the bill did not lie in a list but in the phrase "the same rights ..... as white citizens." Rightly or wrongly the framers assumed that even the lowest common denominator among the states would yield a harvest of rights probably somewhere above the most fundamental.

Political rights were not included. Nor were social. The well-known exchange between Senators Trumbull and Hendricks about the effect of the bill on miscegeration statutes illustrates that. Most Northern, certainly all midwestern states prohibited interracial marriage. Yet this bill appeared to threaten that by extending full contractual rights to black citizens.

Trumbull reassured his worried colleague that the bill did not grant an abstract right to marry but a right to contract and a liability to punishment which was co-extensive with white citizens':

> I beg the Senator for Indiana to read the bill. One of its objects is to secure the same civil rights and subject to the same punishments persons of all races and colors. How does this interfere with the law of Indiana preventing marriages between whites and blacks? Are not both races treated alike by the law of Indiana? Does not the law make it just as much a crime for a white man to marry a black woman as for a black woman to marry a white man, and _vice versa_? ..... Make the penalty the same on all classes of people for the same offence, and then no one can complain.[38]

If this was an invitation to retain certain discriminations by equalising punishments it could only have had any relevance at the interfaces between civil and social rights. The limits to this kind of activity lay not in law but in the old proverb about cutting off one's nose to spite one's face.

The bill brought forth strong passions, not just with respect to the parameters of rights but to the method of protecting them. The United States district courts, "exclusively of the courts of the several States" were given jurisdiction of crimes and offences under the act, and concurrent jurisdiction with the circuit courts where a right was denied or could not be enforced in the state courts. The act transplanted the removal procedures of the 1863 Habeas Corpus Act and made them available to all persons making a claim under the act as well as all personnel who ran foul of state law while trying to enforce it.

On these provisions opponents recited the now very familiar objections that the federal government intended to snatch cases from the states and try them again _de novo_ in the federal courts without regard for state law. Criminal cases were again included under the bill's removal procedure and drew the sharpest reaction around the question of the lack of federal law on murder, arson, theft and so on.[39] All that the law offered as reassurance against filtering a new criminal law into the states by the backdoor was the instruction:

> The jurisdiction in civil and criminal matters hereby conferred on the district and circuit courts of the United States shall be exercised and enforced in conformity with the laws of the United States, so far as such laws are suitable to carry the same into effect; but in all cases where such laws are not adapted to the object, or are deficient in the provisions necessary to furnish suitable remedies and punish offences against law, the common law, as modified and changed by the constitution and statutes of the State wherein the court having jurisdiction of the cause, civil or criminal, is held, so far as the same is not inconsistent with the Constitution and laws of the United States, shall be extended to any govern said courts in the trial and disposition of such cause, and, if of a criminal nature, in the infliction of punishment on the party found guilty.

It was all the reassurance that could be offered under the circumstances and the law had to leave room for manoeuvre on occasions where existing law was at odds with the purposes of the act. If the fears of opponents were not in general well-founded, they were still understandable. The Court in Swift v Tyson had built a whole general law of commerce on such an ambiguity in the Judiciary Act.

The words "exclusively of the courts of the several States" in describing district court jurisdiction under the act also was a source of great anxiety. It seemed further evidence that Republicans had deliberately designed a whole edifice of emancipation, indemnification and now civil rights measures to avoid state courts and state law. Senator Trumbull, however, attempted reassurance on this point too. "Exclusive" jurisdiction, he said, did not mean that in all cases involving a civil right the state courts would be denied jurisdiction.[40] States would continue to legislate freely and their courts take sole jurisdiction provided they respected that equality before the law which the bill demanded. "The bill draws to the Federal Government no power whatever if the States will perform their constitutional obligations" was Trumbull's stock argument.[41] When they did not, however, there was a federal question and the federal courts would have jurisdiction, exclusive of any attempts by States to retain jurisdiction. Far from being a bill to avoid courts, Trumbull insisted, this was a court bill.[42]

The bill's framers were prepared to use a little co-ercion to ensure that the law was executed and that, where appropriate, the federal courts did have exclusive jurisdiction. Under Section 2, judges, or officials or anyone else who deprived a person of his rights or subjected him to different punishments from whites were liable to be fined, or jailed up to a year, or both. Other features were drawn from the 1850 Fugitive Slave Law which commended itself as a workable model of enforcement, shorn of its appalling purpose. Republicans enjoyed the irony of turning slavery's engines to protect freedom.

District attorneys, marshals and deputy marshals, court-appointed commissioners and Freedmen's Bureau officers were "authorized and required" to institute proceedings against violators of the act, at the expense of the United States. Marshals and their deputies were charged with executing all warrants, and were empowered to recruit the help of bystanders, posses and the militia to help enforce them. Fines and imprisonment up to six months awaited anyone who obstructed those who enforced the act, or who attempted to rescue detainees from custody or harbour fugitives from warrants. The kid gloves were off. The curious blend of law and force is well illustrated by the last two sections of the act, one authorising the President to use the army, navy, or militia if need be to prevent violations and enforce the law, the other allowing appeals to the Supreme Court. The sword and the robe sat uneasily side by side.

Democrats were shocked at the idea of putting state judges under such compulsion and subjecting them to possible fines and imprisonment. In the House, Representative Eldridge cast it as a bill which "seeks to lay prostrate at the feet of the Federal Government the judiciary of the States. It not only proposes to enter the States to regulate their police and municipal affairs, but it attempts to destroy the independence of the State judiciary[43]." It was a persistent theme among the bill's opponents in the days between Johnson's veto and the bill's repassage. Representative Lawrence defended the penal sections as extraordinary and only to be justified by the magnitude of the problems and the difficulties of the times. When these abated he hoped they would become redundant.[44] Trumbull also justified penal sanctions against judges who acted "knowingly, viciously, or oppressively" in disregard of the law.[45]

Republicans had simply had enough experience by 1866 to know how state courts could sabotage federal jurisdiction. Suits against federal officers mounted daily. In the South the army had had to resort to protecting itself from harassment by General Orders No.3 under which such prosecutions were effectively discontinued. It reflected the reality of life in the South. The freedmen relied on the protection of the Bureau and the army. The Bureau relied on the army. The army relied on itself. It was not an ideal mutual dependancy and James Wilson preferred law:

> We may provide by law for the same ample protection through the civil courts that now depend on the orders of our military commanders; and I will never consent to any other construction of our Constitution, for that would be the elevation of the military above the civil power.[46]

Legal remedies were for the moment fragile, however. The Habeas Corpus Act offered federal officers removal procedures to take their cases into federal courts but could not compel state courts to comply. If there was to be an alternative to self-help it would have to contemplate being tough on judges.

Representative Cook introduced an amendment to the Habeas Corpus Act on March 13th 1866 just as the Civil Rights Bill emerged from the Judiciary Committee to which it had been re-committed. It made judges liable for damages and double costs if they proceeded with a case after it had been properly removed to a federal court.[47] In the Senate, Clark defended these sanctions because, "We have had about enough of this State authority to teach it to yield respect and obedience to the laws of the United States." His colleague Trumbull cited precedents for penal sanctions against judges, referring to a New York law and to Kent's <u>Commentaries.</u> The amendment was approved on May 11th, 1866. It became woven into the fabric of Trumbull's two bills. The Freedmen's Bureau bill had put Bureau personnel under military protection. The Civil Rights bill explicitly included them and all who enforced it in the removal procedures of the 1863 act "<u>and all acts amendatory thereof.</u>" That the toughening up of the Habeas Corpus Act was related quite deliberately to the purposes of the Civil Rights bill may be deduced from the fact that the words "and all acts amendatory thereof" were only added on March 13th, the same day Cook introduced the Habeas Corpus amendment to the House. The added teeth in the one were intended to be incorporated into the other. It was not, as Democrats frequently charged, all part of a conspiracy to undermine state judiciaries.[48] Senator Cowan referred to "this brood of transferring cases from the State courts to the United States courts[49]." If it was not a conspiracy, it was at least beginning to look more like a plan than earlier, haphazard legislative beginnings. The Republicans were learning from experience and applying what they learned in one context to others. Thus, protection for freedmen, Bureau agents and army officers came to be seen as links in the same jig-saw.

Doubts about the bill, however, were not confined to Democrats or even a handful of conservative Republicans. John Bingham, fully in sympathy with its purposes, doubted whether Congress had the constitutional power to compel states to refrain from discriminating among their inhabitants. His interpretation of the Thirteenth Amendment's enforcement clause was not as expansive as Wilson's and he believed that the bill's objects could only be achieved by a further amendment to the Constitution "expressly prohibiting the States from any such abuse of power in the future." While the bill was still under consideration he attempted to make his objections constructive and worked towards removing some of what he believed were its worst constitutional flaws. Among his specific objections were the lack of provision in the original bill for appeal to the Supreme Court, and to the penal sections which might make it an offence for the Governor of Ohio to obey the laws of his own state. He moved to strike out the broad language of Section 1 ("There shall be no discrimination in civil rights or immunities among citizens of the United States") as well as the penal sections. But his motion to attach these instructions to a motion to re-commit the bill to the Judiciary Committee was defeated on March 9th by 113 votes to 37.[50] All but two of those who voted with him were Republicans, evidence that a significant majority shared his doubts. Bingham was on the prevailing side of the vote to re-commit the bill, however, voting against the majority of his party who feared that a vote to re-commit was a vote to weaken it. The bill returned from committee with some of Bingham's suggestions incorporated. Amendments proposed to strike out the first section and add an addition section allowing a final appeal to the Supreme Court. The penal sections remained. With these changes accepted the bill came to a final vote on March 13th and passed by a resounding 111 votes to 38. Bingham carried his constitutional scruples as far as "Nay." The Senate had already passed it on February 2nd, with only three Republicans in dissent. Even Dixon and Doolittle supported it there, raising high hopes that President Johnson did too.

He did not. Just as Republicans were beginning to build something that looked more than ever before like a planned response to overlapping problems, the demolition man moved in again. Johnson announced his veto on March 27th, and once again the choice of the most provocative ground was his own, rejecting Seward's more moderate draft.

The tone of the message was set by its opening complaint that this bill, which made citizens of Chinamen and gypsies as well as Negroes, discriminated against intelligent and patriotic foreigners, who still had to wait for citizenship. He went on to echo all the objections so lately uttered by the Democrats. Right at the heart of the veto, however, lay his unshakeable belief that the rights covered in the bill were exclusively state business. He acknowledged that there were limitations on state powers. No state could pass a law impairing contracts, bills of attainder or ex post facto laws, or make anything but gold and silver legal tender. But there was nothing to stop them discriminating among their citizens with respect to such matters as property rights. In the "exercise of State policy over matters exclusively affecting the people of each State it had frequently been thought expedient to discriminate between the two races," and miscegenation laws were an example of that. Johnson was clearly not assured by Republican explanations on that point, or on the safe separation of civil and political rights. He objected that if Congress could decide who had the right to hold real estate, testify and so on, then they could also decide who could vote and sit on juries. His was a "thin end of the wedge" argument.

Fears for state judiciaries were high on his list of priorities. The bill "invades the judicial power of the states," depriving state judges of their independence. The penal sections were particularly objectionable in that they punished state officers for faithfully adhering to laws passed by their own legislatures. _De novo_ judgements in federal courts also threatened a situation where "over this vast domain of criminal jurisprudence provided by each state for the protection of its own citizens, and for the punishment of all persons who violate its criminal laws, federal law, wherever it can be made to apply, displaces State law." That was an exercise of judicial power which in Johnson's mind was quite beyond the Constitution.

For the President, "the details of the bill seem fraught with evil." He returned to the theme of the Freedmen's Bureau bill veto that capital and labour could be left to work out a new relationship now that slavery was safely gone. Intervention in the laws of political economy hindered rather than helped that adjustment. The message ended on the most improbable note of all:

> I will cheerfully co-operate with Congress in any measure that may be necessary for the protection of the civil rights of the freedmen, as well as those of all other classes of persons throughout the United States, by judicial process, under equal and impartial laws, in conformity with the provisions of the Federal Constitution.

It was too late for the President to endorse the principle and deny the means to make it a reality. The tenuous line between Johnson and the moderates snapped. In a display of integrity and unity, tinged with disappointment among those who had kept on hoping for more from the President, Congress accomplished a constitutional 'first' by re-passing the bill over the veto. On April 6th it passed the Senate with the required two-thirds majority, aided by the unseating of New Jersey Democrat John P. Stockton and the non-appearance of Dixon.[51] The House needed no aid in its resounding vote of April 9th; 122 to 41. Having stood firm once, it was easier to do so twice, and on July 16th an amended Freedmen's Bureau bill also re-passed. For Johnson - these were the first steps to political suicide. For American citizens - the possibility of equality before the law.

But it was not to be. Far away from Washington it was left to Bureau officers and the army to make sense of citizenship in the chaos of the first days of freedom. General O.O. Howard, Commissioner of the Bureau, later estimated that their courts dealt with 100,000 complaints in 1866.[52] They were mostly petty disputes, more often between blacks than between black and white, but nevertheless testing the meaning of freedom. The judicial work of the Bureau was only a small part of what it did, as one Union officer who served it recalled:

> Indeed a Bureau officer was an official jack-of-all trades. He must understand the Army regulations; he must be able to lead troops on occasion; he must have an idea of civil law; he was a Poor Law Commissioner; he was a statistician. With all this multifarious knowledge, he must be a man of quick common sense, with a special faculty for deciding what not to do. His duties and powers were to a great extent vague, and in general he might be said to do best when he did least.[53]

Too often, however, the inaction of Bureau officers was not a sign that things were going well, but that the civil authorities were once again in uncontested control. There were many reasons which inclined Bureau officers to return jurisdiction to state officials and courts somewhat too precipitously for the good of the freedmen. One was the prevailing antipathy to the enlargement of government in the traditional concerns of the state. The Bureau's leadership shared some of the same assumptions as the Congressional leadership which designed the law. The assistant commissioners were drawn from predominantly Northern, college-educated, native, middle-class, Protestant backgrounds, disposed to believe in economic opportunity and the sufficiency of mere statutary equality.[54] There were civilians and lawyers serving in the Bureau, but lack of funds and available manpower led to the bulk of its personnel being seconded from army service. Few of them were trained in the law, and many regarded the judicial work as a burden best lifted as soon as possible to the state courts.[55] Lack of enthusiasm for the work, their own share of racism, and the sheer magnitude of the problems laid the groundwork for co-operation with local officials, and some even used their authority to help planters regain control over blacks through the enforcement of vagrancy and apprenticeship laws.[56] Even with the will to make the Bureau work effectively in the interests of blacks there was manpower and geography to reckon with. In east central Texas, Bureau agent Charles Culver had 2,800 square miles to look after in three counties, with over 7,500 blacks and a hostile white population over three times larger.[57] If Texas was larger than life it was not so unique in terms of problems.

As much as all these difficulties, however, the Bureau was hamstrung by official policy and a President bent on undermining its work. Under the terms of the act which created the Bureau in 1865 there was no mention of courts. These were set up originally under General Howard's Circular of May 30th 1865. It authorised the Bureau to take jurisdiction of cases where blacks were a party and could not obtain justice either because the courts were not functioning or their testimony was excluded. Right from the beginning Johnson used the order as a means of putting pressure on the states to admit Negro testimony as a means of swiftly regaining control over their judicial business themselves.[58] In Alabama in 1865 General Wagner Swayne invited state judges and magistrates willing to acknowledge freedmen's rights to serve as judicial agents of the Bureau. The policy of transferring jurisdiction was followed elsewhere, even in Mississippi where judges still would not admit black testimony. Army and Bureau personnel who did not relinquish jurisdiction and who fought the black codes, like Thomas Osborn and Thomas Conway got no support or were dismissed. Official policy combined with innate conservatism to frustrate the goal of equality before the law. One of Salmon P. Chase's correspondents wrote from South Carolina, "the Military here, as a general rule do not co-operate with radical men; and the Bureau is a little inclined to conservatism[59]."

By late 1866 state courts had regained jurisdiction. General Howard had awakened to the consequences of that policy a full year earlier when he toured the South and came to the conclusion that justice simply was not being done in the state courts. He collaborated with Trumbull and others in Washington and lobbied for a bill which would enable the Bureau courts to hold on to jurisdiction. But first there was Johnson's veto in February. Then there was his Proclamation of August 20th declaring the return of civil order. Anticipating the Milligan decision he ordered an end to the military trial of civilians, threatening an end to the provost marshal and Bureau courts on which freedmen depended, as well as the military commissions which tried more serious offences. Freedmen's Bureau legislation had finally passed in July 1866. Although similar to Trumbull's original bill it did not authorise penal sanctions against state officials who denied rights under the act, and it still relied heavily on Presidential discretion. Patently the President would use that discretion against rather than for the Bureau. Howard's efforts to re-convene the Bureau courts under a Circular of September 19th, accompanied by a secret letter to the assistant commissioners, was doomed to failure. He withdrew it on December 19th. By that time the Supreme Court had decided Milligan and Johnson used it to justify taking an important case out of Bureau jurisdiction, that of Doctor James Watson of Virginia, accused of killing a Negro. He was subsequently discharged. The state courts were back in business.[60]

It is too easy to draw the conclusion that the Bureau, and the Congress which created it were "tragically limited by the common assumptions of mid-nineteenth-century America" or enmeshed in the "configurations of American government - legal institutions" which made states the centre of the firmament.[61] Many Congressmen and army men were struggling mightily to adapt to new circumstances and there was evidence of lessons learned in the legislation of 1866. They did expect States to go on looking after their citizens, with federal intervention being the exception rather than the norm, but at least in 1866 they were not afraid of a little muscle, either in the law or in the field.

There was courage too, and more than a few heroes. In September 1865, during the first year of the Bureau, an agent in Shreveport, Louisiana, imprisoned the judge, sheriff and all twelve jurors of a local court which had unjustly found against a Negro for stealing a horse.[62] Charles E. Culver, an Illinois volunteer who served the Bureau in Texas in 1867 fined employers for defrauding freedmen and sometimes set aside the rulings of the local courts where they had been ostensibly prejudiced against blacks. On one occasion in September 1867 Culver released all blacks who had been imprisoned for three or more months who were not under a bond of more than five hundred dollars. In January 1866 General Alfred Terry enjoined enforcement of Virginia's vagrancy statutes. In South Carolina in early 1866, General Sickles continued to prohibit state courts from exercising authority over freedmen.

It was dangerous work. Bureau agents and army officers were often the only representatives of federal authority in a hostile area. They walked a tightrope between two civil authorities, the one in Washington anxious for procedure, the other in the States anxious to relieve them of their responsibilities and get on with it themselves. They were expected to shield the freedman from violence "by the book" rather than by the sword, and yet they often did not even have enough resources to protect themselves. Charles E. Culver was shot in November 1867 trying to enforce a local ordinance against carrying weapons in the town of Cotton Gin. The army could not always spare the troops to protect both Negroes and Bureau agents. Yet self-help was usually the only help.

Bureau officers "under military protection and jurisdiction" were entitled to remove suits against them to the federal courts under the Civil Rights Act. Evidence of successful removals is not conspicuous however. This may be because cases did not often emerge from the web of local circumstances, with its overtones of intimidation and sometimes violence. In some instances it may be that cases did not reach the federal courts because the agent depended on military rescue rather than judicial action. This is what happened to one Bureau agent in Texas, and his experience illustrates so many of the problems of enforcement. It was a case about who protects the army for protecting a Freedmen's Bureau agent for protecting freedmen.

General Getty, the commanding officer, instructed General Heintzelman to release Mr. Longworth from civil custody.[63] Longworth was a Bureau Agent who had been "illegally arrested" for acts done under his official capacity. In ordering the release on 29th September 1866, Getty referred to the Army's General Order No.3, ordering the protection of agents, freedmen and others from prosecutions in the state courts. (In later correspondence, the Freedmen's Bureau and Civil Rights Act were cited as additional authority, perhaps illustrating the confusion of men on the spot as to their authority). Heintzelman complied with the order and removed Longworth and all the papers in the case, from local custody. The clerk of the county proceeded to instruct the sheriff to arrest Heintzelman. Heintzelman refused to obey the capias. He appealed to the Adjutant General's office at Galveston saying, "I would not consider my life safe in the hands of the Texas civil authorities[64]." The appeal went right the way up the army echelons. General Grant approved the action, and requested information from the War Department as to whether Heintzelman would be sustained by the Government. The ball passed from one corner to another without anyone picking it up. Stanton wrote to the President for instructions on January 29th.[65] On January 30th, the President instructed Stanton to refer it to the Attorney-General. Meanwhile, events intervened. Whether these events brought comfort to General Heintzelman or not, the Attorney-General's office was at least off the hook, when the case closed with this postscript of 15th July 1868, over a year later:

> Delay and subsequent events supervened and the case is superseded.[66]

In Texas, the Bureau agent was fortunate to have such assistance to hand from the army. Harmony and co-operation could not always be assumed, despite - perhaps even because of - the overlap in personnel. The army was short-staffed for all purposes, and commanders often resented having to allocate men to duties they did not always regard as a priority. Although the Bureau often relied on military commissioners for assistance in trying more serious offences, there were also occasions when jurisdictions clashed, usually between the army's provost courts and the Bureau's courts which dealt with much the same sort of business.[67] For all the procedural jig-saw pieces which Congress had fitted together, in practice the men on the spot dealt with confusion. Indeed the confusion over the boundaries between civil and military "protection" and "jurisdiction" reached all the way back to Washington. Such problems were expected to be of short duration. The real test was when the scaffolding was removed and the Civil Rights Act brought equality under the law to all, black and white, victors and vanquished.

Indeed both the army and the Bureau eagerly awaited the day when federal courts would pick up their burden. In November 1865 Texas commander, General H.G. Wright wrote of the army's limitations in filling the law's gaps, "Cases are constantly arising which are properly referrable to the District U.S. Court, and which call for prompt adjustment; and as they often involve nice points of law, I have not the means for properly deciding them, even if I conceived myself authorized to entertain them[68]." After Johnson effectively cut the feet from under the Bureau courts in 1866, officials turned more and more to the federal courts as the last, best hope for the protection of rights under the Civil Rights Act.

They were to be disappointed. The President had expressed his views in the veto message, and re-passage of the act was not about to make him put his weight, or that of the Attorney-General's office behind it. Everything depended on judicial interpretation, and on the willingness of state courts to play by the rules.

Some state courts delivered surprisingly co-operative opinions, as they had done on the 1863 Habeas Corpus Act. In former Confederate States the highest courts affirmed the Negro's right to testify under the Civil Rights Act, Texas in Ex parte Warren in 1868, Arkansas in the 1869 case of Kelly v The State.[69] Indeed, in this latter case when the court was adjudicating an appeal against a conviction for robbery, on the grounds that black testimony was illegal and the Civil Rights Act unconstitutional, one of the judges, McClure, expressed a startingly optimistic view albeit in a separate opinion. He thought such a case was unlikely to occur in the state again, for the lapse of time and the judgment of other tribunals were moving with "unerring certainty" towards the conclusive establishment of the right of a black man to testify against a white one.

In Smith v Moody, Indiana's highest court sustained the right of a black immigrant plaintiff to sue on a promissory note, despite Indiana's laws denying blacks either entry or contractual capacity.[70] A thornier subject was the marriage contract. Mostly state courts, like Trumbull in the Senate, did not think that laws forbidding interracial marriage contravened the Civil Rights Act. But there was evidence of confusion. In Ellis v The State in 1868 Alabama's Supreme Court reversed a lower court which had found a miscegenation law unconstitutional.[71] The judge reasoned that the Civil Rights Act prohibited discrimination in punishments on grounds of race rather than in the making of race a criteria for the original offence. Four years later, however, the same court changed its mind in Burns v The State when it reversed a judgment against a justice of the peace for solemnising an interracial marriage.[72] Overruling Ellis, Judge B.F. Saffold argued that discriminatory laws had arisen because of the black man's condition and the object of the Civil Rights Act was to end that discrimination and place him on the same footing with white citizens with respect to making contracts, including marriage. In 1877 the pendulum in Alabama had swung back again, however, and the court upheld the conviction of a white woman for marrying a black man, on the grounds of the racial equality of punishment. In Louisiana the same Judge Taliaferro who had denied the validity under the Thirteenth Amendment of promissory notes on slaves also sustained the rights of the children of an interracial marriage to their inheritance.[73] His argument was that the Civil Rights Act had superceded former state laws which had made their marriage illegal. These were unusual holdings and surpassed the expectations of the framers. Much more typical was the opinion of the Indiana judge who held that, "The right, in the states, to regulate and control, to guard, protect and preserve this God-given, civilising and Christianizing institution is of inestimable importance and cannot be surrendered[74]." Next to slavery, marriage was closest to the heart.

Over and above the model behaviour of some state courts in generously interpreting the act without prompting, others also exhibited a willingness to acknowledge the scope of the removal procedures. The opinion of Judge Ogden of the Texas Supreme Court in the 1873 case of Gaines v The State would have been enough to warm the hearts of the Republicans who framed the bill.[75] Allowing a motion for the removal of a case against a Negro on the grounds of local prejudice, he argued that the remedy was not restricted to state action under unequal laws. Texas had equal laws, he said, but there were still plenty of places where a black man could not get justice because of prejudice. He went on, "We think that State courts should be exceedingly cautious in attempting to settle questions of grave importance which belong peculiarly to a different and higher tribunal." When it came their turn, these higher tribunals would not read the Act so generously to reach prejudice in the administration of apparently fair laws, but this state court would at least give them the opportunity. So too would North Carolina's highest court in The State v Dunlap in 1871.[76] Citing Gaines the court endorsed the removal power and argued that Congress intended to reach every case "where, by reason of prejudice in a community or otherwise, a fair and impartial trial cannot be had in the state courts."

Untypical though these state court responses were they require explanation. Before the war, Southern appeal courts maintained some procedural fairness in slave criminal trials, at least in part because it mattered to the South not to be seen to be isolated from humane Western legal traditions. Post-war judges remained in an exposed position, yielding the most visible fruits by which the new tree would be known. New state constitutions in the South lengthened the tenure of judges and attempted to free them from direct popular pressures. Georgia's 1865 constitution provided for the election of judges by the legislature. In 1868 this was changed to put more distance between judges and popular passions. The Governor was to make appointments, for the longer period of twelve years.[77]

Judicial appointments during Reconstruction appear to have been dominated by native whites. Carpetbaggers and scalawags played a prominent part in the highest state judicial offices, while lower court appointments often tended to go to the people who had held them before the war.[78] The lives of some notable carpetbag judges have attracted scholarly attention. Professor Harold Hollingsworth illuminated the career of George Andrews, appointed by the Governor of Tennessee to the state Supreme Court in 1868[79]. He was no dilettante Yankee failure gone South to seek compensation in moral superiority. Nor was he a Republican pawn. His decisions reflect a conscientious search for impartiality and equality before the law. The same may be said of Albion Tourgee who served on North Carolina's Supreme Court from 1868 to 1876 and withstood Klan pressures and vituperative editorial comment to pursue even-handed justice.[80]

Scalawags were more numerous at all levels of state judicial appointments. It is difficult to draw a comprehensive group portrait of them in the absence of fuller information and at a time when historians are still trying to answer the general question, "Who were the scalawags[81]?" It seems likely that they would have come from well-educated, fairly well-off backgrounds and have voted Whig or anti-secession Democrat before the war. Some served the Republicans to keep control of events in local white hands. A few may even have transcended their racial prejudices or simply accepted that with slavery gone, equality before the law would have to be dealt with as a fact of life. At the lower levels of the judiciary information is still more incomplete, but suggestive of the conclusion that it was neither carpetbaggers nor scalawags who got the jobs but local men, repentant or not. There were some exceptions, however, and some state histories may throw light on the interactions and relative proportions of these elements.

In Georgia Governor Bullock appointed Joseph E. Brown as the new Chief Justice. He was not a carpetbagger but a former state judge and Governor. As an ardent champion of states rights in wartime he had been a thorn in the flesh of Jefferson Davis. He was joined on the bench by H.K. McCoy, again a local lawyer, former Unionist and a Republican who had played a part in the constitutional convention. The third judge was Hiram Warner, originally from Massachusetts. He was scarcely a carpetbagger, however, since he moved to Georgia in 1821. Of the three, the Yankee immigrant, if he deserved such a title at all, was the most conservative and often found himself in dissent, as in <u>White v Clements</u> when the court upheld the right of Negroes to hold office. In <u>White v Hart</u> Warner was again in dissent when his colleagues held that the Thirteenth Amendment ended the validity of a promissory note on slaves. This time, however, it was Warner's view which prevailed on the United States Supreme Court when the case was appealed.[82]

The civil courts in South Carolina re-opened after the legislature agreed in October 1866 to admit black testimony, but General Daniel Sickles had to suspend them in April 1867 for failure to do justice. When the Radicals came to power in 1868, however, they reorganised the entire judicial system. They established a new supreme court and multi-county circuit county courts, both of which were to be elected by the legislature, and in 1870 they established a bottom layer of trial courts, over which the Governor had the power of appointment.

The first Radical legislature appointed a black judge to the Supreme Court. Jonathan Jasper Wright was educated in New York and was the first black lawyer to be admitted to the bar in Pennsylvania. He came South with the Freedmen's Bureau and played an active part in the 1868 constitutional convention. He served on the bench from 1870 to 1877 and resigned when the Redeemers gained control. Franklin J. Moses Sr., whose son was Governor from 1872-1874, became Chief Justice. He was a local man who had to wait until Congress removed his political disabilities before he took office in 1868. He went on to serve with some distinction until 1877. A.J. Willard was their carpetbag colleague, a New York lawyer who succeeded Moses as Chief Justice and remained on the bench until 1880. This trio was remarkable for its continuity and balance. It attracted this verdict from Francis Simkins and Robert Woody, "In spite of the fact that the Supreme Court was composed of a Scalawag, a carpetbagger and a Negro, its administration was fair and its decisions equitable[83]."

Circuit court appointments were dominated by locals. Out of eight circuits, six went to native whites who had been respected members of the South Carolina bar. Two were black. Black carpetbagger William Whipper from Michigan was elected to the Charleston Circuit Court but ousted by Democratic opponents before he took office. In the first flush of enthusiasm Radical Governors also appointed blacks to the new trial courts, though these appointees were predictably criticised in the local press as unqualified and of the worst sort. Joel Williamson wryly noted, however, that "the participation of Negores in the judiciary of South Carolina during Reconstruction produced no Scottsboro case in which the defendants were white rather than black, and no Negro, either on or off the bench, was ever heard to declare that the white man had no rights that the Negroes were bound to respect[84]." As in Georgia, however, native whites dominated the upper echelons of the judiciary.

So too in Mississippi.[85] Military Governor Adelbert Ames who made the initial appointments made blacks Justice of the Peace but not judges.

His scalawag successor James L. Alcorn who took office in 1870 made cautious appointments to the Supreme Court. He retained two military appointees, scalawag Ephraim Peyton as Chief Justice and carpetbagger Jonathan Tarbell. He added another scalawag, Horatio F. Simrall who was able, loyal and Republican. As in South Carolina the circuit courts were staffed by natives. There were only two carpetbaggers out of fifteen. Of twenty chancery judges only two were identified as Northern. Not only were nearly all of these judges local, but some had been active Confederates like William Hancock and Jehu Orr. Subsequent Governors had to fight the rising cost of maintaining the judiciary. At quarter of a million dollars a year it was "by far the largest item in the state budget " and savings were made. After Governor Ames fled in 1876 wholesale changes were made in the composition of the judiciary, though Republican Simrall on the Supreme Court survived the transition to become Chief Justice. He was not the only survivor on the Southern state benches.

In Alabama, native whites retained control of the judiciary and again scalawags predominated on the Supreme Court with the appointment of E. Woolsey Peck, Thomas M. Peters and Benjamin F. Saffold. Of circuit court judges and chancellors all but two were native whites. William Woods, later to become a federal circuit judge and later still a Supreme Court Justice was the only notable carpetbag judge. A native of Ohio he had come south as a volunteer in the army and stayed to become a Chancellor in 1868. He was a more distinguished carpetbagger however than his colleague on the federal circuit court, Richard Busteed who faced impeachment in 1874 and resigned, to be replaced by a more distant carpetbagger, John Bruce - from Scotland.[86]

Quality is of course more difficult to define than whether a judge was scalawag or carpetbagger. When Louisiana's Governor Wells appointed a Supreme Court there in March 1865 one of its members, R.J. Jones, was said to be so dim that when he asked to be "qualified," the judge to whom he addressed himself said, "I will swear you in; all hell couldn't qualify you[87]." He died in 1865 and some of the more distinguished decisions of the Louisiana Court thereafter were delivered by his successor, Conservative Unionist James G. Taliaferro. There were some able men on Southern benches, a few of them carpetbaggers and more scalawags. In the middle and lower levels patronage worked to return native ante-bellum lawyers and judges to office. Few blacks were appointed and with the exception of South Carolina's imported Jonathan Jasper Wright, they were at the lowest levels.

Decisions favourable to black civil rights can be discovered and explained but they should not be equated with justice. State supreme courts were the gilt on the gingerbread. They were at the end of the road in the process of obtaining justice in the State. All too often the process never began or was cut off in mid-passage. In a letter to Secretary of War Stanton on January 19th 1867, General Howard of the Freedmen's Bureau was cautious about measuring progress by appeal court decisions:

> I am of the opinion that in the courts of superior jurisdiction, the judges are generally disposed to deal fairly with the Negro, but it is notorious that he stands little or no chance before a magistrate or inferior jurisdiction.[88]

Often there was a tale or two behind apparently well functioning judicial systems in former Confederate States. A Texas judge, Winston Banks, wrote to Washington with the assurance that he was holding court without interruption in his district. Later, when he wrote to General Buell in February 1869, it dawned on him that this statement had been elicited from him by certain persons who were trying to pervert the course of justice. They were attempting to procure the release from federal custody of prisoners charged with the murder of a New York carpetbagger, G.W. Smith, and have the case dealt with in the state courts. It was in their interest to convey a very favourable impression of availability of justice in the district. Judge Banks set the record straight in his letter to Buell. Although he was holding court, it was against a background of lawlessness and intimidation which had forced some of his colleagues to seek military protection. He wrote of the problems he was up against - the scourge of outlaws, whose victims included Union soldiers and the local Freedmen's Bureau agent, the murder of several freedmen, the intimidation of another Bureau agent finally rescued from his office by troops disguised as ordinary citizens, an attack on the home of the Republican candidate to the state convention and the harrying of loyal men. Juries would not bring in guilty verdicts. As a result of this letter, the application to transfer the prisoners to the state court was refused.[89]

The honest endeavours of some state courts to execute the letter and occasionally even the spirit of the law is a very small part of the story. Other state supreme courts interpreted the Civil Rights Act as restrictively as it was possible to do, denying that the Thirteenth Amendment did anything more than end slavery in the technical sense of the right of one man to the labour of another. Bowlin v Commonwealth was the leading case of its kind where the Kentucky Court of Appeals found against the constitutionality of the Civil Rights Act and held that it had no effect on the Kentucky laws which excluded black testimony.[90]

Bigger disappointments in the construction of the act were to come from the federal courts, bigger because these courts were the key to enforcement. It was not so in the beginning. The first two outings of the act in the federal circuit courts brought sympathetic and hopeful constructions. These cases have already been referred to as examples of broad interpretations of the meaning of the Thirteenth Amendment. On circuit in Maryland in 1866 in the case of Turner Chief Justice Chase decided that racially discriminatory apprenticeship indentures violated the Civil Rights Act. The same year his colleague Justice Swayne upheld the constitutionality of the act in U.S. v Rhodes in the circuit court of Kentucky. It was a criminal case. The defendant Rhodes had been found guilty of entering a black woman's house. The issue before the court in this appeal for arrestment of judgment was whether or not the black woman's testimony was legal. Under state law it was not. Counsel for Rhodes argued that in a criminal case the only parties affected were the sovereign state which prosecuted and the defendant. The defendant was white; black testimony was excluded under state law; there was no federal question to trigger jurisdiction. Swayne thought not, and upheld the right of black testimony under the Civil Rights Act. He went on to urge a liberal construction of the act "to carry out the wise and beneficient purposes of Congress in enacting it[91]."

After that the Civil Rights Act was put into cold storage for a century, but not before the Supreme Court had taken some of the stuffing out of it in Blyew. It was a test case, a sequel to Bowlin and U.S. v Rhodes. Kentucky retained its laws excluding black testimony and provoked a crop of removal applications to the federal courts. The legislature passed a resolution directing the Governor to employ counsel to defend Blyew and Kennard, convicted in a federal court of the brutal murder of a black woman on the strength of the testimony of black witnesses. B.H. Bristow, United States Attorney for the district thought it an unfortunate test case, since the co-defendants were clearly guilty.[92] The issue was not their guilt, however, but whether Kentucky's denial of black testimony in the case had raised a federal question under the Civil Rights Act, justifying federal jurisdiction.

Justice Strong for the Supreme Court thought not.[93] The purpose of the Civil Rights Act was to protect coloured persons where a court decision might injuriously affect their personal or property rights. Lucy, the murdered woman, was "beyond" being affected because she was dead. The witnesses themselves were not directly affected. If federal courts could claim jurisdiction of every case where the witnesses happened to be black, it would open the way to depriving states of their rightful criminal jurisdiction on the most tangential of issues. It was left to Justices Swayne and Bradley to lodge vigorous dissents. The Civil Rights Act, they argued, reached situations when blacks or anybody else were unable to enforce their rights (under Section 3), as well as where they were directly denied them (under Section 1). Had Lucy lived she would have been directly affected and the denial of testimony raised a federal question. The fact that she died strengthened rather than weakened the case for federal jurisdiction to avoid a denial of justice.

Blyew might have been a setback, certainly not a rout for the Civil Rights Act. What happened was nothing as direct as a rout but death by association with the Fourteenth Amendment. *Slaughterhouse* was the first of a series of cases to do gratuitous damage to the Civil Rights Act in the course of interpreting the Fourteenth Amendment.[91] The facts of the case are well known. The butchers of New Orleans who challenged Louisiana's grant of a monopoly to the Crescent Livestock Landing and Slaughterhouse claimed that it deprived them of one of their privileges and immunities under the Fourteenth Amendment, that of choosing their livelihood. The Thirteenth Amendment and the Civil Rights Act were thrown in for good measure. Louisiana's Supreme Court rejected their case and upheld the statute conferring the monopoly under the State's police power.

When the case came to the Supreme Court on a writ of error Justice Miller agreed and casually spiked the guns of the Thirteenth Amendment and the Civil Rights by using them as evidence of a unified purpose to liberate slaves rather than enlarge the rights of citizens. The most devastating blow fell on the privileges and immunities of national citizenship. Like everybody else who had ever attempted to say what they were Miller announced the impossibility of precision:

> We may hold ourselves excused from defining the privileges and immunities of citizens of the United States which no State can abridge, until some case involving those privileges may make it necessary to do so.

Nevertheless he too could not resist citing a few, including free access to seaports and land offices, and federal protection on the high seas. It left civil rights where they had been before 1866, stateside. The whole raison d'être of the Thirteenth Amendment, the Civil Rights Act and the Fourteenth Amendment was to give the nation responsibilities for protecting freedom and citizenship rights _in_ the states. Far from driving a wedge between State and national citizenship the Republicans had understood these rights as the common centre of both, and no longer dependent on the one only, the state.

Justice Field wrote in dissent:

> A citizen of a State is now only a citizen of the United States residing in that State. The fundamental rights, privileges, and immunities which belong to him as a free man and a free citizen, now belong to him as a citizen of the United States, and are not dependent upon his citizenship of any State.

and Bradley:

> Equality before the law is undoubtedly one of the privileges and immunities of every citizen.

Even if the court's majority had been prepared to entertain such a view of what Congress intended to do for newly freed blacks, it drew back from the revolutionary implications of what it did for whites. If the nation had the power to interfere in such traditional areas of state power as the regulation of slaughterhouses it posed a much greater threat to the whole balance of federalism than what seemed necessary to root out racially unequal laws. To preserve federalism the Court chose to limit understandings of what the framers intended to "blacks only" and further limit understandings of the nation's role in citizenship for everybody. Curiously it was both a "sell-out" of original intentions and also inspired by some of the same constitutional faiths in state rights which had shaped Republican policy in 1866. The difference was that in 1866 the Republicans believed that federalism could not be preserved _unless_ the nation assumed responsibilities for the protection of substantial privileges and immunities for all citizens. Inviting the states to do the work themselves to avoid having to cross state lines was not in their mind the same thing as "leaving" the states to their pre-war role in the lives of their citizens.

State action also apilled over from the Fourteenth Amendment to the Civil Rights Act. The Supreme Court never denied that the Thirteenth Amendment reached private violations but never harnessed the 1866 act to that purpose until Jones v Alfred Mayer Co. in 1968. On circuit in 1874 it was Bradley's opinion that "it is intended to protect against legal disabilities and legal impediments to the free exercise of the rights secured, and not by private infringements of these rights by prejudice or otherwise, where the laws themselves are impartial and sufficient[95]." In the Civil Rights Cases almost a decade later he confirmed that under the Thirteenth Amendment Congress could reach private violations, but that the 1866 act was "intended to counteract and furnish redress against State laws and proceedings, and customs having the force of law[96]." He would not transplant the key word "prejudice" from the Freedmen's Bureau Act to the Civil Rights Act on the pretext that Trumbull's omission had been due to forgetfulness, or that custom meant the same thing. Congress may have intended more, and Trumbull had been called as a witness for both sides. In Jones v Alfred Mayer Co. in 1968 the Supreme Court per Stewart rediscovered the 1866 Act and claimed to have penetrated the mists of time and neglect to its true original meaning.[97] Considerable reliance was placed on Trumbull's explanations that the bill was intended to break down all discriminations between black and white men and that it applied to everybody, "Not State officers especially, but everybody who violates the law. It is the intention to punish everybody who violates the law." Elsewhere, however, he did say that States could avoid the operation of the act by equalising their laws, seeming to imply that the federal government would not reach behind them to punish unequal administration of the laws or private violations. The act was parented by the Thirteenth Amendment which did, by common consent reach private infringement; it did reach "any person;" it did apply to acts done under law or "custom" if not "prejudice," and custom only becomes "state action" by the inferences of the 1870's rather than the 1860's.

By then the Supreme Court had beached the 1866 Civil Rights Act between two Amendments. The Thirteenth reached private violations, but increasingly limited to a narrowly drawn freedom from bondage. The Fourteenth conferred very limited "privileges and immunities" on national citizens and reached only state action. With the court on such a course the safest berth for an act which spoke of the civil rights pertaining to all citizens and enforceable against all persons was with the judicial baggage of the Fourteenth. By the time of Hodges v United States the process of dislodging the Act from the Thirteenth Amendment and attaching it to the penumbras of the Fourteenth was complete.[98]

The disappointing judicial history of the postwar amendments, and acts 'appropriate' to their enforcement, prompted a group of black lawyers in the 1880's to write a volume lamenting the growing gap between the legislative intention, and the judicial application. They urged a return to the original meaning, which had become obscured in "the silent circumspection with which the courts have walked round the Fourteenth Amendment." But their disappointment was not just in the courts but in the way that both political parties had betrayed the goal of equality before the law. They imagined a conversation between an observer, ignorant of the situation, and a "sarcastic reviewer" who might explain what had happened so:

> You must pardon my mixed metaphors and apparent digression. I wanted to explain to you that, if there is a sick patient in this country, in our opinion, it is the civil rights man; but you see, he does not belong to any of the old nor is he a member of either of the modern great parties of the country, and therefore he cannot legitimately share in the treatment practised by their moderators. One party, for the time being, has placed him in quarantine, in one or another of its judicial harbors, to await the disinfecting process, or the expediences of the future. The other has banished him into an infirmary called the State courts. There he will either die an unnatural death, or if ever under their tyrannical treatment he recovers his health, he will be permitted without further molestation to take up his bed and walk, only because his recovery will be universally accepted as a miraculous interposition of Providence.[99]

Certainly the responsibility for the failure to achieve equality before the law was far flung. It went back through the long history of race prejudice in life and law. Certain pre-conceived notions both about Negro inferiority and about the nature of federalism dogged the experiment. In the framing of the legislation itself, the Republicans went to the very boundaries of their own faith in states rights to make men free and still hung back to make them equal. They would have preferred the states to have spared them the need to intervene by equalising their own laws. They had a naive optimism in the power of equal laws to operate equally on all, underestimating the subtleties of private and public discrimination to circumvent as well as defy the law. These are familiar criticisms, especially from historians who are disappointed in the gap between nineteenth and twentieth century liberalism after the first enthusiasm of recognising shared values and dilemmas.

Interestingly what has survived over a century's ebbing and flowing of commitment to equality is the law itself. It could not have been so badly built. There was a touch of boldness in the Freedmen's Bureau and Civil Rights Acts. The federal courts were to be the regular channel of enforcement. But the Republican framers were so exasperated with defiant state officials and judges that they threatened commissioners, posses, and even military force to compel obedience. They would fine and imprison violators. The law contained more power than anyone was able to use, however. Mostly it was a paper boldness, overwhelmed by violence and prejudice as much as faint-heartedness.

State court judges were seldom called to account. Immediately after the passage of the Civil Rights Act, the legislature of Maryland passed a law to reimburse magistrates and judges for any costs which they incurred for rendering decisions against the act. Only a few anecdotes survive of Southern judges arrested or imprisoned, usually by military authority. H.E. Flack records the case of Judge Abell in Louisiana who was arrested in July 1866 charged with "wickedly, wilfully and with malice aforethought" declaring the Civil Rights Act unconstitutional.[100] Relationships between state and federal courts were strained, but they did not break and judges were not jailed under the act. Eighty years of comity counted for something.

President Johnson offered no help to enforcement, first undermining the Freedmen's Bureau and then allowing the Civil Rights Act to die of neglect. On January 8th 1867, a Senate resolution called for information from the President on violations of the Civil Rights Act, and what steps, if any, had been taken by him to enforce the law and punish the offenders. At the War Department, Stanton showed some energy in collecting information. General Grant sent him a chilling list of offences from his knowledge in the Southern States, including the rape of Negro girls, the murder of freedmen and loyalists, and the murder of a former Bureau agent by a man on whom he had once imposed a fine.[101] And yet, when the Attorney-General, Henry Stanbery, wrote to the President in connection with the same resolution on January 21st, 1867 he had no report in his office of such violations. He cited one case from Georgia, of a black man who was being held to involuntary servitude, without being charged with any crime, but concluded, "I am not advised of any other case which requires Executive action under those sections which have been enumerated, or under any other section of the Civil Rights Bill[102]." It was not that such cases were wanting but even with better information from the Attorney-General's office, Johnson was not disposed to aid the execution of the bills he had vetoed.

Time passed; sectional wounds healed. By the time the federal courts hedged the laws with the judicially created limitations of state action and dual citizenship they reflected the conservatism of changed days rather than imposed it. In 1866, however, the Republicans worked in a different environment, characterised by a sense of learning and moving. Whatever disappointment waited around the corner, they did not carry the burden of knowing about it and it would be hard to look back at their work and join with Albion Tourgee in describing it as he did his own part as "A Fool's Errand."

CONCLUSION

Something had been dreadfully amiss with the Union of 1861. Very soon after the war began, it became clear that there could be no return to "The Union as it was, the Constitution as it is." Events put that beyond free choice. But the relationship between men and events was not so chaotic as to make of the Union and Constitution of 1866 something washed up on the beaches after a great storm. Amidst crowded and pressing legislative timetables the Republicans gained insight into how the choices they made mattered to the kind of Union they wanted to live in after the war. If they were not master-planners of the Union's destiny, they were certainly conscious and intelligent participants.

The end of the war was a time for sermonising about the lessons learned, the point of it all. No cenotaph orator had to look far to justify sacrifice. The Union was preserved; the Constitution was adequate to survival and renewal; four million freed slaves were citizens.[1] There was a sense that these were not the victors' spoils but the nation's new responsibilities. Orestes Browson joined in the spirit of thanksgiving with the thought that the war had brought the nation to maturity, causing it:

> to pass from thoughtless, careless, heedless, reckless adolescence to grave and reflecting manhood. The nation had been suddenly compelled to study itself, and henceforth must act from reflection, understanding, science, statesmanship, not from instinct, impulse, passion or caprice, knowing well what it does and wherefore it does it.[2]

Congress had begun in a muddle, ill-organised and inexpert. The Confiscation debates found them strumbling, divided on the nature of the war and the relationship between the Constitution and the war power; their first steps across state lines to administer the law in newly captured Southern territory were accompanied by much agonising on the point of how to bid military commanders respect some state laws but not others; their first search for the machinery to guarantee personal liberty in hostile state environments was tentative and poorly drafted.

By 1866 Congress was notably more efficient and surefooted. One illustration of their gathering confidence and expertise is the way they transplanted enforcement machinery from one piece of legislation to another. The right of a freedman to a writ of _habeas corpus_ in a federal court was explored in various unsuccessful drafts of confiscation laws and re-appeared in the Wade-Davis Bill. The removal machinery employed to protect federal officers from suits in state courts in the Habeas Corpus Act of 1863 was streamlined and re-employed in the Freedmen's Bureau and Civil Rights laws of 1866. The repugnant 1850 Fugitive Slave Law was the raw material for the enforcement of a better law, the Civil Rights Act of 1866. All this would simply be a curiosity to the student of legislative history if it did not also betoken a cumulative appreciation of the ways in which the problems themselves were interrelated.

That was what was so essentially important about the lessons learned. Along the road from the Crittenden-Johnson resolutions to the Fourteenth Amendment the Republicans realised that there was more to this war than winning. It was not just that they wanted the South to be more like the North but that they wanted the North to be more like the ideal of the free society they were fighting for. The Habeas Corpus Act of 1863, the Civil Rights Act of 1866 and of course the constitutional amendments applied nationwide, not just because the North could not reasonably hold the South to higher standards than their own, but because they were needed nationwide. If State sovereignty was a Southern problem states rights were not. During the war there were plenty of demonstrations that federal officers in Pennsylvania, New York or Kentucky were as vulnerable to hostile state processes as they were in the returning South; after the war there were Chinese in California and blacks in the Midwest who could not successfully assert their right to testify against whites. A great deal of debating time on these measures was taken up arguing their effects on Northern jurisdictions. Supporters and opponents were equally alive to the sensitivities of their constituents in areas of traditional state business, especially criminal law and the law of private property. The oft-quoted assurances of Lyman Trumbull and others that the new laws would have no effect on states whose own laws measured up to them should not be understood as invitations to self-satisfaction or token compliance. The North knew that it had work to do also.

In racial matters, Northern self-reconstruction was far from wholehearted and intrastate battles for black suffrage were bitter and mostly unsuccessful before the Fifteenth Amendment. Nonetheless the majority of Northern states were more receptive to the idea of equality before the law with respect to civil rights and took steps to put their own houses in order. While they waved the bloody shirt they also removed the most glaring inequalities in their own laws and in a few cases, as in Massachusetts, Iowa and Pennsylvania advanced beyond that to public accommodation laws and desegregated streetcars. It was a start and perhaps Northerners listened to Trumbull's assurances more with growing self-confidence and good intentions than with smugness.

Disappointment and a sense of failure still stalk our memories of the First Reconstruction however. Historians persist in writing more "ifs and but fors" in the book about what didn't happen. If land had been vigorously confiscated and equitably distributed to give blacks a solid economic reenforcement to political power; if the Republicans had been able to transcend their state-centred assumptions about federalism sufficiently to centralise power and equip an effective bureaucracy; if the Supreme Court had been appointed by the editors of the Liberator rather than mere Republican Presidents; if the Republicans had been tougher and held the South in limbo until it was truly repentant and re-educated. If wishes were horses beggars would ride.

To offer the sad consolation that second class citizenship was better than slavery or that Reconstruction left a marvellous constitutional legacy for later generations if they had the will to use it invites reproach. More was on offer in 1866. The Republicans had made the discovery that the Union's only hope was to free itself from the ways in which slavery's cancer had metastised into so many aspects of the nation's political and institutional life just as it had into the real lives of freed slaves. Black and white interests were truly one for the moment and if the Republicans were prepared to go as far for the freedman as they would for the Union, then it was still quite a distance and getting further all the time. It took them from grudging acceptance of confiscation-as-emancipation all the way to economic, political and even some social rights for blacks. If in the process they did not transcend their own racial prejudices or surmount their states-rights constitutionalism they were not paralysed by them either.

As early as 1866 Frederick Douglass questioned whether it was possible to achieve an equality of rights without making more radical changes in the way Americans perceived the role of states in the federal system:

> The Civil Rights and the Freedmen's Bureau Bill and the proposed constitutional amendments, with the amendment already adopted and recognised as the law of the land, do not reach the difficulty and cannot, unless the whole structure of the government is changed from a government by States to something like a despotic central government, with power to control even the municipal regulations of States,

> and to make them conform to its own despotic will. While there remains such an idea as the right of each state to control its local affairs - an idea, by the way, more deeply rooted in the minds of men of all sections of the country than perhaps any other political idea - no general assertion of human rights can be of any practical value.[3]

Douglass offered an alternative to the unacceptable. Give black men the vote. They would rather take their share in making the laws than be the deserving subject of laws made by others. It was an argument which Republicans also targetted at conservatives whose fears of centralisation were even greater than their fears of black voters. Carl Schurz put it this way:

> Far from desiring centralization repugnant to the genius of this country, it is in the distinct interest of local self-government and legitimate states rights that we urge these propositions, and nothing can be more certain than this is the only way in which a dangerous centralization of power in the hands of our general government can be prevented.[4]

Only a year earlier the Civil Rights and Freedmen's Bureau Acts had been a safer haven for the party's moderates and conservatives than black suffrage. It was too late to use suffrage as a means of abandonning blacks to sink or swim in the states. By 1866 the Republicans had already made citizenship permanent federal business. Republicans intended neither centralisation nor abandonment but a golden means of local self-government connected to the nation by main arteries of law and process.

Leaving the states the closest and primary relationship to the everyday incidents of citizenship was not necessarily an inherent weakness in the plan. Standards of citizenship offered by states to their white citizens, with the exceptions noted in Chapter 6, were not believed to be so minimal that extending them to blacks would fall short of real freedom - especially after they were enfranchised. For the shortfalls and exceptions the federal government offered superior rights and remedies. It set standards, forbade certain state conduct, threatened state officers with fines and jail for their failures, empowered Congress to pass appropriate legislation and bid the nation's courts to represent federal justice to the individual in the States. It was a mixture of blackmail and bullying which had much to commend it in such a decentralised society. It did, however, rely upon a continuous and vigilant Northern commitment as well as Southern re-education to freedom's ways. Without evidence of either, there were very many ways that states could make an empty shell of equal laws.

Judicial cases which surfaced from the depths of the states had to be awaited and patiently litigated. Most never made it that far. Meanwhile life went on and the police power did not stand still to await the result. Wendell Phillips made this observation about the judicial power to enforce the Thirteenth Amendment:

> Many abolitionists have said that, "with the prohibition of chattel slavery, and an abolitionist for the Chief Justice, the negro is safe." How unwise! On the other side the State fence is Robert Small and Governor Aiken. On this side is Salmon P. Chase and the Federal Constitution. Why, if Governor Aiken has got any brains, he can grind Robert Small to powder in nine hundred and ninety nine different ways without trespassing on the Anti-Slavery Amendment; and until he does, Salmon P. Chase cannot interfere.[5]

Even with the will to pursue federal laws vigorously the federal courts were institutionally weak in the face of subterfuge, malice and massive resistance. In the beginning they tried, perhaps sharing the confidence of the legislature in time, law, and their own key educative function. In the 1860's the lower federal courts on the front line of Reconstruction kept faith with Congressional intentions in interpreting the Habeas Corpus Act, the Thirteenth Amendment and the Civil Rights Act.

The Supreme Court's Slaughterhouse opinion signalled retreat. It was not a planned and orderly one at first and it left the field strewn with dicta affirming equality under the law even as its underpinnings were being removed.[6] Enough was left to account for the occasional broad constructions which survived in some federal and even state courts in the 1870's. But there was a growing gap between original legislative intentions and judicial applications. There was no way that the Supreme Court's rationale for denying black testimony in Blyew accorded with Republican intentions; no way that Justice Miller's Slaughterhouse understanding of citizenship could be squared with Congress's; no way that the road to reaching private acts of discrimination could have been closed off by reference to the original meaning of the Thirteenth Amendment; no way that the words "only" or "restricted to" could have found their way into the relationship between the Civil Rights Act and the two constitutional amendments it linked.

The Court was responding to the felt needs of the 1870's rather than the framers' intent, and these needs were more white than black. Preserving the Union remained the priority of bench and bar, and it was not difficult for them to believe that they were true to original intentions. In 1866, however, the Republicans had believed that the Union's safe future depended upon making quite substantial changes in the relationship between state and nation and nation and individual, on making blacks citizens and on guaranteeing all American citizens equality before the law in the enjoyment of their civil rights. A decade later the preservation of the Union could be and was being achieved without making individual civil rights its centrepiece. Indeed the new community of white interests upon which it rested could be jeopardised rather than cemented by incursions into state police power on behalf of white butchers in New Orleans, would-be women lawyers in Illinois or new black citizens. The realisation of just how far the new constitutional order could radically change relationships between states and their citizens of both races and even genders prompted the Court to limit its reach to blacks only, to freedom "only," and to state violations only. So successfully did the Supreme Court erect these barriers and so close to events as to convey the impression of sharing in original understandings, that subsequent generations forgot that there was life before Slaughterhouse.

White Americans did benefit from Reconstruction. Appomattox generated a spirit of reform at state as well as national level, North as well as South.[7] Northern states spawned new boards of health, bureaus of statistics and charity boards; legislatures financed new schools and state universities and internal improvement; reform efforts centred on labour legislation and sometimes liquor regulation. Even women, deliberately excluded from the benefits of national Reconstruction, made some state gains on both sides of Mason-Dixon. A series of bills in Massachusetts after 1869 liberalised divorce and gave women the right to sue and be sued and contract for family necessities. In 1874 the law placed women on an equal footing with their husbands with respect to real property and allowed them to enter contracts without their husbands' consent. Other Northern States followed similar courses. In the South, nine new state constitutions guaranteed women some property and contractual rights, though these often simply codified changes which had already taken place or were, as in South Carolina, in effect debt relief measures to exempt a wife's property from liability for her husband's debts in hard times.[8] Women, like black men, were the beneficiaries of these rare moments when justice and expediency were thrown into each others company.

The expansion of federal court jurisdiction was one of the Republicans most important achievements and lasting benefits. The courts became very busy indeed as a result of removal legislation. Long after beleaguered federal officers, Bureau agents and blacks had ceased to be their clients they became the channels of the nation's business in the states and the link which had once been missing between state, nation and individual. Through them the nation sent out roots to the states establishing its presence there and offering a forum for the resolution of disputes and the enforcement of the nation's laws.

Making the nation's authority credible in the states was not a selfless patriotic endeavour or a disinterested academic exercise. The national authority served the interests of those who held the reins of power. Emancipation, confiscation, indemnification and civil rights were what Republicans chose to make federal court business in the 1860's. The machinery would equally well serve the business and commercial needs of the reconstructed nation in the following decades. The Republicans wanted to ensure that federalism would go on being responsive to the needs of a free, expanding democracy in which the will of the dominant majority expressed nationally was obeyed locally. It was not so in 1860. In 1866, with the foundations laid, the prospects were brighter.

APPENDIX

(a) An Act to confiscate Property used for Insurrectionary Purposes. August 6th, 1861.

Be it enacted by the Senate and House of Representatives of the United States of America in Congress assembled, That if, during the present or any future insurrection against the Government of the United States, after the President of the United States shall have declared, by proclamation, that the laws of the United States are opposed, and the execution thereof obstructed by combinations too powerful to be suppressed by the ordinary course of judicial proceedings, or by the power vested in the marshals by law, any person or persons, his, her or their agent, attorney, or employe, shall purchase or acquire, sell or give any property of whatsoever kind or description with intent to use or employ the same, or suffer the same to be used or employed in aiding, abetting, or promoting such insurrection or resistance to the laws, or any person or persons engaged therein; or if any person or persons, being the owner or owners of any such property, shall knowingly use or employ, or consent to the use or employment of the same as aforesaid, all such property is hereby declared to be lawful subject of prize and capture wherever found; and it shall be the duty of the President of the United States to cause the same to be seized, confiscated and condemned.

2. And be it further enacted, That such prizes and capture shall be condemned in the district or circuit court of the United States having jurisdiction of the amount, or in admiralty in any district in which the same may be seized to which they may be taken and proceedings first instituted.

3. And be it further enacted, That the Attorney-General, or any district attorney of the United States in which said property may at the time be, may institute proceedings of condemnation, and in such case they shall be wholly for the benefit of the United States; or any person may file an information with such attorney, in which case the proceedings shall be for the use of the informer and the United States in equal parts.

4. And be it further enacted, That whenever hereafter, during the present insurrection against the Government of the United States, any person claimed to be held to labor or service under the law of any State, shall be required or permitted by the person to whom such labor or service is claimed to be due, or by the lawful agent of such person, to take up arms against the United States, or shall be required or permitted by the person to whom such labor or service is claimed to be due, or

his lawful agent, to work or be employed in or upon any fort, navy yard, dock, armory, ship, entrenchment or in any military or naval service whatsoever, against the Government and lawful authority of the United States, then, and in every such case, the person to whom such labor or service is claimed to be due shall forfeit his claim to such labor, and law of the State or of the United States to the contrary notwithstanding. Any whenever thereafter the person claiming such labor or service shall seek to enforce his claim, it shall be a full and sufficient answer to such claim that the person whose service or labor is claimed had been employed in hostile service against the Government of the United States, contrary to the provisions of this Act.

(b) An Act to suppress Insurrection, to punish Treason and Rebellion, to seize and confiscate the Property of Rebels, and for other purposes. July 17th, 1862.

Be it enacted by the Senate and House of Representatives of the United States of America in Congress assembled, That every person who shall hereafter commit the crime of treason against the United States, and shall be adjudged guilty thereof, shall suffer death, and all his slaves, if any, shall be declared and made free; or, at the discretion of the court, he shall be imprisoned for not less than five years and fined not less than ten thousand dollars, and all his slaves, if any, shall be declared and made free; said fine shall be levied and collected on any or all the property, real and personal, excluding slaves, of which the said person so convicted was the owner at the time of committing the said crime, any sale or conveyance to the contrary notwithstanding.

2. Any be it further enacted, That if any person shall hereafter incite, set on foot, assist, or engage in any rebellion or insurrection against the authority of the United States, or the laws thereof, or shall give aid or comfort thereto, or shall engage in, or give aid and comfort to, any such existing rebellion or insurrection, and be convicted thereof, such person shall be punished by imprisonment for a period not exceeding ten years; or by a fine not exceeding ten thousand dollars, and by the liberation of all his slaves, if any he have; or by both of said punishments, at the discretion of the court.

3. And be it further enacted, That every person guilty of either of the offences described in this act shall be forever incapable and disqualified to hold any office under the United States.

4. And be it further enacted, That this act shall not be construed in any way to affect or alter the prosecution, conviction, or punishment of any person or persons guilty of treason against the United States before the passage of this act, unless such person is convicted under this act.

5. And be it further enacted, That, to ensure the speedy termination of the present rebellion, it shall be the duty of the President of the United States to cause the seizure of all the estate and property, money, stocks, credits, and effects of the persons hereinafter named in this section, and to apply and use the same and the proceeds thereof for the support of the Army of the United States, that is to say:

First. Of any person hereafter acting as an officer of the army or navy of the rebels in arms against the Government of the United States.

Secondly. Of any person hereafter acting as president, vice president, member of congress, judge of any court, cabinet officer, foreign minister, commissioners or consul of the so-called confederate States of America.

Thirdly. Of any person acting as governor of a State, member of a convention or legislature, or judge of any court of any of the so-called confederate States of America.

Fourthly. Of any person who, having held an office of honor, trust, or profit in the United States, shall hereafter hold an office in the so-called confederate States of America.

Fifthly. Of any person hereafter holding any office or agency under the government of the so-called confederate States of America, or under any of the several states of the said confederacy, or the laws thereof, whether such office or agency be national, State, or municipal in its name or character; Provided, That the persons thirdly, fourthly, and fifthly above described shall have accepted their appointment or election since the date of the pretended ordinance of secession of the State, or shall have taken an oath of allegiance to, or to support the constitution of the so-called confederate States.

Sixthly. Of any person who, owning property in any loyal State or Territory of the United States, or in the District of Columbia, shall hereafter assist and give aid and comfort to such rebellion; and all sales, transfers, or conveyances of any such property, shall be null and void; and it shall be a sufficient bar to any suit brought by such person for the possession or the use of such property, or any of it, to allege and prove that he is one of the persons described in this section.

6. And be it further enacted, That if any person within any State or Territory of the United States, other than those named as aforesaid, after the passage of this act, being engaged in armed rebellion against the Government of the United States, or aiding or abetting such rebellion, shall not, within sixty days after public warning and proclamation duly given and made by the President of the United States, cease to aid, countenance, and abet such rebellion, and return to his allegiance to the United States, all the estate and property, moneys,

stocks, and credits of such person shall be liable to seizure as aforesaid, and it shall be the duty of the President to seize and use them as aforesaid or the proceeds thereof. And all sales, transfers, or conveyances of any such property after the expiration of the said sixty days from the date of such warning and proclamation shall be null and void; and it shall be a sufficient bar to any suit brought by such person for the possession or the use of such property, or any of it, to allege and prove that he is one of the persons described in this section.

7. And be it further enacted, That to secure the condemnation and sale of any such property, after the same shall have been seized, so that it may be made available for the purpose aforesaid, proceedings in rem shall be instituted in the name of the United States in any district court thereof, or in any territorial court, or in the United States district court for the District of Columbia, within which the property above described, or any part thereof, may be found, or into which the same, if movable, may first be brought, which proceedings shall conform as nearly as may be to proceedings in admiralty or revenue cases and if said property, whether real or personal, shall be found to have belonged to a person engaged in rebellion, or who has given aid or comfort thereto, the same shall be condemned as enemies' property and become the property of the United States, and may be disposed of as the court shall decree and the proceeds thereof paid into the Treasury of the United States for the purposes aforesaid.

8. And be it further enacted, That the several courts aforesaid shall have power to make such orders, establish such forms of decree and sale, and direct such deeds and conveyances to be executed and delivered by the marshals thereof where real estate shall be the subject of sale, as shall fitly and efficiently effect the purposes of this act, and vest in the purchasers of such property good and valid titles thereto. And the said courts shall have powers to allow such fees and charges of their officers as shall be reasonable and proper in the premises.

9. And be it further enacted, That all slaves of persons who shall hereafter be engaged in rebellion against the Government of the United States, or who shall in any way give aid or comfort thereto, escaping from such persons and taking refuge within the lines of the Army; and all slaves captured from such persons or deserted by them and coming into the control of the Government of the United States; and all slaves of such

persons found on (or) being within any place occupied by rebel forces and afterwards occupied by the forces of the United States, shall be deemed captives of war, and shall be forever free of their servitude, and not again held as slaves.

10. And be it further enacted, That no slave escaping into any State, Territory, or the District of Columbia, from any other State, shall be delivered up, or in any way impeded or hindered of his liberty, except for crime, or some offense against the laws, unless the person claiming said fugitive shall first make oath that the person to whom the labor or service of such fugitive is alleged to be due is his lawful owner, and has not borne arms against the United States in the present rebellion, nor in any way given aid and comfort thereto; and no person engaged in the military or naval service of the United States shall, under any pretense whatever, assume to decide on the validity of the claim of any person to the service or labor of any other person, or surrender up any such person to the claimant, on pain of being dismissed from the service.

11. And be it further enacted, That the President of the United States is authorized to employ as many persons of African descent as he may deem necessary and proper for the suppression of this rebellion, and for this purpose he may organize and use them in such manner as he may judge best for the public welfare.

12. And be it further enacted, That the President of the United States is hereby authorized to make provision for the transportation, colonization, and settlement, in some tropical country beyond the limits of the United States, of such persons of the African race, made free by the provisions of this act, as may be willing to emigrate, having first obtained the consent of the Government of said country to their protection and settlement within the same, with all the rights and privileges of freemen.

13. And be it further enacted, That the President is hereby authorized, at any time hereafter, by proclamation, to extend to persons who may have participated in the existing rebellion in any State or part thereof, pardon and amnesty, with such exceptions and at such time and on such conditions as he may deem expedient for the public welfare.

14. And be it further enacted, That the courts of the United States shall have full power to institute proceedings, make orders and decrees, issue process, and do all other things necessary to carry this act into effect.

(c) An Act relating to Habeas Corpus, and regulating Judicial Proceedings in Certain Cases.
March 3rd, 1863.

Be it enacted by the Senate and House of Representatives of the United States of America in Congress assembled, That, during the present rebellion, the President of the United States, whenever, in his judgment, the public safety may require it, **is authorized to** suspend the privilege of the writ of habeas corpus in any case throughout the United States, or any part thereof. And whenever and wherever the said privilege shall be suspended, as aforesaid, no military or other officer shall be compelled, in answer to any writ of habeas corpus, to return the body of any person or persons detained by him by authority of the President; but upon the certificate, under oath, of the officer having charge of any one so detained that such person is detained by him as a prisoner under authority of the President, further proceedings under the writ of habeas corpus shall be suspended by the judge or court having issued the said writ, so long as said suspension by the President shall remain in force, and said rebellion continue.

2. And be it further enacted, That the Secretary of State and the Secretary of War be, and they are hereby, directed, as soon as may be practicable, to furnish to the judges of the circuit and district courts of the United States and of the District of Columbia a list of the names of all persons, citizens of states in which the administration of the laws has continued unimpaired in the said Federal courts, who are now, or may hereafter be, held as prisoners of the United States, by order or authority of the President of the United States or either of said Secretaries, in any fort, arsenal, or other place, as state or political prisoners, or otherwise than as prisoners of war; the said list to contain the names of all those who reside in the respective jurisdictions of said judges, or who may be deemed by the said Secretaries, or either of them, to have violated any law of the United States in any of said jurisdictions, and also the date of each arrest; the Secretary of State to furnish a list of such persons as are imprisoned by the orders or authority of the President, acting through the State Department, and the Secretary of War a list of such as are imprisoned by the order or authority of the President, acting through the Department of War. And in all cases where a grand jury, having attended any of said courts having jurisdiction in the premises, after the passage of this act, and after the furnishing of said list, as

aforesaid, has terminated its session without finding an indictment or presentment, or other proceeding against any such person, it shall be the duty of the judge or said court forthwith to make an order that any such prisoner desiring a discharge from said imprisonment be brought before him to be discharged; and every officer of the United States having custody of such prisoner is hereby directed immediately to obey and execute said judge's order; and in case he shall delay or refuse so to do, he shall be subject to indictment for a misdemeanor, and be punished by a fine of not less than five hundred dollars and imprisonment in the common jail for a period not less than six months, in the discretion of the court: Provided, however, That no person shall be discharged by virtue of the provisions of this act until after he or she shall have taken an oath of allegiance to the Government of the United States and to support the Constitution thereof: and that he or she will not hereafter in any way encourage or give aid and comfort to the present rebellion, or the supporters thereof: And provided, also, That the judge or court before whom such persons may be brought, before discharging him or her from imprisonment, shall have power, on examination of the case, and, if the public safety shall require it, shall be required to cause him or her to enter into recognizance, with or without surety, in a sum to be fixed by said judge or court, to keep the peace and be of good behaviour towards the United States and its citizens, and from time to time, and at such times as such judge or court may direct, appear before said judge or court to be further dealt with, according to law, as the circumstances may require. And it shall be the duty of the district attorney of the United States to attend such examination before the judge.

3. And be it further enacted, That in case any of such prisoners shall be under indictment or presentment for any offence against the laws of the United States, and by existing laws bail or a recognizance may be taken for the appearance for trial of such person, it shall be the duty of said judge at once to discharge such person upon bail or recognizance for trial as aforesaid. And in case the said Secretaries of State and War shall for any reason refuse or omit to furnish the said list of persons held as prisoners as aforesaid at the time of the passage of this act within twenty days thereafter, and of such persons as hereafter may be arrested within twenty days from the time of the arrest, any citizen may, after a grand jury shall have terminated its session without finding an indictment or presentment, as provided in the second section

of this act, by a petition alleging the facts aforesaid touching any of the persons so as aforesaid imprisoned, supported by the oath of such petitioner or any other credible person, obtain and be entitled to have the said judge's order to discharge such prisoner on the same terms and conditions prescribed in the second section of this act: Provided, however, That the said judge shall be satisfied such allegations are true.

4. And be it further enacted, That any order of the President, or under his authority, made at any time during the existence of the present rebellion, shall be a defence in all courts to any action or prosecution, civil or criminal, pending, or to be commenced, for any search, seizure, arrest, or imprisonment, made, done, or committed, or acts omitted to be done, under and by virtue of such order, or under color of any law of Congress, and such defence may be made by special plea, or under the general issue.

5. And be it further enacted, That if any suit or prosecution, civil or criminal, has been or shall be commenced in any state court against any officer, civil or military, or against any other person, for any arrest or imprisonment made, or other trespasses or wrongs done or committed, or any act omitted to be done, at any time during the present rebellion, by virtue or under color of any authority derived from or exercised by or under the President of the United States, or any act of Congress, and the defendant shall, at the time of entering his appearance in such court, or if such appearance shall have been entered before the passage of this act, then at the next session of the court in which such suit or prosecution is pending, file a petition, stating the facts and verified by affidavit, for the removal of the cause for trial at the next circuit court of the United States, to be holden in the district where the suit is pending, and offer good and sufficient surety for his filing in such court, on the first day of its session, copies of such process and other proceedings against him, and also for his appearing in such court and entering special bail in the cause, if special bail was originally required therein. It shall then be the duty of the state court to accept the surety and proceed no further in the cause or prosecution, and the bail that shall have been originally taken shall be discharged. And such copies being filed as aforesaid in such court of the United States, the cause shall proceed therein in the same manner as if it had been brought in

said court by original process, whatever may be the amount in dispute or the damages claimed, or whatever the citizenship of the parties, any former law to the contrary notwithstanding. And any attachment of the goods or estate of the defendant by the original process shall hold the goods or estate so attached to answer the final judgment in the same manner as by the laws of such state they would have been holden to answer final judgment had it been rendered in the court in which the suit or prosecution was commenced. And it shall be lawful in any such action or prosecution which may be now pending, or hereafter commenced, before any state court whatever, for any cause aforesaid, after final judgment, for either party to remove and transfer, by appeal, such case during the session or term of said court at which the same shall have taken place, from such court to the next circuit court of the United States to be held in the district in which such appeal shall be taken, in manner aforesaid. And it shall be the duty of the person taking such appeal to produce and file in the said circuit court attested copies of the process, proceedings, and judgment in such cause; and it shall also be competent for either party, within six months after the rendition of a judgment in any such cause, by writ of error or other process, to remove the same to the circuit court of the United States of that district in which such judgment shall have been rendered; and the said circuit court shall thereupon proceed to try and determine the facts and the law in such action, in the same manner as if the same had been there originally commenced, the judgment in such case notwithstanding. And any bail which may have been taken, or property attached, shall be holden on the final judgment of the said circuit court in such action, in the same manner as if no such removal and transfer had been made, as aforesaid. And the state court, from which any such action, civil or criminal, may be removed and transferred as aforesaid, upon the parties giving good and sufficient security for the prosecution thereof, shall allow the same to be removed and transferred, and proceed no further in the case: Provided, however, That if the party aforesaid shall fail duly to enter the removal and transfer, as aforesaid, in the circuit court of the United States, agreeably to this act, the state court, by which judgment shall have been rendered, and from which the transfer and removal shall have been made, as aforesaid, shall be authorized, on motion for that purpose, to issue execution, and to carry into effect any such judgment, the same as if no such removal and transfer had been made. And provided also, That no such appeal or writ of error shall be allowed in any criminal action or prosecution where final judgment shall have been rendered in favor of the defendant or respondent by the state court. And if in any suit hereafter commenced the plaintiff is nonsuited or judgment pass against him, the defendant shall recover double costs.

6. And be it further enacted, That any suit or prosecution described in this act, in which final judgment may be rendered in the circuit court, may be carried by writ of error to the supreme court, whatever may be the amount of said judgment.

7. And be it further enacted, That no suit or prosecution, civil or criminal, shall be maintained for any arrest or imprisonment made, or other trespasses or wrongs done or committed, or act omitted to be done, at any time during the present rebellion, by virtue or under color of any authority derived from or exercised by or under the President of the United States, or by or under any act of Congress, unless the same shall have been commenced within two years next after such arrest, imprisonment, trespass, or wrong may have been done or committed or act may have been omitted to be done: Provided, That in no case shall the limitation herein provided commence to run until the passage of this act, so that no party shall, by virtue of this act, be debarred of his remedy by suit or prosecution until two years from and after the passage of this act.

(d) An Act to guarantee to certain States whose governments have been usurped or overthrown a republican form of government.
July 2nd, 1864. Pocket-vetoed, July 8th, 1864.

Be it enacted by the Senate and House of Representatives of the United States of America in Congress assembled, That in the States declared in rebellion against the United States the President shall, by and with the advice and consent of the Senate, appoint for each a provisional governor, whose pay and emoluments shall not exceed that of a brigadier-general of volunteers, who shall be charged with the civil administration of such State until a State government therein shall be recognized as hereinafter provided.

2. And be it further enacted, That so soon as the military resistance to the United States shall have been suppressed in any such State and the people thereof shall have sufficiently returned to their obedience to the Constitution and the laws of the United States the provisional governor shall direct the marshal of the United States, as speedily as may be, to name a sufficient number of deputies, and to enroll all white male citizens of the United States resident in the State in their respective counties, and to request each one to take the oath to support the Constitution of the United States, and in his enrollment to designate those who take and those who refuse to take that oath, which rolls shall be forthwith returned to the provisional governor; and if the persons taking that oath shall amount to a majority of the persons enrolled in the State, he shall, be proclamation, invite the loyal people of the State to elect delegates to a convention charged to declare the will of the people of the State relative to the re-establishment of a State government, subject to and in conformity with the Constitution of the United States.

3. And be it further enacted, That the convention shall consist of as many members as both houses of the last constitutional State legislature, apportioned by the provisional governor among the counties, parishes or district of the State, in proportion to the white population returned as electors by the marshal in compliance with the provisions of this act. The provisional governor shall, be proclamation, declare the number of delegates to be elected by each county, parish, or election district; name a day of election not less than thirty days thereafter; designate the places of voting in each county, parish or district, conforming as

nearly as may be convenient to the places used in the State elections next preceding the rebellion; appoint one or more commissioners to hold the election at each place of voting, and provide an adequate force to keep the peace during the election.

4. And be it further enacted, That the delegates shall be elected by the loyal white male citizens of the United States of the age of 21 years, and resident at the time in the county, parish, or district in which they shall offer to vote, and enrolled as aforesaid, or absent in the military service of the United States, and who shall take and subscribe the oath of allegiance to the United States in the form contained in the act of Congress of July 2nd 1862; and all such citizens of the United States who are in the military service of the United States shall vote at the headquarters of their respective commands, under such regulations as may be prescribed by the provisional governor for the taking and return of their votes; but no person who has held or exercised any office, civil or military, State or Confederate, under the rebel usurpation, or who has voluntarily borne arms against the United States, shall vote or be eligible to be elected as delegate at such election.

5. And be it further enacted, That the said commissioners, or either of them, shall hold the election in conformity with this act, and, so far as may be consistent therewith, shall proceed in the manner used in the State prior to the rebellion. The oath of allegiance shall be taken and subscribed on the poll book by every voter in the form above prescribed, but every person known by or proved to the commissioners to have held or exercised any office, civil or military, State or Confederate, under the rebel usurpation, or to have voluntarily borne arms against the United States, shall be excluded though he offer to take the oath; and in case any person who shall have borne arms against the United States shall offer to vote, he shall be deemed to have borne arms voluntarily unless he shall prove the contrary by the testimony of a qualified voter. The poll book, showing the name and oath of each voter, shall be returned to the provisional governor by the commissioners of election, or the one acting, and the provisional governor shall canvass such returns and declare the person having the highest number of votes elected.

6. And be it further enacted, That the provisional governor shall, by proclamation, convene the delegates elected as aforesaid at the capital

of the State on a day not more than three months after the election, giving at least thirty days' notice of such day. In case the said capital shall in his judgment be unfit, he shall in his proclamation appoint another place, He shall preside over the deliberations of the convention and administer to each delegate, before taking his seat in the convention, the oath of allegiance to the United States in the form above prescribed.

7. And be it further enacted, That the convention shall declare on behalf of the people of the State their submission to the Constitution and laws of the United States, and shall adopt the following provisions, hereby prescribed by the United States in the execution of the constitutional duty to guarantee a republican form of government to every State, and incorporate them in the constitution of the State; that is to say:

First. No person who has held or exercised any office, civil or military (except offices merely ministerial and military offices below the grade of colonel), State or Confederate, under the usurping power, shall vote for or be a member of the legislature or governor.

Second. Involuntary servitude is forever prohibited, and the freedom of all persons is guaranteed in said State.

Third. No debt, State or Confederate, created by or under the sanction of the usurping power shall be recognized or paid by the State.

8. And be it further enacted, That when the convention shall have adopted those provisions it shall proceed to re-establish a republican form of government and ordain a constitution containing those provisions, which when adopted, the convention shall by ordinance provide for submitting to the people of the State entitled to vote under this law, at an election to be held in the manner prescribed by the act for the election of delegates, but at a time and place named by the convention, at which election the said electors, and none others, shall vote directly for or against such Constitution and form of State government. And the returns of said election shall be made to the provisional governor, who shall canvass the same in the presence of the electors, and if a majority of the votes cast shall be for the constitution and form of government, he shall certify the same, with a copy thereof, to the President of the United States, who, after obtaining the assent of Congress, shall, by

proclamation, recognize the government so established, and none other, as the constitutional government of the State; and from the date of such recognition, and not before, Senators and Representatives and electors for President and Vice-President may be elected in such State, according to the laws of the State and of the United States.

9. And be it further enacted, That if the convention shall refuse to re-establish the State government on the conditions aforesaid the provisional governor shall declare it dissolved; but it shall be for the duty of the President, whenever he shall have reason to believe that a sufficient number of people of the State entitled to vote under this act, in number not less than a majority of those enrolled as aforesaid, are willing to re-establish a State government on the conditions aforesaid, to direct the provisional governor to order another election of delegates to a convention for the purpose and in the manner prescribed in this act, and to proceed in all respects as hereinbefore provided, either to dissolve the convention or to certify the State government re-established by it to the President.

10. And be it further enacted, That until the United States shall have recognized a republican form of State government the provisional governor in each of said States shall see that this act and the laws of the United States and the laws of the State in force when the State government was overthrown by the rebellion are faithfully executed within the State; but no law or usage whereby any person was heretofore held in involuntary servitude shall be recognized or enforced by any court or officer in such State; and the laws for the trial and punishment of white persons shall extend to all persons, and jurors shall have the qualifications of voters under this law for delegates to the convention. The President shall appoint such officers provided for by the laws of the State when its government was overthrown as he may find necessary to the civil administration of the State, all which officers shall be entitled to receive the fees and emoluments provided by the State laws for such officers.

11. And be it further enacted, That until the recognition of a State government as aforesaid the provisional governor shall, under such regulations as he may prescribe, cause to be assessed, levied, and collected, for the year 1864 and every year thereafter, the taxes provided by the laws of such State to be levied during the fiscal year preceding the overthrow of the State government thereof, in the manner

prescribed by the laws of the State, as nearly as may be; and the officers appointed as aforesaid are vested with all powers of levying and collecting such taxes, by distress or sale, as were vested in any officers or tribunal of the State government aforesaid for those purposes. The proceeds of such taxes shall be accounted for to the provisional governor and be by him applied to the expenses of the administration of the laws in such State, subject to the direction of the President, and the surplus shall be deposited in the Treasury of the United States to the credit of such State, to be paid to the State upon an appropriation therefor to be made when a republican form of government shall be recognized therein by the United States.

12. And be it further enacted, That all persons held to involuntary servitude or labor in the State aforesaid are hereby emancipated and discharged therefrom, and they and their posterity shall be forever free. And if any such persons or their posterity shall be restrained of liberty under pretense of any claim to such service or labor, the courts of the United States shall, on habeas corpus, discharge them.

13. And be it further enacted, That if any person declared free by this act, or any law of the United States or any proclamation of the President, be restrained of liberty with intent to be held in or reduced to involuntary servitude or labor, the person convicted before a court of competent jurisdiction of such act shall be punished by fine of not less than $1,500 and be imprisoned not less than five nor more than twenty years.

14. And be it further enacted, That every person who shall hereafter hold or exercise any office, civil or military (except offices merely ministerial and military offices below the grade of colonel), in the rebel service, State or Confederate, is hereby declared not to be a citizen of the United States.

(e) An Act to amend an act entitled "An act to establish a Bureau for the relief of Freedmen and Refugees," and for other purposes. February 9th, 1866. Vetoed, February 19th.

Be it enacted by the Senate and House of Representatives of the United States of America in Congress assembled, That the act to establish a bureau for the relief of freedmen and refugees, approved March three, eighteen hundred and sixty-five, shall continue in force until otherwise provided by law, and shall extend to refugees and freedmen in all parts of the United States; and the President may divide the section of country containing such refugees and freedmen into districts, each containing one or more States, not to exceed twelve in number, and, by and with the advice and consent of the Senate, appoint an assistant commissioner for each of said districts, who shall give like bond, receive the compensation, and perform the duties prescribed by this and the act to which this is an amendment or said bureau may, in the discretion of the President, be placed under a commissioner and assistant commissioners, to be detailed from the army; in which event each officer so assigned to duty shall serve without increase of pay or allowances.

2. And be it further enacted, That the commissioner, with the approval of the President, and when the same shall be necessary for the operations of the bureau, may divide each district into a number of sub-districts, not to exceed the number of counties or parishes in such district, and shall assign to each sub-district at least one agent, either a citizen, officer of the army, or enlisted man, who, if an officer, shall serve without additional compensation or allowance, and if a citizen or enlisted man, shall receive a salary of not less than five hundred dollars nor more than twelve hundred dollars annually, according to the services rendered, in full compensation for such services; and such agent shall, before entering on the duties of his office, take the oath prescribed in the first section of the act to which this is an amendment. And the commissioner may, when the same shall be necessary, assign to each assistant commissioner not exceeding three clerks, and to each of said agents one clerk, at an annual salary not exceeding one thousand dollars each, provided suitable clerks cannot be detailed from the army. And the President of the United States, through the War Department and the commissioner, shall extend military jurisdiction and protection

over all employes, agents, and officers of this bureau in the exercise of the duties imposed or authorized by this act or the act to which this is additional.

3. And be it further enacted, That the Secretary of War may direct such issues of provisions, clothing, fuel and other supplies, including medical stores and transportation, and afford such aid, medical or otherwise, as he may deem needful for the immediate and temporary shelter and supply of destitute and suffering refugees and freedmen, their wives and children, under such rules and regulations as he may direct: Provided, That no person shall be deemed "destitute," "suffering," or "dependent upon the Government for support," within the meaning of this act, who, being able to find employment, could by proper industry and exertion avoid such destitution, suffering, or dependence.

4. And be it further enacted, That the President is hereby authorized to reserve from sale, or from settlement, under the homestead or pre-emption laws, and to set apart for the use of freedmen and loyal refugees, unoccupied public lands in Florida, Mississippi, Alabama, Louisiana, and Arkansas, not exceeding in all three millions of acres of good land; and the commissioner, under the direction of the President, shall cause the same from time to time to be allotted and assigned, in parcels not exceeding forty acres each, to the loyal refugees and freedmen, who shall be protected in the use and enjoyment thereof for such term of time and at such annual rent as may be agreed on between the commissioner and such refugees or freedmen. The rental shall be based upon a valuation of the land, to be ascertained in such manner as the commissioner may, under the direction of the President, by regulation prescribe. At the end of such term, or sooner, if the commissioner shall assent thereto, the occupants of any parcels so assigned, their heirs and assigns, may purchase the land and receive a title thereto from the United States in fee, upon paying therefor the value of the land ascertained as aforesaid.

5. And be it further enacted, That the occupants of land under Major General Sherman's special field order, dated at Savannah, January sixteen, eighteen hundred and sixty-five, are hereby confirmed in their possession for the period of three years from the date of said order, and no person shall be disturbed in or ousted from said possession during said three years, unless a settlement shall be made with said occupant, by the former

owner, his heirs or assigns, satisfactory to the commissioner of the Freedmen's Bureau: Provided, That whenever the former owners of lands occupied under General Sherman's field order shall make application for restoration of said lands, the commissioner is hereby authorized, upon the agreement and with the written consent of said occupants, to procure other lands for them by rent or purchase, not exceeding forty acres for each occupant, upon the terms and conditions named in section four of this act, or to set apart for them, out of the public lands assigned for that purpose in section four of this act, forty acres each, upon the same terms and conditions.

6. And be it further enacted, That the commissioner shall, under the direction of the President, procure in the name of the United States by grant or purchase, such lands within the districts aforesaid as may be required for refugees and freedmen dependent on the Government for support; and he shall provide or cause to be erected suitable buildings for asylums and schools. But no such purchase shall be made, nor contract for the same entered into, nor other expense incurred, until after appropriations shall have been provided by Congress for such purposes. And no payment shall be made for lands purchased under this section, except for asylums and schools, from any moneys, not specifically appropriated therefor. And the commissioner shall cause such lands from time to time to be valued, allotted, assigned, and sold in manner and form provided in the fourth section of this act, at a price not less than the cost thereof to the United States.

7. And be it further enacted, That whenever in any State or district in which the ordinary course of judicial proceedings has been interrupted by the rebellion, and wherein, in consequence of any State or local law, ordinance, police or other regulation, custom, or prejudice, any of the civil rights or immunities belonging to white persons, including the right to make and enforce contracts, to sue, be parties, and give evidence, to inherit, purchase, lease, sell, hold and convey real and personal property, and to have full and equal benefit of all laws and proceedings for the security of person and estate, including the constitutional right of bearing arms, are refused or denied to negroes, mulattoes, freedmen, refugees, or any other persons, on account of race, color, or any previous condition of slavery or involuntary servitude, or wherein they or any of them are subjected to any other or different punishment, pains, or penalties, for the commission of any act or offence

than are prescribed for white persons committing like acts or offences, it shall be the duty of the President of the United States, through the commissioner, to extend military protection and jurisdiction over all cases affecting such persons so discriminated against.

8. And be it further enacted, That any person who, under color of any State or local law, ordinance, police, or other regulation or custom, shall, in any State or district in which the ordinary course of judicial proceedings has been interrupted by the rebellion, subject, or cause to be subjected, any negro, mulatto, freedman, refugee, or other person, on account of race or color, or any previous condition of slavery or involuntary servitude, or for any other cause, to the deprivation of any civil right secured to white persons, or to any other or different punishment than white persons are subject to for the commission of like acts or offences, shall be deemed guilty of a misdemeanour, and be punished by fine not exceeding one thousand dollars, or imprisonment not exceeding one year, or both; and it shall be the duty of the officers and agents of this bureau to take jurisdiction of, and hear and determine all offences committed against the provisions of this action, and also of all cases affecting negroes, mulattoes, freedmen, refugees, or other persons who are discriminated against in any of the particulars mentioned in the preceding section of this act, under such rules and regulations as the President of the United States, through the War Department, shall prescribe. The jurisdiction conferred by this and the preceding section on the officers and agents of this bureau shall cease and determine whenever the discrimination on account of which it is conferred ceases, and in no event to be exercised in any State in which the ordinary course of judicial proceedings has not been interrupted by the rebellion, nor in any such State after said State shall have been fully restored in all its constitutional relations to the United States, and the courts of the State and of the United States within the same are not disturbed or stopped in the peaceable course of justice.

9. And be it further enacted, That all acts, or parts of acts, inconsistent with the provisions of this act, are hereby repealed.

An Act to continue in force and to amend "An Act to establish a Bureau for the Relief of Freedmen and Refugees," and for other Purposes.
July 16th, 1866

Be it enacted, That the act to establish a bureau for the relief of freedmen and refugees, approved March third, eighteen hundred and sixty-five, shall continue in force for the term of two years from and after the passage of this act.

2. And be it further enacted, That the supervision and care of said bureau shall extend to all loyal refugees and freedmen, so far as the same shall be necessary to enable them as speedily as practicable to become self-supporting citizens of the United States, and to aid them in making the freedom conferred by proclamation of the commander-in-chief, by emancipation under the laws of States, and by constitutional amendment, available to them and beneficial to the republic.

3. And be it further enacted, That the President shall, by and with the advice and consent of the Senate, appoint two assistant commissioners, in addition to those authorized by the act to which this is an amendment, ... and each of the assistant commissioners of the bureau shall have charge of one district containing such refugees or freedmen, to be assigned him by the commissioner with the approval of the President. And the commissioner shall, under the direction of the President, and so far as the same shall be, in his judgment, necessary for the efficient and economical administration of the affairs of the bureau, appoint such agents, clerks, and assistants as may be required for the proper conduct of the bureau. Military officers or enlisted men may be detailed for service and assigned to duty under this act; and the President may, if in his judgment safe and judicious so to do, detail from the army all the officers and agents of this bureau; but no officer so assigned shall have increase of pay or allowances ....And it shall be the duty of the commissioner, when it can be done consistently with public interest, to appoint, as assistant commissioners, agents, and clerks, such men as have proved their loyalty by faithful service in the armies of the Union during the rebellion. And all persons appointed to service under this act and the act to which this is an amendment, shall be so far deemed in the military service of the United States as to be under the military jurisdiction, and entitled to the military

protection of the government while in discharge of the duties of their office.

4. Officers of veteran reserve corps now in the bureau may be retained.

5. And be it further enacted, That the second section of the act to which this is an amendment shall be deemed to authorize the Secretary of War to issue such medical stores or other supplies and transportation, and afford such medical or other aid as here may be needful for the purposes named in said section: Provided, That no person shall be deemed "destitute," "suffering," or "dependent upon the government for support," within the meaning of this act, who is able to find employment, and could, by proper industry or exertion, avoid such destitution, suffering, or dependence.

Sections 6–11 relate to the disposition of certain lands in South Carolina and Georgia.

12. And be it further enacted, That the commissioner shall have power to seize, hold, use, lease, or sell all buildings and tenements, and any lands appertaining to the same, or otherwise, formerly held under color of title by the late so-called confederate states, and not heretofore disposed of by the United States, and any buildings or lands held in trust for the same by any person or persons, and to use the same or appropriate the proceeds derived therefrom to the education of the freed people; and whenever the bureau shall cease to exist, such of so-called confederate states as shall have made provision for the education of their citizens without distinction of color shall receive the sum remaining unexpended of such sales or rentals, which shall be distributed among said states for educational purposes in proportion to their population.

13. And be it further enacted, That the commissioner of this bureau shall at all times co-operate with private benevolent associations of citizens in aid of freedmen, and with agents and teachers, duly accredited and appointed by them, and shall hire or provide by lease buildings for purposes of education whenever such association shall, without cost to the government, provide suitable teachers and means of instruction; and he shall furnish such protection as may be required for the safe conduct of such schools.

14. And be it further enacted, That in every State or district where the ordinary course of judicial proceedings has been interrupted by the rebellion, and until the same shall be fully restored, and in every State or district whose constitutional relations to the government have been practically discontinued by the rebellion, and until such State shall have been restored in such relations, and shall be duly represented in the Congress of the United States, the right to make and enforce contracts, to sue, be parties, and give evidence, to inherit, purchase, lease, sell, hold, and convey real and personal property, and to have full and equal benefit of all laws and proceedings concerning personal liberty, personal security, and the acquisition, enjoyment, and disposition of estate, real and personal, including the constitutional right to bear arms, shall be secured to and enjoyed by all the citizens of such State or district without respect to race or color, or previous condition of slavery. And whenever in either of said States or districts the ordinary course of judicial proceedings has been interrupted by the rebellion, and until the same shall be fully restored, and until such State shall have been restored in its constitutional relations to the government, and shall be duly represented in the Congress of the United States, the President shall, through the commissioner and the officers of the bureau, and under such rules and regulations as the President, through the Secretary of War, shall prescribe, extend military protection and have military jurisdiction over all cases and questions concerning the free enjoyment of such immunities and rights, and no penalty or punishment for any violation of law shall be imposed or permitted because of race or color, or previous condition of slavery, other or greater than the penalty or punishment to which white persons may be liable by law for the like offence. But the jurisdiction conferred by this section upon the officers of the bureau shall not exist in any State where the ordinary course of judicial proceedings has not been interrupted by the rebellion, and shall cease in every State when the courts of the State and the United States are not distrubed in the peaceable course of justice, and after such State shall be fully restored in its constitutional relations to the government, and shall be duly represented in the Congress of the United States.

15 And be it further enacted, That all officers, agents, and employes of this bureau, before entering upon the duties of their office shall take the oath prescribed in the first section of the act to which this is an amendment; and all acts or parts of acts inconsistent with the provisions of this act are hereby repealed.

(f) An Act to protect all Persons in the United States in their Civil Rights, and furnish the Means of their Vindication. April 9th, 1866.

Be it enacted by the Senate and House of Representatives of the United States of America in Congress assembled, That all persons born in the United States and not subject to any foreign power, excluding Indians not taxed, are hereby declared to be citizens of the United States; and such citizens, of every race and color, without regard to any previous condition of slavery or involuntary servitude, except as a punishment for crime whereof the party shall have been duly convicted, shall have the same right, in every State and Territory in the United States, to make and enforce contracts, to sue, be parties, and give evidence, to inherit, purchase, lease, sell, hold, and convey real and personal property, and to full and equal benefit of all laws and proceedings for the security of person and property, as is enjoyed by white citizens, and shall be subject to like punishment, pains, and penalties, and to none other, any law, statute, ordinance, regulation, or custom, to the contrary notwithstanding.

2. And be it further enacted, That any person who, under color of any law, statute, ordinance, regulation, or custom, shall subject, or cause to be subjected, any inhabitant of any State or Territory to the deprivation of any right secured or protected by this act, or to different punishment, pains, or penalties on account of such person having at any time been held in a condition of slavery or involuntary servitude, except as a punishment for crime whereof the party shall have been duly convicted, or by reason of his color or race, than is prescribed for the punishment of white persons, shall be deemed guilty of a misdemeanour, and, on conviction, shall be punished by fine not exceeding one thousand dollars, or imprisonment not exceeding one year, or both, in the discretion of the court.

3. And be it further enacted, That the district courts of the United States, within their respective districts, shall have, exclusively of the courts of the several States, cognizance of all crimes and offences committed against the provisions of this act, and also, concurrently with the circuit courts of the United States, of all causes, civil and criminal affecting persons who are denied or cannot enforce in the courts

or judicial tribunals of the State or locality where they may be any of the rights secured to them by the first section of this act; and if any suit or prosecution, civil or criminal has been or shall be commenced in any State court, against any such person, for any cause whatsoever, or against any officer, civil or military, or other person, for any arrest or imprisonment, trespasses, or wrongs done or committed by virtue or under color of authority derived from this act or the act establishing a Bureau for the relief of Freedmen and Refugees, and all acts amendatory thereof, or for refusing to do any act upon the ground that it would be inconsistent with this act, such defendant shall have the right to remove such cause for trial to the proper district or circuit court in the manner prescribed by the "Act relating to habeas corpus and regulating judicial proceedings in certain cases," approved March three, eighteen hundred and sixty-three, and all acts amendatory thereof. The jurisdiction in civil and criminal matters hereby conferred on the district and circuit courts of the United States shall be exercised and enforced in conformity with the laws of the United States, so far as such laws are suitable to carry the same into effect; but in all cases where such laws are not adapted to the object, or are deficient in the provisions necessary to furnish suitable remedies and punish offences against law, the common law, as modified and changed by the constitution and statutes of the State wherein the court having jurisdiction of the cause, civil or criminal, is held, so far as the same is not inconsistent with the Constitution and laws of the United States, shall be extended to and govern said courts in the trial and disposition of such cause, and, if of a criminal nature, in the infliction of punishment on the party found guilty.

4. And be it further enacted, That the district attorneys, marshals, and deputy marshals of the United States, the commissioners appointed by the circuit and territorial courts of the United States, with powers of arresting, imprisoning or bailing offenders against the laws of the United States, the officers and agents of the Freedmen's Bureau, and every other officer who may be specially empowered by the President of the United States, shall be, and they are hereby, specially authorized and required, at the expense of the United States, to institute proceedings against all and every person who shall violate the provisions of this act, and cause him or them to be

arrested and imprisoned, or bailed, as the case may be, for trial before such court of the United States or territorial court as by this act has cognizance of the offence. And with a view to affording reasonable protection to all persons in their constitutional rights of equality before the law, without distinction of race or color, or previous condition of slavery or involuntary servitude, except as a punishment for crime, whereof the party shall have been duly convicted, and to the prompt discharge of the duties of this act, it shall be the duty of the circuit courts of the United States, and the superior courts of the Territories of the United States, from time to time, to increase the number of commissioners, so as to afford a speedy and convenient means for the arrest and examination of persons charged with a violation of this act; and such commissioners are hereby authorized and required to exercise and discharge all the powers and duties conferred on them by this act, and the same duties with regard to offences created by this act, as they are authorized by law to exercise with regard to other offences against the laws of the United States.

5. And be it further enacted, That it shall be the duty of all marshals and deputy marshals to obey and execute all warrants and precepts issued under the provisions of this act, when to them directed; and should any marshal or deputy marshal refuse to receive such warrant or other process when tendered, or to use all proper means diligently to execute the same, he shall, on conviction thereof, be fined in the sum of one thousand dollars, to the use of the person upon whom the accused is alleged to have committed the offence. And the better to enable the said commissioners to execute their duties faithfully and efficiently, in conformity with the Constitution of the United States and the requirements of this act, they are hereby authorized and empowered, within their counties respectively, to appoint, in writing, under their hands, any one or more suitable persons from time to time, to execute all such warrants and other process as may be issued by them in the lawful performance of their respective duties; and the persons so appointed to execute any warrant or process as aforesaid shall have authority to summon and call to their aid the bystanders or posse comitatus of the proper county, or such portion of the land or naval forces of the United States, or of the militia, as may be necessary to the performance of the duty with which they are charged, and to insure a faithful observance of the clause of the Constitution which prohibits slavery, in conformity with the

provisions of this act; and said warrants shall run and be executed by said officers anywhere in the State or Territory within which they are issued.

6. And be it further enacted, That any person who shall knowingly and wilfully obstruct, hinder, or prevent any officer, or other person charged with the execution of any warrant or process issued under the provisions of this act, or any person or persons lawfully assisting him or them, from arresting any person for whose apprehension such warrant or process may have been issued, or shall rescue or attempt to rescue such person from the custody of the officer, other person or persons, or those lawfully assisting as aforesaid, when so arrested pursuant to the authority herein given and declared, or shall aid, abet, or assist any person so arrested as aforesaid, directly or indirectly, to escape from the custody of the officer or other person legally authorized as aforesaid, or shall harbor or conceal any person for whose arrest a warrant or process shall have been issued as aforesaid, so as to prevent his discovery and arrest after notice or knowledge of the fact that a warrant has been issued for the apprehension of such person, shall, for either of said offenses, be subject to a fine not exceeding one thousand dollars, and imprisonment not exceeding six months, by indictment and conviction before the district court of the United States for the district in which said offence may have been committed, or before the proper court of criminal jurisdiction, if committed within any one of the organized Territories of the United States.

7. And be it further enacted, That the district attorneys, the marshals, their deputies, and the clerks of the said district and territorial courts shall be paid for their services the like fees as may be allowed to them for similar services in other cases; and in all cases where the proceedings are before a commissioner, he shall be entitled to a fee of ten dollars in full for his services in each case, inclusive of all services incident to such arrest and examination. The person or persons authorized to execute the process to be issued by such commissioners for the arrest of offenders against the provisions of this act shall be entitled to a fee of five dollars for each person he or they may arrest and take before any such commissioner as aforesaid, with such other fees as may be deemed reasonable by such commissioner for such other additional services as may be necessarily performed by him or them, such as attending at the examination, keeping the prisoner in custody, and providing him with food and lodging during his detention, and until the final determination of such

commissioner, and in general for performing such other duties as may be required in the premises; such fees to be made up in conformity with the fees usually charged by the officers of the courts of justice within the proper district or county, as nearly as may be practicable, and paid out of the Treasury of the United States on the certificate of the judge of the district within which the arrest is made, and to be recoverable from the defendant as part of the judgment in case of conviction.

8. And be it further enacted, That whenever the President of the United States shall have reason to believe that offenses have been or are likely to be committed against the provisions of this act within any judicial district, it shall be lawful for him, in his discretion, to direct the judge, marshal, and district attorney of such district to attend at such place within the district, and for such time as he may designate, for the purpose of the more speedy arrest and trial of persons charged with a violation of this act; and it shall be the duty of every judge or other officer, when any such requisition shall be received by him, to attend at the place and for the time therein designated.

9. And be it further enacted, That it shall be lawful for the President of the United States, or such person as he may empower for that purpose, to employ such part of the land or naval forces of the United States, or of the militia, as shall be necessary to prevent the violation and enforce the due execution of this act.

10. And be it further enacted, That upon all questions of law arising in any case under the provisions of this act a final appeal may be taken to the Supreme Court of the United States.

Notes: Chapter 1

1. E.L. Godkin, "The Constitution and its Defects," North American Review, July 1864, p.122.

2. Quoted in Harold M. Hyman (ed.), The Radical Republicans and Reconstruction 1861-1870 (N.Y., 1967), p.28.

3. Arthur Bestor, "The American Civil War as a Constitutional Crisis," American Historical Review, Vol. ixix, Jan. 1964 makes a persuasive argument.

4. The best discussion of constitutional choices among antislavery groups is in William Wiecek, The Sources of Antislavery Constitutionalism in America, 1760-1848 (Ithaca, 1977).

5. See also Eric Foner, Politics and Ideology in the Age of the Civil War (N.Y., 1980).

6. Jacobus TenBroek, The Antislavery Origins of the Fourteenth Amendment, (Berkeley, 1951) and Howard J. Graham, Everyman's Constitution, (Madison, 1968).

7. Barron v Baltimore, 7 Pet. (32 U.S.) 243 (1833).

8. For the view that some early substantive content attached to due process through the protection of vested property rights see Edward S. Corwin, "The Higher Law Background of American Constitutional Law," 42, Harvard Law Review (1928) and "The Doctrine of Due Process of Law Before the Civil War, " 24 Harvard Law Review (1911).

9. Morton J. Horwitz, The Transformation of American Law (Cambridge, 1977) noted these developments.

10. Scholars have attempted to fit both the slavery decisions of the Supreme Court and antislavery constitutional thought into a pattern of development from instrumentalism to postwar formalism. Some confusion arises however because instrumentalism and formalism often seem to co-exist in mid-century, and judicial insistence that they follow "positive law" may be a feature of both! See William E. Nelson, The Roots of Bureaucracy (Cambridge, 1982) and "The Impact of the Antislavery Movement Upon Styles of Judicial Reasoning in Nineteenth Century America," 87 Harvard Law Review (1974).

11. The best discussion of these decisions is by William M. Wiecek in "Slavery and Abolition Before the United States Supreme Court, 1820-1860," 65 Journal of American History (1979) and in William Wiecek and Harold Hyman, Equal Justice Under Law 1835-1875, (N.Y., 1982).

12. Nelson, op. cit.

13. Roger M. Cover, Justice Accused: Antislavery and the Jucidial Process (New Haven, 1975), p.6. Perhaps the nearest any court came to their position was Lemuel Shaw's opinion in Commonwealth v Aves 35 Mass. 193 (1836).

14. This relationship between public opinion and antislavery constitutional ideas in areas of abolitionist strength remains one of the most important discoveries of Howard Graham's in Everyman's Constitution. He places Bingham in this context in "The Conspiracy Theory of the Fourteenth Amendment," Yale Law Journal, 1938.

15. Godkin, op. cit, p.122. John C. Hurd makes a rather similar point with respect to the Constitution, that it had been regarded as an object of legal knowledge to be referred to like a statute, rather than as the instrument of a living political compact. Hurd, "Theories of Reconstruction," American Law Review, Vol.1 (1867).

16. Compiled from A Biographical Congressional Dictionary 1744-1911, (Washington, 1913).

17. Donald G. Morgan, Congress and the Constitution: A Study of Responsibility (Cambridge, 1966) argues that one of the effects of the growing importance of committees was that Congress abdicated some of its collective responsibilities to harmonise legislation with the Constitution to them.

18. Leonard Curry, Blueprint for Modern America (Nashville, 1968), Chapter 1.

19. The best historiographical essay is Harold M. Hyman's introduction to The Radical Republicans and Reconstruction 1861-1870, itself a significant contribution to the revision of old attitudes.

20. Of particular interest are Michael L. Benedict, A Compromise of Principle: Congressional Republicans and Reconstruction, 1863-1869 (N.Y., 1974); Glenn M. Linden, Politics or Principle: Congressional Voting on the Civil War Amendments and Pro-Negro Measures, 1838-1869 (Seattle, 1976) and Allan Bogue, The Earnest Men: Republicans of the Civil War Senate (N.Y., 1981).

21. Cong. Globe, 37 Cong., 2 sess. p.570, Jan.28th 1863.

22. Benedict, Compromise of Principle, pp.24-27.

23. Cong. Globe, 3 sess., pp.1064-1066, Feb. 18th 1863.

24. David Donald, "The Radicals and Lincoln" in Lincoln Reconsidered (N.Y., 1961), p.126.

25. Roy P. Baster (ed.), Collected Works of Abraham Lincoln (N.Y., 1953, 9 vols.) V, pp.333-339. Hereafter cited as Lincoln, Works.

26. Ibid., IV, p.426, July 4th 1861.

27. Ibid., VII, pp.259-260, March 21st, 1864.

28. Ibid., V, pp.51-53. The Lincoln Works abound in similar affirmations of the importance of Union. See also K. Stampp, "The Concept of a Perpetual Union," Journal of American History, (1978).

29. Philip S. Paludan, "The American Civil War Considered as a Crisis in Law and Order" 77 American Historical Review, 1972.

30. The idea is well expressed by Senator Morrill, Cong. Globe, 37 Cong., 2 sess. pp. 1074-1077, March 5th 1862, Thaddeus Stevens, Ibid., pp. 439-441, Jan. 22nd 1862 and in George Julian's many Speeches on Political Questions (N.Y., 1872) but the ideas are pervasive. A recent article by Peyton McCrary catches the reforming impulse nicely, "The Party of Revolution: Republican Ideas about Politics and Social Change, 1862-1867" Civil War History, Dec. 1984.

31. Cong. Globe, 2 sess. p.2274, May 22nd 1862.

32. Eric Foner, Free Soil, Free Labor, Free Men: The Ideology of the Republican Party Before the Civil War (N.Y., 1970).

33. Quoted by Henry C. Wright in the Liberator, October 7th 1864.

34. Cong. Globe, 37 Cong., 2 sess. p.1107, March 6th 1862.

35. Frederick Douglass, "Reconstruction," Atlantic Monthly Dec. 1866, p.764.

36. Martin F. Conway to the Editor of the New York Tribune, 29th May 1863, quoted in the Liberator, June 12th 1863.

37. David Donald, in The Politics of Reconstruction (Baton Rouge, 1965) found a statistical correlation between radicalism and safe seats.

38. George Selden Henry, Jr. Radical Republican Policy Toward the Negro During Reconstruction 1862-1872 (Unpublished Ph.D. Dissertation, Yale University, 1963).

39. William H. Lofton, "Northern Labor and the Negro During the Civil War," Journal of Negro History, July 1949.

40. Cong. Globe, 37 Cong. 2 sess. pp.439-441, Jan. 22nd 1862; Ibid. p.596, Jan. 31st 1862.

41. The new public opinion was reflected in this statement from the N.Y. Tribune in the winter of 1861 - "this is no longer a question of morals, but one of common sense and common safety." Quoted in the Liberator, Nov. 22nd 1861.

42. James E. Sefton, The United States Army and Reconstruction (Baton Rouge, 1977) explores the role played by the army while Harold M. Hyman, A More Perfect Union (N.Y., 1973) assesses the constitutional interplay between Congress and army, and again in Wiecek and Hyman, Equal Justice Under Law.

43. Cong. Globe, 37 Cong. 2 sess., p.499

44. Ibid., p. 329, Jan. 14th 1862.

45. James G. Randall, no friend of "emergency" legislation which denied civil liberties found the Lincoln Administration on the whole careful. Randall, Constitutional Problems Under Lincoln rev. ed. (Urbana, 1964).

46. Harold Hyman, A More Perfect Union is the leading authority on the dimensions of adequacy constitutionalism.

47. Michael L. Benedict, "Preserving the Constitution: The Conservative Basis of Reconstruct," _Journal of American History_ (1974), **Daniel Elazar, "The Civil War and the Preservation of Federalism"** 1 _Publius_ (1970).

48. In George L. Stearns, _The Equality of All Men Before the Law Claimed and Defended: In Speeches by William D. Kelley, Wendell Phillips, and Frederick Douglass_ (Boston, 1865) p.37.

49. The phrase is Alfred Kelly's.

50. Wallace D. Farnham, "The Weakened Spring of Government: A Study in Nineteenth Century American History" _American Historical Review_, April 1963 also takes the view that in terms of administrative centralisation "the war brought fewer changes than it is now fashionable to believe."

51. Charles Warren, _The Supreme Court in United States History_ (Boston, 1960).

52. Stanley J. Kutler, _Judicial Power and Reconstruction Politics_ (Chicago, 1968), Harold Hyman, _A More Perfect Union_ (N.Y., 1973), William Wiecek, "The Reconstruction of Federal Judicial Power, 1863-1875," _American Journal of Legal History_, 1969.

53. Hyman and Wiecek, _Equal Justice Under Law_, p.71, Carl B. Swisher, The Taney Period: 1836-1864, (Holmes Devise History of the Supreme Court, N.Y., 1974) also documents its achievements.

54. Hyman and Wiecek, p.85.

55. See William Wiecek, "Slavery and Abolition Before the United States Supreme Court," 65 _Journal of American History_ (1979).

56. _Cong. Globe_, 37 Cong., 2 sess. p.500, Jan. 27th 1862.

57. See David M. Silver, _Lincoln's Supreme Court_ (Urbana, 1956).

58. F. Frankfurter and J. Landis, _The Business of the Supreme Court: A Study in the Federal Judicial System_ (N.Y., 1928), p.64.

59. Kermit L. Hall, "The Civil War Era as a Crucible for Nationalizing the Lower Federal Courts," 7 _Prologue_, 1975.

60. _Ibid._, p.186. Neither the Harris Bill of 1866 which did not pass Congress, nor the Trumbull Bill which became the Judiciary Act of 1869 met the need for more district courts.

61. Charles Warren makes a succinct analysis of the interactions in "Federal and State Court Interference," _Harvard Law Review_, Jan.1930 and "Federal Criminal Laws and the State Courts," _Harvard Law Review_, March 1925.

62. Thomson, "Abuses of the Writ of Habeas Corpus," _American Law Review_ quoted in Warren, "Federal and State Court Interference" p.353

63. Quoted in _The Albany Law Journal_, March 19th 1870, p.219.

64. John F. Dillon, "A Century of American Law" 13 *New York Bar Assoc. Journal* (1890), p.251. For contemporary criticisms see also Daniel Chamberlain, *The State Judiciary, Its Place in the American System* (N.Y., 1889) and George C. Barret, "The Administration of Criminal Justice," *Journal of Social Science, Transactions of the American Assoc.* Vol. 2, 1870.

65. Simeon E. Baldwin, "Recent Changes in Our State Constitutions," Journal of Social Science, *Transactions of the American Assoc.*, Vol. 10, 1879.

66. James Schouler, *Constitutional Studies, State and Federal* (N.Y., 1897).

67. A.E. Keir Nash, "Fairness and Formalism in the Trials of Blacks in the State Supreme Courts of the Old South," *Virginia Law Review*, Feb. 1970. Although Michael Hindus finds a harsher record in South Carolina he too notes the difference between local and state supreme courts. M. Hindus, "Black Justice Under White Law: Criminal Prosecution of Blacks in antebellum South Carolina," *Journal of American History*, Dec. 1976.

68. Mark Tushnet argues for putting this in a perspective of white interests in "Approaches to the Study of the Law of Slavery," 25 *Civil War History* (1979) and *The American Law of Slavery* 1810-1860 (Princeton, 1981).

69. Ralph A. Wooster, *Planters, Politicians and Plain Folk: Court House and State House in the Upper South, 1850-1860* (Knoxville, 1975).

70. Kermit Hall, "Constitutional Machinery and Judicial Professionalism" in Gerald W. Gawalt, *The New High Priests: Lawyers in Post-Civil War America* (Greenwood, 1984). Among his interesting statistics he finds that 31.5 percent of federal judges compared with 23.9 percent of state appellate judges had either graduated from or attended a law school. 80.9 percent of state judges had held previous judicial and/or public legal posts where only 45.3 percent of federal judges had done so, tending to serve in other public offices. State judges were younger on election (50.9 years) than federal judges on appointment (59.8 years). State judges had briefer careers on the bench (8.9 years compared with 18.2).

71. Kermit L. Hall, "Social Backgrounds and Judicial Recruitment: A Nineteenth Century Perspective on the Lower Federal Judiciary" 29 *Western Political Quarterly* (1976).

72. Harold M. Hollingsworth, "George Andrews, Carpetbagger," 28 *Tennessee Historical Quarterly*, 1969.

73. Albion W. Tourgee, *A Fool's Errand* ed. by John Hope Franklin (Cambridge, 1961).

74. W. Raymond Blackard, "The Demoralization of the Legal Profession in Nineteenth Century America," 16 *Tenn.Law Review*, 1940.

75. Perry Miller, The Life of the Mind in America (N.Y., 1965), pp.134-143.

76. Maxwell Bloomfield, American Lawyers in a Changing Society (Cambridge, 1976).

77. The new professionalism is recorded by John A. Matzko, "The Best Men of the Bar: The Founding of the American Bar Association," in Gawalt, The New High Priests.

78. Bloomfield, American Lawyers in a Changing Society, Ch.8.

79. Ibid., Ch.9. The publication of such a treatise as that by the Brotherhood of Liberty, Justice and Jurisprudence (N.Y., 1969 reprint of 1889 ed.) also suggests the existence of civil rights minded black lawyers.

80. Gilbert Pillsbury to Salmon P. Chase, Sept. 24th 1867, Chase Papers, L.C. Vol. 99 F. 14959.

81. Hugh L. Bond to Salmon P. Chase, Nov. 13th 1865, Chase Papers, L.C. Vol. 96 F. 14355

Notes: Chapter 2

1. John Sherman, Recollections of Forty Years in the House, Senate and Cabinet (2 vols., Chicago, 1895), vol.1, pp.314-315.

2. James G. Randall, Constitutional Problems Under Lincoln, (revd. ed. Urbana, 1964).

3. For confirmation of this view see John D. Syrett, The Confiscation Acts: Efforts at Reconstruction During the Civil War, (Unpublished Ph.D., Univ. of Wisconsin, 1971).

4. Albert G. Riddle, Recollections of War Times. Reminiscences of Men and Events in Washington 1860-1865 (N.Y., 1895), p.75.

5. Brown v U.S. 8 Cranch 143.

6. The Prize Cases 67 U.S. 635

7. Leading speeches to this effect are by Lyman Trumbull, Cong. Globe, 37th Cong., 2 sess., 942-944 (Feb. 25th, 1862), and Thomas Eliot, Ibid., p.2235 (May 20th, 1862).

8. Representative arguments illustrating the conservative constitutional case are those of Edgar Cowan, Ibid., pp.1050-1053 (March 4th, 1862) and Orville Browning, Ibid., pp.1136-1141 (March 10th, 1862).

9. William Whiting, War Powers Under the Constitution (Boston, 1871) p.60.

10. Asked by Fernando Beaman among others, Cong. Globe, 2 sess., app. pp.203-205 (May 24th, 1862).

11. Ibid., p.1763 (April 22nd, 1862).

12. Defenders of the same procedure in the second Confiscation Act often made the point that there had been no objection to it in August 1861. Representative B.F. Thomas, who had been on the Judiciary Committee then and voted for it, opposed it in 1862, making the point that under the August act, the guilty predicament of property actually used in rebellion would be self-evident. Ibid., app. p.202 (May 20th, 1862).

13. The amendment passed on July 22nd. Cong. Globe, 1 sess., p.218 (July 22nd, 1861); Ten Eyck's speech, Ibid., p.219 (July 22nd, 1861) and McClernand's, Ibid., p.411 (August 2nd, 1861).

14. Ibid., p.410 (August 2nd, 1861).

15. 12 U.S. Stat. 319.

16. Cong. Globe, 37th Cong., 1 sess., p.219 (July 22nd, 1861).

17. Henry D. Shapiro, Confiscation of Confederate Property in the North (N.Y., 1952) pp.15-26 and Syrett, The Confiscation Acts.

18. Cong. Globe, 37th Cong., 2 sess., p.2203 (May 19th, 1862).

19. Edward L. Pierce, "The Contrabands at Fortress Monroe," Atlantic Monthly, November 1861.

20. Benjamin P. Thomas and Harold M. Hyman, Stanton: The Life and Times of Lincoln's Secretary of War (N.Y., 1962), pp.234-246.

21. James G. Blaine in Twenty Years of Congress (2 vol., Norwich 1884) believes this was a reason for the passage of a sterner bill in the North in 1862.

22. Cong. Globe, 37th Cong., 2 sess., app. p.180 (May 23rd, 1862), Ibid., pp.2990-2992 (June 28th, 1862).

23. Roy P. Basler (ed.), Collected Works of Abraham Lincoln (9 vols., New Brunswick, 1953), IV pp.531-533, September 22nd, 1861.

24. Proclamation to the border states, Ibid., V pp.145-146, March 6th, 1862; revocation of Hunter's proclamation, Ibid., V pp.222-223, May 19th, 1862.

25. Miller v U.S. 78 U.S. 268 (1870).

26. 12 U.S. Stat. 589.

27. Cong. Globe, 37th Cong., 2 sess., pp.942-943, February 25th, 1862. The text of S 151 is printed in the Globe, Ibid., p.1758 (April 22nd, 1862).

28. The Palmyra 12 Wheaton 1 (1827).

29. Cong. Globe, 37th Cong., 2 sess., p.944 (February 25th, 1862).

30. Expanded in speeches by Cowan, Ibid., p.1053 (March 4th, 1862); Browning, pp.1136-1137 (March 10th, 1862) and Collamer, pp.1808-1810 (April 24th, 1862).

31. Anon., "The Power of Congress to Confiscate and Emancipate," 24 Monthly Law Reporter, June 1862.

32. See comments by Browning, 37th Cong., 2 sess., p.1859 (April 29th, 1862); Collamer, Ibid., pp.1808-1810 (April 24th, 1862); Davis, p.1762 (April 22nd, 1862) and Cowan, pp.2959-2963 (July 27th, 1862).

33. Ibid., p.1157 (March 11th, 1862).

34. See especially the speech by Democrat Henderson, Ibid., p.1573 (April 8th, 1862) and Republican Cowan, Ibid., pp.1052-1053 (March 4th, 1862).

35. A recurrent theme in conservative speeches, but well expressed by Browning, Ibid., pp.1136-1137 (March 10th, 1862).

36. Ibid., pp.1714-1720 (April 18th, 1862).

37. William Whiting, War Powers pp.27-28.

38. Cong. Globe, 37th Cong., 2 sess., p.1897 (May 1st, 1862).

39. Whiting, War Powers p.50

40. Anon., "The Right to Confiscate and Emancipate" 24 <u>Monthly Law Reporter</u>, September 1862, p.648.

41. <u>Cong. Globe</u>, 37th Cong., 2 sess., pp.2188-2196 (May 19th, 1862).

42. <u>Ibid.</u>, p.1720 (April 18th, 1862).

43. <u>Ibid.</u>, pp.1074-1077 (March 5th, 1862).

44. <u>Ibid.</u>, p.1715 (April 18th, 1862).

45. Sumner to John Bright, March 13th 1865, printed in Edward L. Pierce, <u>Memoirs and Letters of Charles Sumner</u> (4 vols., London, 1878) IV p.229.

46. <u>Cong. Globe</u>, 37th Cong., 2 sess., pp.1136-1137 (March 10th, 1862).

47. <u>Ibid.</u>, p.1811 (April 24th, 1862).

48. <u>Ibid.</u>, pp.1714-1720 (April 18th, 1862).

49. <u>Ibid.</u>, pp.2188-2196 (May 19th, 1862).

50. Senator Carlile commented to this effect, <u>Ibid.</u>, p.1885 (April 30th, 1862).

51. Joel Parker, "Constitutional Law," <u>North American Review</u> April 1862.

52. <u>Cong. Globe</u>,37th Cong., 2 sess., p.1812 (April 24th, 1862). He was referring to similar wording in a bill which he had offered as a substitute.

53. <u>Ibid.</u>, p.946 (February 25th, 1862).

54. <u>Ibid.</u>, p.1604 (April 10th, 1862).

55. <u>Ibid.</u>, p.945 (February 25th, 1862).

56. <u>Ibid.</u>, p.1604 (April 10th, 1862). Willey later withdrew the proposal. See also Doolittle's proposal and speech in favour of colinisation, <u>Ibid.</u>, app. pp.94-101 (April 11th, 1862).

57. Sherman's substitute bill is printed in the <u>Globe</u>, p.1604 (April 10th), Harris' p.1655 (April 14th), Collamer's p.1814 (April 24th) and Cowan's informal proposal, p.1870 (April 30th, 1862).

58. <u>Ibid.</u>, p.1959 (May 6th, 1862).

59. Theodore C. Pease and James G. Randall (eds.), <u>The Diary of Orville Hickman Browning</u> (2 vols., Springfield, 1929) I p.534.

60. Cowan made two such proposals, <u>Cong. Globe</u>, 37th Cong., 2 sess., p.1846 (April 28th) and p.1856. The motion was defeated on April 30th by 22 votes to 18, <u>Ibid.</u>, p.1886. The final vote to refer it there was 24 in favour, 14 (all Republicans) against, <u>Ibid.</u>, p.1965 (May 6th, 1862). Though Charles Sumner came round to the idea that it was a necessary move in view of the mass of alternatives, Trumbull had no faith in the venture and refused to serve on the committee. He was replaced by Harlan. <u>Ibid.</u>, p.1991 (May 7th, 1862).

61. The bill is printed in the Globe, p.2165 (May 16th, 1862).

62. Comments by Trumbull, Ibid., p.2226 (May 20th, 1962) and Wade, Ibid., p.2203 (May 19th, 1862).

63. Ibid., p.2172 (May 16th, 1862).

64. Report on the Impeachment of Judge West H. Humphreys, House Reports No. 44, 37th Cong., 2 sess., Vol.3 and articles of impeachment, House Miscellaneous Documents No.76, 37th Cong., 2 sess.

65. Cong. Globe, 37th Cong., 2 sess., pp.2253-2254 (May 21st, 1862). The Senate voted 33 to 9 to take up consideration of a tax bill instead.

66. Ibid., p.1303 (March 20th, 1862).

67. Ibid., p.1768 (April 22nd, 1862). Bingham objected that his bill was about persons, not property.

68. Ibid., p.1789 (April 23rd, 1862).

69. Ibid., p.1793 (April 23rd, 1862).

70. Ibid., p.1771 (April 22nd, 1862) and p.1788 (April 23rd, 1862).

71. The vote was taken on April 24th, Ibid., p.1820. The new committee had several strong friends of confiscation: Eliot, Hutchins, Beaman, Sedgwick and Noell (usefully from the border states).

72. Printed Ibid., pp.2232-2233 (May 20th, 1862).

73. Among the more specific speeches on these legal points are those by Eliot, Ibid., pp.2233-2237 (May 20th), Noell's, pp.2237-2240, and Babbitt's, app. pp.166-168 (May 22nd, 1862).

74. Ibid., app. p.220 (May 24th, 1862).

75. Sargent, Loomis and Arnold all cited this evidence, Ibid., app. pp.175-179, 179-182, 182-184 (May 23rd, 1862).

76. Ibid., pp.2360-2361 (May 26th, 1862).

77. Ibid., p.2363 (May 26th, 1862).

78. Printed Ibid., pp.2232-2233 (May 20th, 1862).

79. Ibid., app. p.209 (May 26th, 1862).

80. Ibid., app. pp.148-150 (May 22nd, 1862).

81. Ibid., app. p.193 (May 24th, 1862).

82. Ibid., p.2361 (May 26th, 1862).

83. Ibid., app. pp.191-193 (May 24th, 1862).

84. Walton's bill, Ibid., p.2362 (May 26th, 1862) and his comments on the need for legal procedures, Ibid., app. p.264 (May 24th, 1862) and the vote on the bill, Ibid., p.2362 (May 26th, 1862).

85. Text and vote, <u>Ibid.</u>, p.2793 (June 18th, 1862).

86. <u>Ibid.</u>, pp.2919-2924 (June 25th), 3000-3002 (June 28th), 2971-2972 and 2963-2965 (June 27th).

87. <u>Ibid.</u>, p.2995 (June 28th, 1862).

88. <u>Ibid.</u>, p.3000 (June 28th), p.3006 (June 30th).

89. <u>Ibid.</u>, p.3006 (June 30th).

90. The House refused on July 3rd, <u>Ibid.</u>, pp.3106-3107 and the Senate on July 8th, p.3166. The House concurred by 84 votes to 42 on July 11th, pp.3267-3268 and the Senate the following day, p.3276.

91. Randall, <u>Constitutional Problems</u> pp.359-363.

92. Donald Morgan, <u>Congress and the Constitution: A Study of Responsibility</u> (Cambridge, 1966) makes a similar point.

93. Joshua Tevis' to Hon. James Speed, <u>Attorney-Generals Papers</u>, Record Group 60, Nat.Archives, Letters Received (Kentucky).

94. Lincoln, <u>Works</u> V p.325, July 15th, 1862.

95. Browning, <u>Diary</u> p.558.

96. <u>Cong. Globe</u>, 37th Cong., 2 sess., p.3374 (July 16th,1862).

97. <u>Ibid.</u>, pp.2972-2973 (June 27th, 1862).

98. <u>Ibid.</u>, p.3380 (July 16th, 1862).

99. <u>Ibid.</u>, p.3383 (July 16th, 1862).

100. Lincoln, <u>Works</u> V pp.328-331 (July 17th, 1862).

101. A "Radical Abolitionist" in the <u>Liberator</u>, August 22nd, 1862.

102. Lincoln, <u>Works</u> V pp.336-337, 341, 433-436, VI pp.28-30.

103. <u>Ibid.</u>, V pp.419-425.

104. <u>Cong. Globe</u>, 37th Cong., 2 sess., p.2300 (May 22nd, 1862).

105. The problems of enforcement are documented in James G. Randall, "Some Legal Aspects of the Confiscation Acts," <u>A.H.R.</u>, October 1912, H. Shapiro, <u>Confiscation of Confederate Property in the North</u> (N.Y., 1962) and Syrett, <u>Confiscation Acts</u>.

106. Attoeney-General Bates to R.J. Lackey, district attorney for the western district of Missouri, January 19th, 1863, <u>Attorney-Generals Papers</u>, Letterbook 4. A typical letter of advice was sent to James Broadhead, also in Missouri explaining his reluctance to prosecute, <u>Ibid.</u>, April 10th, 1862.

107. Bates to Richard Dana, E.D. Smith, George Coffey and William Price, <u>Attorney-Generals Papers</u>, Letterbook 4, 1st December, 1862.

108. *Miller v United States*, 78 U.S. 268, The Confiscation Cases, 87 U.S. 92. Syrett, *Confiscation* contains the best analysis.

109. *Tyler v Defrees* 78 U.S. 331.

110. *Union Insurance Co. v U.S.* 6 Wall. 759, Armstrong's Foundry, 6 Wall. 767.

111. 87 U.S. 92.

112. *McVeigh v U.S.* 78 U.S. 259.

113. Cf. *Armstrong's Foundry* and the *Confiscation Cases* on the effect of pardon and the role of the jury.

114. J. Hubley Ashton to the district attorneys in Missouri advising restraint, April 22nd, 1865, *Attorney-Generals Papers*, Letterbook D, and Henry Stanbery to Bennett Pike, August 14th, 1866, Letterbook F.

115. Randall, *Constitutional Problems* pp.288-291.

116. Bank's general orders 71 and 76. *War of the Rebellion: Official Records of the Union and Confederate Armies* (128 vols., 1180-1901) Vol.15 pp.571-575.

117. Bates to Benjamin H. Smith, district attorney, Virginia, March 1862, *Attorney-Generals Papers*, Letterbook 4.

118. Bates to Stanton, January 21st, 1863, *Ibid.*

119. *Official Records of the Rebellion* Ser. III, Vol.4 pp.407-408, 413-415.

120. Bates to Stanton, April 7th, 1864, *Attorney-Generals Papers*, Letterbook 5.

121. John C. Underwood to Salmon P. Chase, April 28th, 1865. *Chase Papers* L.C.

122. James Speed to L.H. Chandler, district attorney, Norfolk, Virginia, July 15th, 1865. *Attorney-Generals Papers*, Letterbook Vol.E.

123. *Armstrong's Foundry*, 6 Wall. 767.

124. *The Confiscation Cases*, 87 U.S. 92.

125. James Speed to C.W. Hall, U.S. attorney, Knoxville, Tenn., January 11th, 1866, *Attorney-Generals Papers*, Letterbook, Vol.E.

126. William K. Evarts to U.S. District Attorneys, March 2nd, 1869, *Attorney-Generals Papers*, Letters sent.

127. Syrett, *Confiscation Acts*, p.109.

128. H.W. Davis to Mrs. S.F. DuPont, quoted in Herman Belz, "Protection of Personal Liberty in Republican Legislation of 1862," 42 *Journal of Southern History*, August 1976. Professor Belz also concludes that guaranteeing personal liberty had to take its place lower down the scale of priorities than victory and emancipation.

Notes: Chapter 3

1. James G. Randall, Constitutional Problems pp.193-194.

2. Felix Frankfurter and James M. Landis, The Business of the Supreme Court: A Study in the Federal Judicial System (N.Y. 1927), p.2.

3. In "New Light on the History of the Federal Judiciary Act of 1789," 37 Harvard Law Review (1924), Charles Warren documents the areas of compromise which had to be made with states rights. See also John Norton Pomeroy, An Introduction to the Constitutional Law of the United States (9th ed., Boston, 1886) pp.621-622.

4. Daniel H. Chamberlain, "The State Judiciary. Its Place in the American Constitutional System" in Constitutional History of the United States as Seen in the Development of American Law (N.Y., 1889).

5. The subtleties are explored by Charles Warren, "Federal and State Court Interference" Harvard Law Review (1930).

6. 1 Stat. 335, Section 5.

7. In Groves v Slaughter, 16 Peters (40 U.S.) 449 (1841) the Supreme Court construed the constitution of Missouri as affecting the validity of a note given for the purchase of slaves imported to that State, since there were no state decisions on the point at the time. Even after the state courts rendered decisions contrary to Groves v Slaughter the Supreme Court did not say that it was bound to follow them. Justice Grier in Pease v Peck, 18 Howard (59 U.S.) 595 said, "when the decisions of the state court are not consistent, we do not feel bound to follow the last, if it is contrary to our convictions."

8. For a fuller discussion of Swift v Tyson 16 Pet. (41 U.S.) 1 (1842) see Mitchell Wendell, Relations Between the Federal and State Courts (Unpublished Ph.D. dissertation, Columbia University, 1949) pp. 115-128, and Hyman and Wiecek, Equal Justice pp.71-73. It was reversed in Eerie Railroad Co. v Tompkins 304 U.S. 64 (1938).

9. William F. Duker, A Constitutional History of Habeas Corpus (Westport, 1980) Chapter 1. He regards Taney's reasoning in rejection of the right in Ableman as faulty.

10. Ableman v Booth 21 How. (62 U.S.) 506 (1859) cf Hyman and Wiecek's conclusion, Equal Justice p.201 with Duker's supra p.149.

11. There had been another occasion when the removal power was invoked, in 1842 to take alien defendants who claimed the protection of the law of nations into federal courts. This was in the wake of the McLeod murder case. Again in 1855 the Senate had considered legislation to remove cases against fugitive slave commissioners into the federal courts. It was unsuccessful. See Harold M. Hyman, A More Perfect Union (N.Y., 1973), Ch. XV. The acts are those of February 4th, 1815, 3 Stat. 195 and March 2nd, 1833, 4 Stat. 632.

12. Wendell, Federal and State Courts p.26.

13. The acts are listed in Frankfurter and Landis, The Business of the Supreme Court pp.61–67 and discussed in the context of Reconstruction objectives by Stanley I. Kutler, Judicial Power and Reconstruction Politics (Chicago, 1968) and William M. Wiecek, "The Reconstruction of Federal Judicial Power" American Journal of Legal History (1969).

14. The Attorney-General upheld the President's right to make the suspension, 11 Opinions 297. Horace Binney's pamphlet, The Privilege of the Writ of Habeas Corpus Under the Constitution (2nd ed. Philadelphia, 1862) confirmed this view and sparked off a vigorcus debate, joined by many outstanding jurists and politicians. Sydney G. Fisher's reply, "The Suspension of Habeas Corpus During the War of the Rebellion" Political Science Quarterly, Sept. 1888 was a powerful argument for Congressional authority.

15. Cong. Globe 37th Cong., 3 sess., pp.534–535 (January 27th, 1863).

16. Leading comments by Senators Powell and Bayard, Ibid., pp.535–537.

17. Edward Bates to Lyman Trumbull, January 7th, 1863, Attorney-Generals Papers Letterbook 4 pp.310–311, Record Group 60, National Archives. Harold Hyman, A More Perfect Union has an excellent account of the subtleties in the relationship between civil and military authorities, and Congress's twin needs to both control and protect the army.

18. Cong. Globe, 37th Cong., 3 sess., p.529 (January 27th, 1863).

19. Ibid., pp.20–22 (Dec. 8th, 1862).

20. Ibid., pp.165–166 (Dec. 22nd, 1862).

21. Ibid., p.321 (Jan. 16th, 1863).

22. Ibid., pp.534–535 (Jan. 27th, 1863).

23. Charles Warren, "Federal Criminal Laws and the State Courts" 38 Harvard Law Review 1925 traces the history of several federal laws in which state courts applied penalties for crimes of embezzlement, robberty of the mails etc. Fears that the federal courts might develop a federal common law of crimes were probably groundless in that the states had won that battle in colonial times.

24. Cong. Globe, 33 Cong., 2 sess., App. p.211, quoted in Warren, "Federal Criminal Laws."

25. Cong. Globe, 37 Cong., 3 sess., pp.534–535 (January 27th, 1863).

26. Ibid.

27. Ibid., p.535 (January 27th, 1863). Charles Warren writes that the state courts had begun to object to sharing the load of federal criminal jurisdiction, especially if the law was unpopular. He cites cases in Connecticut, Kentucky and Missouri in the late 1820's and early 1830's that "no respectable Government ever yet undertook to execute the criminal code of another." In Prigg v Pennsylvania in 1842, 16 Peters 539, the Supreme Court held that the states could not be compelled to enforce such laws. Warren, "Federal Criminal Laws," pp.580–581.

28. Tennessee v Davis 100 U.S. 257 (1879).

29. Cong. Globe, 37 Cong., 3 sess., p.537 (January 27th, 1863).

30. Ibid., p.539.

31. The Justices v Murray 9 Wall. (76 U.S.) 274 (1869). When the case was in the circuit court, in Murray v Patrie Fed.Cas. 9, 967 (1866) the judgment had gone the other way. There Judge Nelson had cited Martin v Hunter, 1 Wheat. (14 U.S.) 346 and Osborn v Bank of U.S. 9 Wheat. (22 U.S.) 821 as authority for the correctness of removals after, as well as before judgment.

32. Cong. Globe, 37 Cong., 3 sess., p.538 (January 27th, 1863).

33. Ibid., p.1067 (February 18th, 1863).

34. Ibid., p.536 (January 27th, 1863).

35. Ibid., pp. 529-534 (January 27th, 1863). A similar connection was made by Representative Stiles in the House, pp.1087-1088 (February 19th, 1863). The jurist B.R. Curtis also warned that indemnification for emergency actions threatened to make them permanent, "They establish a system. They do not relate to some instant emergency - they cover an indefinite future." B.R. Curtis, Executive Powers (Boston, 1862).

36. Cong. Globe, 37 Cong., 3 sess., pp.529-534 (January 27th, 1863).

37. Ibid., pp.1064-1069, 1083-1086, and 1074-1080 (February 18th, 1863).

38. Ibid., pp.1080-1083.

39. Ibid., p.554 (January 27th, 1863).

40. Ibid., p.1107 (February 19th, 1863). The lack of debate makes it difficult to isolate their specific objections.

41. Ibid., p.1479 (March 2nd, 1863).

42. Ibid., p.1477 (March 2nd, 1863).

43. Randall, Constitutional Problems p.197.

44. Eifort v Bevins 1 Bush. 460 (1866).

45. Griffin v Wilcox 21 Indiana 370 (1863). See also Short v Wilson 1 Bush 350 and Hogue v Penn. 3 Bush 663.

46. Mitchell v Harmony 13 Howard (54 U.S.) 115 (1851).

47. Skeen v Huntington 25 Ind. 510 (1865).

48. 1 Bush 350 (1866).

49. Commonwealth v Palmer 2 Bush 570 (1866).

50. See Smith v Brazelton, 48 Tenn. 44, Cummings v Driggs, 48 Tenn. 67, Wright v Winningham, 49 Tenn. 254, Price v Poynter, 1 Bush 387, Terrill v Rankin, 2 Bush 453 and Lewis v McGuire, 3 Bush 202 (Judge Williams followed Terrill.)

51. Farmer v Lewis 1 Bush 66 (1866).

52. Discussed in Randall, Constitutional Problems p.197.

53. According to Henry C. Black, A Treatise on the Laws and Practice Governing the Removal of Causes (St. Paul, 1898) pp.312-313 this was the correct behaviour: "Issues of fact upon the petition cannot be raised in the state court. That court must take the facts to be as they are stated in the record and the petition; it has no jurisdiction to pass upon any such questions; that is the exclusive province of the federal court." On the other hand, "the mere filing of a petition for the removal of a suit which is not removable does not work a transfer." A case must be made which, prima facie, shows that the petitioner has a right to transfer. The federal court also had to decide if its own jurisdiction attaches to the cause by reason of proper steps having been taken to remove the cause, so that, "the decision of the state court is not conclusive."

54. Kulp v Ricketts 5 Philadelphia 305 (1863).

55. Jones v Seward as reported in Edward McPherson, The Political History of the United States During the Great Rebellion. (Washington, 1865) pp.185-187.

56. Edwards v Ward 2 Bush 606 (1866).

57. McCormick v Humphrey 27 Ind. 144 (1866).

58. The State v Fairfield Co. Common Pleas 15 Ohio St. (1864).

59. Col. B.H. Bristow, Asst. U.S. Attorney, Ky. to Hon. James Speed, February 9th, 1866, Letters Received, Attorney-Generals Papers, National Archives.

60. Cf. Robertson: opinion in Short v Wilson 1 Bush 350 with Williams' in Edwards v Ward 2 Bush 606.

61. Pennsylvania Conscription Cases 45 Pa. 238.

62. Walker v Crane Fed. Cas. 17067 (1865) is cited by James Sefton, The United States Army and Reconstruction, as an instance in which a civilian plaintiff in Vermont was awarded $1,000 damages in a suit against a provost marshal for false arrest after the case had been removed.

63. McCall v McDowell Fed. Cas. 8673, again a case of a civilian plaintiff awarded damages in the federal court.

64. Bean v Beckwith 85 U.S. 515 (1873). Bean was charged with enticing soldiers to desert. Beckwith, as provost marshal, claimed authority for his arrest under Presidential authority i.e. by reason of his office. Justice Field held the plea defective but the Supreme Court later ordered a re-trial in Beckwith v Bean 98 U.S. 289 (1878).

65. McKee v Rains 77 U.S. 22 (1869). A case against McKee for eviction had gone against him in the state court. A petition for removal filed, but the U.S. circuit court had remanded the case back to the state court. McKee brought a writ of error. Chase said that the fatal objection to McKee's application for removal was that it was made after final judgment in the state court.

66. The Mayor v Cooper 73 U.S. 247 (1867).
Other federal cases which took a broad view of the act include Hodgson v Millward Fed. Cas. 6 568, Murray v Patrie Fed. Cas 9 967 (1866), Clark v Dick 5 Fed. Cas 865 (1870), Beard v Burt 95 U.S. 434 (1877), Mitchell v Clark 110 U.S. 633 (1883).

67. 110 U.S. 633 (1883).

68. The problem of enforcement was discussed by Henry C. Black's Treatise, Ch.15. It was his opinion that further proceedings in a state court were void after removal was authorised. If the state court did proceed, the defendant could defend his case without forfeiting his right to trial in a federal court when jurisdiction could be asserted. If the case went against him he could take it to the Supreme Court on a writ of error or file a transcript of the record in the U.S. circuit court and require the plaintiff to litigate there even while proceedings were going on in the state court. In special circumstances, he concluded, an injunction to the State Court would be admissable.

69. Gordon v Longest 41 U.S. 97 (1842). The Supreme Court ordered the state court to release the record to the appropriate federal court.

70. Fisk v Union Pacific Fed. Cas. 4 827 (1869).

71. In re Farrand Fed. Cas. 4 678 (1867) the federal officer was jailed after he refused to hand over a recruit in answer to a habeas writ from a state court.

72. Bates, Diary pp.306-307.

73. Ibid., p.307.

74. In re Spangler 11 Mich. 298 (1863).

75. In re Oliver 17 Wisc. 681 (1864), In re Shirk 5 Philadelphia 333 (1863).

76. In re Tarble 25 Wisc. 390 (1870).

77. This was In re Reynolds, Fed. Cas. 11 721, in the N.Y. circuit court in 1867. Here the judge was of the opinion that the state courts have jurisdiction to issue a writ inquiring into the cause of the prisoner's detention and may discharge him if it appears that he was illegally held. Reynolds was discharged by the federal court.

78. In re Farrand Fed. Cas. 4 678 (1867).

79. In re Tarble 80 U.S. 397 (1871).

80. John A. Rawlins to the Attorney-General, May 11th, 1869, Correspondence Between War Department and Attorney-General V.9 Attorney-Generals Papers, General U.S. Grant to Henry Stanbery, February 13th, 1868, Ibid., Edwin Stanton to James Speed, December 29th, 1865.

81. **Belknap to Attorney-General, December 14th, 1870, Attorney-Generals Papers.**

82. D.H. Starbuck to J. Hubley Ashton, October 8th, 1866, Attorney-Generals Papers, Letters received.

83. *Ibid.*, John M. Palmer to the Sheriff of Hart County, January 27th, 1866.

84. *Ibid.*, John M. Palmer to the Adjutant-General, January 27th, 1866.

85. *Ibid.*, Adjutant-General Holt to the Attorney-General, February 8th, 1866.

86. *Ibid.*, H.H. Harrison, U.S. district attorney, to James Speed, March 2nd, 1866.

87. *Cong. Globe*, 39 Cong., 1 sess., p.1368, March 13th, 1866.

88. *Ibid.*, pp.1387-1388 (March 14th, 1866).

89. *Ibid.*, pp.1423-1425 (March 15th, 1866).

90. *Ibid.*, p.1526 (March 20th, 1866).

91. *Ibid.*, p.1530 (March 20th, 1866).

92. *Ibid.*, p.2052 (April 20th, 1866).

93. *Ibid.*, pp.2053-2054 (April 20th, 1866).

94. *Ibid.*, p.2054 (April 20th, 1866).

95. *Ibid.*, pp.2055-2056 (April 20th, 1866).

96. *Ibid.*, p.2059.

97. Speeches by Williams, *Ibid.*, p.2055, Trumbull, pp.2055-2056, Howard, pp.2060-2061 and Johnson, pp.2061-2062 were the most notable.

98. *Ibid.*, p.2066.

Notes: Chapter 4

1. T. Harry Williams, Lincoln and the Radicals (Madison, 1941) p.296. James G. Randall presents a similar view of the bill's political context in The Civil War and Reconstruction (Boston, 1953).

2. Welles, Diary II pp.95-96.

3. Cong. Globe, 38th Cong., 1 sess., p.1829 (April 23rd, 1864).

4. John G. Nicolay and John Hay, Abraham Lincoln: A History (10 vols., N.Y., 1917) Vol.9 pp.113-115 discuss the background of the Blair-Davis feud in Maryland politics.

5. Among many works which now recognise some of these similarities see Benedict, Compromise of Principle, op.cit. and LaWanda Cox, Lincoln and Black Freedom (Columbia S.C., 1981) and especially Herman Belz, Reconstructing the Union: Theory and Practice During the Civil War (N.Y., 1969).

6. Lincoln, Works VII pp.433-434, July 8th, 1864.

7. The text of the Manifesto is reprinted in full in Harold M. Hyman (ed.,) The Radical Republicans and Reconstruction, 1861-1870 (Indianapolis, N.Y., 1964), pp.137-147.

8. Herman Belz's excellent volume, Reconstructing the Union is unparalleled in unravelling the complex legislative and political history of these measures.

9. Charles Sumner, "Our Domestic Relations: Power of Congress over the Rebel States," Atlantic Monthly Vol.XII October 1863, p.499.

10. Cong. Globe, 37th Cong., 1 sess., p.209 (July 19th, 1861). The resolutions have to be used very cautiously. The first part of the resolution apportioned blame for the rebellion on Southern disunionists. The seventeen House Republicans who abstained from that part of the resolution disavowing any purpose to interfere with established institutions had voted in favour of the first part. Some known anti-slavery advocates, like Beaman, voted for both parts. Its terms were loose enough to cover most consciences, and it was not the time to say more with the military and political outlook so uncertain. They never claimed to begin with anything as strong as a "purpose." See Belz, Reconstructing the Union, Ch.1 for fuller discussion.

11. Ibid., p.337 (July 30th, 1861).

12. Speeches by Trumbull, Ibid., p.337 and Baker, pp.378-379 (August 1st, 1861) emphasise that these were Congressional concerns and should not be "left to the Executive as Commander-in-Chief."

13. Cong. Globe, 37th Cong., 2 sess., p.1193 (March 12th, 1862).

14. Ibid., p.1204 (March 12th, 1862).

15. Ibid., pp.1551-1552 (April 4th, 1862).

16. Herman Belz, Reconstructing the Union, pp.62-83 contains a full discussion of territorialisation and charts the shift away from it in favour of the guarantee clause.

17. LaWanda Cox, Lincoln and Black Freedom, argues that Lincoln did not lag behind Congress in these matters but kept pace.

18. The best discussions of theoretical alternatives are Belz, op.cit., Michael Les Benedict, "Preserving the Constitution: The Conservative Basis of Reconstruction," Journal of American History, 1974, and William Wiecek, The Guarantee Clause of the U.S. Constitution (Ithaca, 1972). The Harris bill is printed in Cong. Globe, 37th Cong., 2 sess., p.3138 (July 7th, 1862).

19. Cong. Globe, 37th Cong., 2 sess., p.3139 (July 7th, 1862).

20. Ibid., p.3140 (July 7th, 1862).

21. Ibid., p.3146 (July 7th, 1862).

22. Ibid., p.3142 (July 7th, 1862).

23. Infra Ch.III

24. Lincoln, Works V pp.504-505.

25. Lincoln, Works VI pp.364-365 (August 5th, 1863).

26. Ibid.

27. Ibid., VII pp.1-2 (November 5th, 1863).

28. Ibid., VI p.440 (September 11th, 1863).

29. Ibid., VI pp.407-409 (August 26th, 1863). Lincoln's demonstrated ability to "grow" in these matters, toward suffrage and civil rights is well documented by Harold Hyman, "Lincoln's Reconstruction: Neither Failure of Vision Nor Vision of Failure" (The Third Annual McMurtry Lecture, Indiana 1980).

30. The resolution to seat representatives from Louisiana passed on February 17th, Cong. Globe, 37th Cong., 3 sess., p.1036.

31. Ibid., pp.862-866 (February 11th, 1863).

32. Ibid., pp.859-860 (February 10th, 1863).

33. Ibid., p. 1033 (February 17th, 1863).

34. Ibid., p.1509

35. Lincoln, Works VII pp.54-56, December 8th, 1863.

36. In Nicolay and Hay, Abraham Lincoln, Vol.9, p.109.

37. Charles Sumner, "Our Domestic Relations" Atlantic Monthly October 1863.

38. Edward L. Pierce, Memoirs and Letters of Charles Sumner (4 vols., London, 1878) IV p.216, Sumner to Bright, December 15th, 1863.

39. LaWanda Cox, Lincoln and Black Freedom stresses the constructive aspects of Reconstruction in Louisiana and its open-endedness with respect to suffrage and civil rights. Michael Les Benedict, A Compromise and Principle, Ch.3, doubts how well informed Congressmen were about events in Louisiana in early 1864, or how universal distrust was for the leaders who were emerging there.

40. Harold M. Hyman, "Deceit in Dixie," Civil War History, March 1957, p.71.

41. Belz, Reconstructing the Union is authoritative on its genetic inheritance.

42. Davis to Wade, June 21st, 1864, Wade Papers, quoted in Belz, Reconstructing the Union, p.216.

43. Cong. Globe, 38th Cong., 1 sess., p.1247 (March 22nd, 1864). Similar points were made by Boutwell, pp.2102-2105 (May 4th) and Donnelly, pp.2036-2039 (May 2nd).

44. Ibid., App. p.84 (March 22nd, 1864).

45. Ibid., p. 1246 (March 22nd, 1864).

46. Ibid., App. pp.84-85 (March 22nd, 1864).

47. Ibid., App. p. 84 (March 22nd, 1864).

48. Ibid., p. 1739 (April 19th, 1864).

49. Ibid., p. 2039 (May 2nd, 1864).

50. Ibid., p. 2107 (May 4th, 1864).

51. Ibid., p. 1346 (March 30th, 1864) and Senate vote (22 to 17 in favour of Wilkinson's amendment), Ibid., p.1361 (March 31st). The House vote was 85 to 54 against concurring in the Senate version, Ibid., p.1652 (April 15th).

52. Ibid., pp.2107-2108 (May 4th, 1864). The majority for the bill was 73 to 59 against.

53. Eben G. Scott in Reconstruction During the Civil War in the United States (Boston & N.Y., 1895) p.301 carries the story that there was a deliberate attempt to prevent the bill coming up earlier so that Lincoln would not have to exercise an official veto over it. Senator Doolittle had apparently written to a member of General Banks' staff in Louisiana to this effect. The story is unconfirmed.

54. Cong. Globe, 38th Cong., 1 sess., p.3449 (July 1st, 1864). Wade explained that he would rather the amendment was not adopted since it might mean sacrificing the bill.

55. Ibid., p.3449 (July 1st, 1864). There is no evidence that support had been planned for it as an alternative, but it looked rather like a "maverick" which slipped in unexpectedly. At most it indicates a lack of wild enthusiasm for the bill, which in the House was described only as "the best we can get."

56. Ibid., p.3461 (July 1st, 1864).

57. Ibid., pp.3460-3461 (July 1st, 1864).

58. The vote was 18 for, 14 against, with the high absentee figure of 17. It was the end of session. Enthusiasms waned. Ibid., p.3491 (July 2nd, 1864).

59. Quoted in Nicolay and Hay, Abraham Lincoln Vol.9, p.120.

60. Lincoln, Works VII pp.433-434, July 8th, 1964.

61. Albert G. Riddle, Recollections of War Times (N.Y., 1895) p.305.

62. Quoted in The Liberator, September 16th, 1864.

63. David Donald (ed.,) Inside Lincoln's Cabinet: The Civil War Diary of Salmon P. Chase (N.Y., 1954) pp.230-232.

64. George W. Julian, Political Recollections, 1840-1872 (Chicago, 1884) p.247.

65. John Sherman, Recollections of Forty Years in the House, Senate, and Cabinet (2 vols., Chicago, 1895) I p.361.

66. Cong. Globe, 38th Cong., 2 sess., p.280 (January 16th, 1865).

67. Ibid., pp.281-291 (January 16th, 1865).

68. See Eliot's remarks, Ibid., p.298 (January 17th, 1865), and Dawes', p.935 (February 20th, 1865).

69. Ibid., p.234 (January 12th, 1865).

70. Ibid., pp.934-937 (February 20th, 1865).

71. The bill was postponed on January 17th by a vote of 103 to 34, Ibid., p.301. The whole subject, including substitutes by Wilson and Eliot was tabled on February 22nd by 80 votes to 65, pp.1102-1103.

72. Ibid., p.970 (February 21st, 1865).

Notes: Chapter 5

1. Cong. Globe, 39th Cong., 1 sess., p.499 (January 30th, 1866). Democratic Senator Saulsbury, among others, expressed similar views, pp. 476-480 (January 29th).

2. Ibid., p.322 (January 19th, 1866).

3. Charge to the Grand Jury, 30 Fed.Cas. 18, 260 (1875).

4. U.S. v Rhodes Fed.Cas. 16, 151 (1866).

5. Jacobus tenBroek, Equal Under Law (N.Y., 1965). Mark A. DeWolfe Howe, "Federalism and Civil Rights," Massachusetts Historical Society Proceedings (1965) also takes a substantive view of the amendment. But see Charles Fairman, History of the Supreme Court of the United States Vol.6. Reconstruction and Reunion, 1864-88 (N.Y., 1971), and Herman Belz, Emancipation and Equal Rights (N.Y., 1978) for the view that the Republicans worked within the limitations of states rights constitutionalism. Hyman and Wiecek, Equal Justice Under Law (1982) revive interest in the Thirteenth Amendment's organic potential. A welcome addition to the literature on the Amendment is Sydney G. Buchanan, "The Quest for Freedom: A Legal History of the Thirteenth Amendment," published serially in Vol. 12-13 of Houston Law Review.

6. Fairman, op.cit., p.1156.

7. Ibid., p.1157 - Representative Wilson said that the proposition "introduces no intricate question of constitutional law for discussion," Senator Henderson, "We give him no right except his freedom, and leave the rest to the States."

8. Note, "The New Thirteenth Amendment: A Preliminary Analysis," 82 Harvard Law Review (1969) p.1299.

9. Cong. Globe, 38th Cong., 1 sess., p.1246 (March 22nd, 1864).

10. Cornelius Cole, Memoirs (N.Y., 1908) p.221.

11. Senator Trumbull's speech on the amendment resolution sums up most of these doubts on the legality of the proclamation. Cong. Globe, 38th Cong., 1 sess., pp.1313-1314 (March 28th, 1864).

12. Lincoln, Works V pp.328-331 (July 17th, 1862), VII, pp.433-434 (July 8th, 1864).

13. Ibid., VI pp.438-439 (September 2nd, 1863).

14. Ibid., VIII pp.254-255 (February 1st, 1865).

15. Aaron A. Ferris, "The Validity of the Emancipation Edict," 131 North American Review (1882). See also the Richard Dana contribution to the exchange in the same volume.

16. Compare Trumbull's views on ratification, <u>Cong. Globe</u>, 38th Cong., 1 sess., pp.1313–1314 (March 28th, 1864) with those of James Ashley, pp.138–141 (January 6th, 1865).

17. <u>Ibid.</u>, 1 sess., pp.1456–1458 (April 7th, 1864). See also comments by Powell, pp.1444–1447 (April 6th) and Davis pp.1489–1490 (April 8th).

18. <u>Ibid.</u>, pp.1367–1370 (March 31st, 1864).

19. <u>Ibid.</u>, pp.1419–1424 (April 5th, 1864).

20. <u>Ibid.</u>, pp.2989–2991 (June 15th, 1864). See also Speeches by James Harlan, p.1439 (28th March, 1864) and Henry Wilson, <u>Ibid.</u>, p.1332 to the same effect.

21. <u>Ibid.</u>, p.1482 (April 8th, 1864). This represented an alteration from his original wording, "Everywhere within the limits of the United States, and of each State or Territory thereof, all persons are equal before the law, so that no person can hold another as a slave," pp.521–522 (February 8th, 1864).

22. <u>Ibid.</u>, pp.1479–1483 (April 8th, 1864).

23. Sumner had begun his campaign to secure the right of testimony in the federal courts as early as the Confiscation debate, when the question of the freedmen's judicial defence of his status arose. See <u>infra</u>. The federal courts applied the forum states laws and rules of decision, and continued to do so, but they admitted black testimony where they could in the District of Columbia in slavery cases, April 1862, and in July 1864 in issues arising under an appropriation act. For Sumner's part see Charles Sumner, <u>Works</u> (15 vols., Boston, 1870–73) VII pp.443–444, 502–503 and VIII pp.176–216.

24. <u>Cong. Globe</u>, 38th Cong., 1 sess., pp.1479–1483 (April 8th, 1864).

25. <u>Bowlin v Commonwealth</u> 65 Ky.5 (1867).

26. <u>Cong. Globe</u>, 38th Cong., 1 sess., p.1488 (April 8th, 1864).

27. <u>Ibid.</u>, pp.1488–1489 (April 8th, 1864).

28. <u>Ibid.</u>, 39th Cong., 1 sess., pp.503–504 (January 30th, 1866).

29. It was not the only time in the debate when the rights of women, or the possible effect of laws on marriage and family were urged as a limitation. Democrats regularly compared slavery with marriage as a state institution, immune from interference, and Republican legislators seemed anxious to draw the line at that. For full discussion of the point see Patricia Lucie, "On Being a Free Person and a Citizen by Constitutional Amendment," 12 <u>Journal of American Studies</u> (1978).

30. Bates, <u>Diary</u> p.330 (February 10th, 1864).

31. <u>Ibid.</u>, p.407 (September 11th, 1864).

32. <u>Cong. Globe</u>, 38th Cong., 1 sess., pp.2981–2983 (June 15th, 1864).

33. <u>Ibid.</u>, pp.2986–2987 (June 15th, 1864).

34. Jacobus tenBroek, <u>The Antislavery Origins of the Fourteenth Amendment</u> Berkeley, 1951) pp.147–148.

35. Hyman and Wiecek, _Equal Justice Under Law_ (1982) Chapter 11, "The Fourteenth Amendment in Light of the Thirteenth: Not Cramped by the Old Technicalities," is quite convincing on the organic nature of their intentions.

36. _Cong. Globe_, 38th Cong., 1 sess., p.2010 (April 30th, 1864).

37. _Ibid._, 2 sess., p.143 (January 6th, 1865).

38. _Ibid._, pp.1459–1465, as quoted in Fairman, _Reconstruction and Union_ p.1143, though his use of it was to argue a limited reach of the amendment.

39. _Cong. Globe_, 39th Cong., 1 sess., p.600 (February 2nd, 1866), "The bill draws to the Federal government no power whatever if the States will perform their constitutional obligations."

40. These examples are drawn from contributions to James C. Mohr (ed.), _Radical Republicans in the North_ (Baltimore, 1976).

41. Pomeroy, _Introduction to the Constitutional History of the United States_ (9th ed., N.Y., 1886) pp.127–128.

42. Sumner introduced the proposal on February 6th, 1865, _Works_, IX p.236.

43. _Cong. Globe_, 38th Cong., 1 sess., p.1370 (March 31st, 1864).

44. Lincoln, _Works_ VII p.443 (July 16th, 1864), p.451 (July 18th), p.461 (July 25th), pp.482–483 (August 6th), pp.489–490 (August 9th), pp.517–518 (August 24th), pp.499–501 (August 17th) and Vol.VIII, pp.1–2 (September 12th) documents Lincoln's resolve on this point.

45. Samuel S. Cox, _Three Decades of Federal Legislation_ (Providence, 1886) pp.327–329.

46. _Works_, VIII p.149. James G. Blaine believed that Lincoln's support was crucial at the margins. Blaine, _Twenty Years of Congress_ (Norwich, 1884) pp.533–536.

47. Cox, _Three Decades_, p.326.

48. Blaine, _Twenty Years_, p.536.

49. Cole, _Memoirs_, p.221, Blaine, _Twenty Years_, p.538.

50. Charles A. Dana, _Recollections of the Civil War_ (N.Y., 1898) pp.174–177.

51. Cox, _Three Decades_, pp.327–329.

52. Albert G. Riddle, _Recollections_, pp.324–325.

53. LaWanda and John H. Cox, _Politics, Principle and Prejudice, 1865–1866_ (N.Y., 1963) p.42.

54. The correspondence is quoted and discussed in Howard Devon Hamilton, _The Legislative and Judicial History of the Thirteenth Amendment_ (Urbana, 1950).

55. Dana, Recollections pp.174-177. Nevada was admitted on October 31st, 1864 and ratified the amendment on February 16th, 1865.

56. McElvain v Mudd 44 Ala. 48 (1870) - though in other cases it was also argued that the Proclamation was what had interfered with the contract, e.g. Dorris v Grace 24 Ark. 326 (1866).

57. Jacoway v Denton 25 Ark. 665. Other cases include Hand v Armstrong 34 Ga. 232, Walker v Gatlin 12 Fla. 1, Blease Baxter v Pratt 3 S.C. 513, Thomas v Porter 3 Bush 177, Porter v Ralston 6 Bush 665, Haskill v Sevier 25 Ark. 152.

58. Roundtree v Baker 52 Ill. 241.

59. Wainwright v Bridges 19 La.Ann. 234 and Austin v Sandel 19 La.Ann 309 Georgia's highest court took a similar line in White v Hart 39 Ga. 306 and Shorter v Cobb 39 Ga. 285.

60. White v Hart 13 Wall. (80 U.S.) 646, and Osborn v Nicholson 13 Wall. (80 U.S.) 654.

61. Paradoxically, to uphold the contracts made under ante bellum law it was necessary to override new state constitutions and state court constructions of them, raising issues of comity. Jacoway v Denton had been argued only upon the issue of the construction of the state constitution, and the Supreme Court declined jurisdiction to review for that reason. The result accorded with its own decision in Osborn v Nicholson. But in Boyce v Tabb in 1873, the case was appealed after the Louisiana Supreme Court had found against the validity of slave contracts on a construction of its own constitution. When the plaintiff in error argued that the Supreme Court was bound to respect that construction under Clause 34 of the Judiciary Act, Justice Davis held that the rule did not apply to questions "of a general nature not based on local statute or usage nor any rule of law affecting title to land or settled rules of property."

62. Parish v Hill 63 Ky. 396. Similar opinions were given in Neely v Merrill 9 Bush 346 and Todd v Trott 64 N.C. 280.

63. Farmer's Bank of Kentucky v Johnson 4 Bush 411.

64. John Jay to Salmon P. Chase, January 5th, 1867, Chase Papers, L.C. V 98 f 14727.

65. U.S. v Rhodes Fed.Cas. 16, 151.

66. In re Turner Fed.Cas. 14, 427.

67. In the case of Jones v Alfred H. Mayor Co. 392 U.S. 409 (1968). In many respects Stewart's opinion and Harlan's dissent were echoes of the divisions in Congress and on the Court a hundred years earlier. See Fairman, Reunion and Reconstruction for a critical view of the result and compare with R. Kohl, "The Civil Rights Act of 1866. Its Hour Came Round at Last" 55 Virginia Law Review (1969).

68. Blyew v U.S. 13 Wall. (80 U.S.) 581. As a result of this case the legislature altered the law to admit black testimony. See V.B. Howard, "The Black Testimony Controversy in Kentucky 1866-1872" 58 Journal of Negro History (1973).

69. <u>The Slaughterhouse Cases</u> 83 U.S. 36 (1873).

70. Field's overall strategy was to detach the 1866 Civil Rights Act from the Thirteenth Amendment and bring it within the Fourteenth Amendment's 'state action' limitation. See Hyman and Wiecek, <u>Equal Justice</u> pp.473-475, and <u>infra</u> Chapter 7.

71. <u>U.S. v Hall</u> 26 Fed.Cas. 79 (1871).

72. In <u>U.S. v Cruikshank</u> Fed.Cas. 14, 897 (1874). The case was appealed to the Supreme Court on a certificate of division after Bradley disagreed with Woods. In <u>U.S. v Cruikshank</u> 92 U.S. 542 (1876) a unanimous court held the indictments defective for want of showing the conspiracy was to prevent the exercise of a federal right, an "attribute of national citizenship," rather than to prevent persons meeting for any purpose whatsoever. Two blacks had been lynched. The Court, per Waite, did not rule out circumstances in which private action would be reached, however.

73. <u>U.S. v Harris</u> 106 U.S. 629 (1882), and see Wood's opinion in <u>LeGrand v U.S.</u> 12 F. 577.

74. <u>The People v Brady</u> 40 Cal. 198 (1870).

75. <u>Texas v Gaines</u> Fed.Cas. 13, 847 (1874), cited and followed in Louisiana ex rel. <u>Moncure v Dubuclet</u> Fed.Cas. 8, 588 (1877).

76. <u>Ex parte Wells</u> Fed.Cas. 17, 386.
It was also the view of Harlan and White more recently in <u>Jones v Alfred H. Mayer Co.</u> 392 U.S. 409 (1968).

77. <u>Civil Rights Cases</u> 109 U.S. 3 (1883).

78. <u>U.S. v Morris</u> 125 F 322.

79. <u>Hodges v U.S.</u> 203 U.S. 1 (1906).

80. <u>In re Sah Quah</u> 31 F 327 (1886).

81. <u>Butler v Perry</u> 240 U.S. 328 (1916).

82. <u>Clyatt v U.S.</u> 197 U.S. 207 (1905) and <u>Bailey v Alabama</u> 219 U.S. 219 (1911).

Notes: Chapter 6

1. *Opinions of the Attorneys General of the United States* Vol.10 p.383. See also John Norton Pomeroy's discussion of the problem in *Constitutional Law* Vol.1 pp.68-69 and Simeon E. Baldwin, "The Citizen of the United States," *Yale Law Journal* 1893.

2. In 1821, Attorney-General William Wirt, discussing the question of the eligibility of a free coloured man to command a coasting vessel, gave the opinion that a free Negro was not a citizen *Opinions* I p.506. In 1843, however, Attorney-General Legare reached the opposite conclusion in his opinion on a statute for the pre-emption of public lands by citizens of the United States. *Ibid.*, IV p.506. Bates himself gave the opinion that all persons born within the limits of the United States were citizens, owing allegiance to the United States in return for protection. *Ibid.*, X p.382; *Dred Scott v Sanford* 19 How. 393 (1857). State court opinions on free black citizenship are discussed *infra*.

3. *Passenger Cases* 7 Howard (48 U.S.) 283 (1849).

4. Hyman and Wiecek, *Equal Justice* p.182. Don E. Fehrenbacher, *The Dred Scott Case: Its Significance in American Law and Politics* (N.Y., 1978) Ch.13 is a superb analysis of the flaws in Taney's reasoning.

5. John P. Roche, *Courts and Rights: The American Judiciary in Action* (N.Y., 1961) and Edward S. Corwin, *Liberty Against Government: The Rise, Flowering and Decline of a Famous Juridical Concept* (Baton Rouge, 1948).

6. Hamilton and Madison knew the dangers and warned of them in the *Federalist Papers*.

7. Charles Warren, "Federal Criminal Laws and the State Courts" 38 *Harvard Law Review* (1925). Recent work suggests, however, that the lower federal courts had more business, including criminal than has been supposed, Mary K. Bronsteel Tachau, *Federal Courts in the Early Republic, Kentucky 1789-1816* (Princeton, 1978).

8. Jacob W. Landynski, *Search and Seizure and the Supreme Court* (Baltimore, 1966) p.49. For the extent, or lack of it of federal criminal law see Joel P. Bishop, *Commentaries on the Criminal Law* (5th ed., Boston 1872) pp.179-180.

9. Leonard Levy, *Legacy of Suppression* (N.Y., 1960) argues a restricted interpretation of the First Amendment, and that Jeffersonian opponents of the Sedition Act went beyond original understandings in arguing a right to freedom of discussion.

10. Hyman and Wiecek, *Equal Justice* pp.118-119.

11. *Barron v Baltimore* 7 Pet. (32 U.S.) 243 (1833) William W. Crosskey, *Politics and the Constitution in the History of the United States* (Chicago, 1953) offers a different view and so of course did radical antislavery theorists.

12. Pomeroy, *Constitutional Law* I p.151. The states had organic laws and bills of rights too, as discussed *infra*.

13. The literature on antislavery uses of the privileges and immunities clause, and the Bill of Rights as sources of rights pertaining to all citizens of the nation is extensive. See Howard J. Graham, Everyman's Constitution (Madison, 1968), Jacobus tenBroek, The Antislavery Origins of the Fourteenth Amendment (Berkeley, 1951), William Wiecek, The Sources of Antislavery Constitutionalism in America (Ithaca, 1977) and William Nelson, "The Impact of the Antislavery Movement Upon Styles of Judicial Reasoning" 87 Harvard Law Review 1974. Abolitionists were certainly familiar with Dred Scott, though it is unlikely that Barron v Baltimore reached popular awareness.

14. James H. Kettner, The Development of American Citizenship, 1608–1870 Ch.9 explores some of these possibilities in the case law.

15. Corfield v Coryell 4 Wash. C.C. 371 (1823). See also The State v Medbury 3 R.I. 138 (1855) confirming that a statute forbidding the taking of oysters and shellfish from the state's waters or shores was not a violation of the comity clause.

16. Counsel's argument in Minor v Happersett 21 Wall. 162 (1875).

17. Cong. Globe, 39th Cong., 1 sess., pp.474–476 and p.599.

18. Raoul Berger, Government by Judiciary (Cambridge, 1977) p.31.

19. Charles Fairman, Reconstruction and Reunion p.1123 argues that the comity clause had a limited meaning and that in giving it such a broad one "Justice Washington's words, as reported, far overleaped his thought."

20. Campbell v Morris 3 H. McH. 535 (1797), Abbot v Bayley 6 Pick. 89 (1827), Wiley v Parmer 14 Ala. 627 (1848), Kettner Op. Cit offers others.

21. Amy v Smith 1 Litt (Ky) 326 (1822) and The State v Claiborne 1 Meigs (Tenn.) 331 (1838), discussed infra.

22. Davis v Pierse 7 Minn. 13 (1862).

23. Crandall v The State 10 Conn. 339 (1834).

24. John Randolph Tucker, Address Delivered Before the Phoenix and Philomatheon Societies of William and Mary College (Richmond, 1854) p.10.

25. Lawrence M. Friedman, A History of American Law (N.Y., 1973) p.103. The constitutions are collected in Francis N. Thorpe, The Federal and State Constitutions, Colonial Charters and Other Organic Laws (7 vols., Washington, 1909). They are compared in Frederic J. Stimson, The Law of the Federal and State Constitutions of lthe United States (Boston, 1908).

26. Benjamin F. Wright, American Interpretations of Natural Law (Cambridge, 1931) p.185.

27. Leonard Levy, Origins of the Fifth Amendment (N.Y., 1968) p.415.

28. Thomas McIntyre Cooley, A Treatise on the Constitutional Limitations Which Rest Upon the Legislative Power of the States of the American Union (DaCapo reprint, N.Y., 1972) p.182. See also John W. Cary, "Limitations of the Legislative Power in Respect to Personal Rights and Private Property," Reports of the American Bar Association, Vol.X (1892).

29. James W. Hurst, Law and Conditions of Freedom in the Nineteenth Century United States (Madison, 1967) pioneered efforts to understand the role played by law in actively expanding individual choice.

30. Calder v Bull 3 Dall. (3 U.S.) 386 (1798) Justice Iredell, in dissent, argued that the Court was not empowered to defeat the intention of the legislature, except on specific constitutional grounds.

31. Fletcher v Peck 6 Cranch (10 U.S.) 87 (1810), Dartmouth College v Woodward 4 Wheat. (17 U.S.) 518 (1819).

32. Roger M. Cover, Justice Accused (New Haven, 1975) argues that judges avoided natural law as a basis for constitutional decision in preference for a "will-less" role in applying positive law but not that the natural law tradition was unimportant.

33. Hyman and Wiecek, Equal Justice Chapter 2 is the basis for this argument, and William E. Nelson, The Roots of American Bureaucracy (Cambridge, 1982) Ch.1.

34. The origins and development of substantive due process from these pre-war roots is analysed by Edward S. Corwin, in "The Doctrine of Due Process of Law Before the Civil War," 24 Harvard Law Review (1911). Due process was understood primarily in procedural rather than substantive terms before the war, outside of the antislavery constitutionalists who argued that the Fifth Amendment was a source of substantive power against slavery. The very uncertain beginnings of the doctrine in Holboken and Wynehamer were carefully restricted to property. Dred Scott is not thought to be a landmark in these developments but "almost a throwaway line." Hyman and Wiecek, Equal Justice p.187.

35. Morton J. Horwitz, The Transformation of American Law, 1780-1860 (Cambridge, 1977) discovered the extent to which judges played a self-conscious role in releasing new economic energies.

36. Friedman, History of American Law pp.107-108.

37. T.D. Woolsey, "Nature and Sphere of Police Powers," Journal of Social Science, Transactions of the American Assoc., Vol.3, 1871 and Eugene McQuillon, "Some Observations on State Laws and Municipal Ordinances" 64 Central Law Journal.

38. In Cooley, Limitations, p.573.

39. Woolsey, Op.cit.,

40. Nelson M. Blake, The Road to Reno (Greenwood Reprint, Westport 1977) p.151.

41. In Philip Foner (ed.) Frederick Douglass on Women's Rights (Westport, 1976) p.76.

42. Richard B. Morris, Studies in the History of American Law (N.Y., 1930).

43. Peggy A. Rabkin, Fathers to Daughters: The Legal Foundation of Female Emancipation (Westport, 1980), Patricia Lucie, "Marriage and Law Reform in Nineteenth Century America" in Elizabeth Craik (ed.), Marriage and Property (Aberdeen, 1984), Friedman, History of American Law p.186.

44. Cong. Globe, 39th Cong., 1 sess., pp.1063-1064 (Feb. 27th, 1866), discussed further in Patricia Lucie, "On Being a Free Person and a Citizen by Constitutional Amendment" 12 Journal of American Studies (1978).

45. The ones which follow are based on Leon Litwak, North of Slavery (Chicago, 1961), and Chief Justice Taney's opinion in Dred Scott!

46. Ira Berlin, Slaves Without Masters: The Free Negro in the Antebellum South (N.Y., 1974) p.49.

47. Ibid., p.97.

48. The inner contradictions are explored by J.R. Pole, The Pursuit of Equality in American History (Berkeley, 1978) and Kettner, Op.cit.

49. Amy v Smith 1 Litt. (Ky.) 326 (1822).

50. The State v Claiborne 1 Meigs 331 (1838).

51. The State v Manuel 20 N.C. 144 (1838). The legislature passed an act the same year which resolved the matter by making all persons liable to jail for non-payment of fines. The Court recommended that Manuel's case should be disposed of under the new law.

52. These examples are drawn from Cooley, Limitations, Chapters 12 and 13.

53. Connecticut had no guarantee against double jeopardy. See Charles Fairman and Stanley Morrison, The Fourteenth Amendment and the Bill of Rights: The Incorporation Theory (DaCapo reprint, N.Y., 1970) p.162.

54. Ibid., The incorporation debate goes on, denied by Raoul Berger in Government by Judiciary, but ably revitalised by Michael Kent Curtis in "The Bill of Rights as a Limitation on State Authority: A Reply to Professor Berger." 16 Wake Forest Law Review (1980).

Notes: Chapter 7

1. Quoted in Lawanda and John Cox, Politics, Principle, and Prejudice, 1865–1866 (N.Y., 1963) p.166.

2. Michael Les Benedict, A Compromise of Principle (N.Y., 1974) argues that the Centrists changed their minds on suffrage in response to these events and opted for a "conservative Reconstruction."

3. Mississippi of course had not ratified the Thirteenth Amendment.

4. Cong.Globe, 39th Cong., 1 sess., p.322 (January 19th, 1866) for comment to this effect by Trumbull in the Senate, and p.1118 (March 1st) by Wilson in the House.

5. Ibid., p.503 (January 30th, 1866).

6. Ibid., p.1151 (March 2nd, 1866).

7. Trumbull had discussed them with Johnson, shown him drafts. See Patrick W. Riddleberger, 1866: The Critical Year Revisited (Carbondale, 1979) Ch.4.

8. Donald G. Nieman, To Set the Law in Motion: The Freedmen's Bureau and the Legal Rights of Blacks, 1865–1868 (N.Y., 1979) Ch.4 argues that Howard was by the end of 1865 prepared to take a more advanced position than Trumbull and the Republicans, advocating a bill which would reach discrimination in administering the law. Congress's constitutional conservatism "kept them from taking action as radical as that recommended by Howard. See also William S. McFeely, Yankee Stepfather (New Haven, 1968) pp.190–199 for a view of Howard's role which puts less distance between him and Trumbull.

9. Cong. Globe, 39th Cong., 1 sess., pp.314–319 (January 19th, 1866).

10. Ibid., p.323 (January 19th, 1866).

11. Ibid., p.345 (January 22nd, 1866).

12. Ibid., p.374.

13. Ibid., p.348.

14. Ibid., p.421 (January 25th, 1866).

15. Ibid., p.517 (January 30th).

16. Ignatius Donnelly was a prominent enthusiast for freedmen's education, pp.585–589.

17. Ibid., p.631 (February 3rd).

18. Ibid., p.688 (February 6th). The House had amended the bill to apply only to places where the writ of habeas corpus had been suspended on February 1st, 1866. Trumbull, however, clearly believed that it was important that its relief features and coverage of Bureau agents by military jurisdiction and protection should apply nationwide. The Senate struck out the House amendment, p.747 (February 8th) and the House agreed, p.775 (February 9th).

19. William R. Brock, An American Crisis: Congress and Reconstruction, 1865–1867 (N.Y., 1963) pp.105–106.

20. Cong. Globe, 39th Cong., 1 sess., pp.936–943 (February 20th).

21. Benedict, Compromise of Principle, pp.155–156.

22. Cong. Globe, 39th Cong., 1 sess., p.363 (January 23rd).

23. Robert L. Kohl, "The Civil Rights Act of 1866, Its Hour Came Round at Last" Virginia Law Review March 1969 argued in support of Justice Potter Stewart's broad view of the act in reaching private action. Charles Fairman, Reconstruction and Reunion takes the Court's use of history apart and argues a more limited application to discrimination under hostile state laws.

24. Speeches centring on these connections, include Morrill's remarks, Cong. Globe, 39th Cong., 1 sess., pp.570–571 (February 1st), Thayer, pp.1151–1154 (March 2nd), Broomall, p.1263 (March 8th) and Shellabarger, pp.1293–1294 (March 9th). Trumbull argued Congressional power over citizenship was derived from its constitutional power of naturalisation.

25. Ibid., pp.474–476 (January 29th, 1866).

26. Ibid., app. p.157.

27. Herman Belz, A New Birth of Freedom: The Republican Party and Freedmen's Rights, 1861–1866 (Westport, 1976), p.164.

28. Some Republicans did put more emphasis on the existence of a discernible body of "national" citizenship rights. Representative William Lawrence of Ohio spoke of such in connection with the Civil Rights Act, Cong. Globe, 39th Cong., 1 sess., pp.1832–1837 (April 7th, 1866). On the whole, however, much of what they said straddled the 'organic' and the 'absolute' approaches.

29. Ibid., p.597 (February 2nd).

30. Ibid., p.1258 (March 8th).

31. Ibid., p.475 (January 29th).

32. Ibid., p.606 (February 2nd).

33. Ibid., p.1151 (March 8th).

34. Ibid., pp.1115–1119 (March 1st).

35. For a discussion of Bingham's position see Robert A. Burt, "Miranda and a Morgantic Marriage," 1969 Supreme Court Review and Fairman, Reconstruction and Reunion p.1191–1193. Cong. Globe, 39th Cong., 1 sess., p.1366 (March 13th).

36. George S. Boutwell, Speeches and Papers Relating to the Rebellion and the Overthrow of Slavery (2 vols., Boston, 1867) p.522. This was in contrast however to the clearer separation made by moderates like Trumbull.

37. Cong. Globe, 39th Cong., 1 sess., p.606 (February 2nd) and p.1162 (March 2nd).

38. Ibid., p.322 (January 19th, 1866).

39. Ibid., pp.476-480 (January 29th), pp.595-599 (February 2nd).

40. Ibid., pp.1755-1761 (April 4th, 1866).

41. Ibid., p.600 (February 2nd, 1866).

42. Ibid., p.605.

43. Ibid., p.1154 (March 2nd, 1866).

44. Ibid., pp.1832-1837 (April 7th, 1866).

45. Ibid., pp.1755-1761 (April 4th, 1866).

46. Ibid., p.1119 (March 1st, 1866).

47. See Chapter 3 for fuller discussion of its legislative history.

48. Garret Davis was particularly voluble on that point and attempted unsuccessfully to strike out the section in the Freedmen's Bureau bill conferring 'military protection' on Bureau personnel. Cong. Globe, 39th Cong., 1 sess., p.347 (January 22nd, 1866).

49. Ibid., p.2057 (April 20th, 1866).

50. Ibid., p.1276. The Thirty-seven were predominantly, though not entirely moderates and conservatives.

51. Ibid., p.1809 (April 6th, 1866). Stockton had been elected as a senator for New Jersey, despite Republican efforts there to prevent it. His victory had depended on a change of rules to allow for election by a plurality rather than a majority and it was successfully contested in the Senate. For the suspense caused by the ailing Dixon's failure to appear see Benedict, Compromise of Principle p.165.

52. George R. Bentley, A History of the Freedmen's Bureau (Philadelphia, 1955) p.155.

53. John William De Forext, A Union Officer in the Reconstruction, ed. James H. Croushore and David Morris (New Haven, 1948) pp.41-42.

54. James Oakes, "A Failure of Vision: The Collapse of the Freedmen's Bureau Courts" 25 Civil War History (1979). Also W.McFeeley, Yankee Stepfather.

55. J. Thomas May's portrait, "The Freedmen's Bureau at the Local Level: A Study of a Louisiana Agent" Louisiana History IX (1968) illustrates the dilemma of a well-intentioned agent who was not impressed by the standard of local justice but never called in the troops or challenged the civil authorities. In his eyes the immediate priority was the regeneration of agriculture.

56. John David Smith, "More than Slaves, Less than Freedmen: The "Share Wages" Labor System during Reconstruction," Civil War History (1980).

57. James Smallwood, "Charles E. Culver, A Reconstruction Agent in Texas: The Work of Local Freedmen's Agents and the Black Community," Civil War History (Dec. 1981).

58. Donald G. Nieman, To Set the Law in Motion Ch.1.

59. Gilbert Pillsbury to Salmon P. Chase, September 24th, 1867, Chase Papers, L.C. V. 99 f.14959.

60. In fact, Ex parte Milligan did not deal with military trial of civilians in the South at all, but President and Congress made that inference. See Hyman and Wiecek, Equal Justice pp.381-385.

61. Phrases drawn from Oakes, "Failure of Vision" and Nieman, To Set the Law in Motion.

62. Recorded in Bentley, A History of the Freedmen's Bureau, p.155.

63. Breut.Maj.Gen. Getty to Breut.Maj.Gen. Heintzelman, September 29th, 1866, Attorney-Generals Papers, Nat. Archives, Record Group 60.

64. Heintzelman to the Acting Asst.Adjt.Gen., Galveston, December 22nd, 1866, Ibid.

65. Stanton to Johnson, January 29th, 1866, Ibid.

66. Stanton to Henry Stanbery, January 30th, 1866, Ibid., endorsed on July 15th, closing the case.

67. Discords are documented by James E. Sefton, The United States Army and Reconstruction, 1865-1877 (Baton Rouge, 1967) Ch.2, "Working With (and Against) the Provisional Governors."

68. Quoted Ibid., at 41, Genl. H.G. Wright to AAG Div. Gulf, Nov.20, 1865, original in Sheridan Papers.

69. Ex Parte Warren 31 Tex. 143 (1868), Kelly v The State 25 Ark. 392 (1869).

70. Smith v Moody 26 Ind. 299 (1866).

71. Ellis v The State 42 Ala. 525 (1868).

72. Burns v The State 48 Ala. 195 (1872).

73. Hart v Hose 26 La Ann. 90 (1874).

74. The State v Gibson 36 Ind. 389 (1871); also Green v The State 58 Ala. 190 (1877).

75. Gaines v The State 39 Tex. 606 (1873). On appeal, however, Justice Bradley on circuit rejected the argument that the Civil Rights Act reached discriminatory conduct based on "prejudice."

76. The State v Dunlop 65 N.C. 491 (1871).

77. C. Mildred Thompson, Reconstruction in Georgia (N.Y., 1915) pp.352-360.

78. Michael Perman, Reunion Without Compromise: The South and Reconstruction (Cambridge, 1973) pp.110-121 discusses patronage considerations with respect to judicial appointments.

79. Harold M. Hollingsworth, "George Andrews, Carpetbagger," Tennessee Historical Quarterly Vol.28 (1969).

80. Otto H. Olsen, Carpetbagger's Crusade: The Life of Albion Winegar Tourgee (Baltimore, 1965) pp.143-155.

81. James A. Baggett "Origins of Upper South Scalawag Leadership," 29 Civil War History (March 1983) concludes that at least in the Upper South the Scalawags were men of property and government experience though of lower social standing than their political enemies. cf A. Trelouse, "Who Were the Scalawags?" Journal of Southern History, November 1963.

Richard C. Hume examines a group of active carpetbaggers in Southern conventions, "Carpetbaggers in the Reconstruction South: A Group Portrait of Outside Whites in the "Black and Tan" Constitutional Conventions," Journal of American History Vol.64 (1977) and finds that a much smaller proportion went on to serve in state judiciaries than in Reconstruction legislatures.

82. C. Mildred Thompson, Reconstruction in Georgia, Ethel K. Ware, A Constitutional History of Georgia (N.Y., 1947).

83. Francis B. Simkins and Robert H. Woody, South Carolina During Reconstruction (Chapel Hill, 1932) p.144.

84. Joel Williamson, After Slavery: The Negro in South Carolina During Reconstruction (Chapel Hill, 1965) p.333.

85. This account is based on William C. Harris, The Day of the Carpetbagger: Republican Reconstruction in Mississippi (Baton Rouge, 1979).

86. Sarah Woodfall Wiggins, The Scalawag in Alabama Politics (Alabama, 1977).

87. Quoted in John Rose Ficklen, History of Reconstruction in Louisiana (Baltimore, 1910) p.96, n.4.

88. In Bentley, A History of the Freedmen's Bureau.

89. Winston Banks to General George P. Buell, February 1st, 1869, Attorney-Generals Papers, Nat. Archives, Record Group 60.

90. Bowlin v Commonwealth 65 Ky. (2 Bush) 5 (1867).

91. In re Turner, Fed.Cas. 14, 247 (1867), U.S. v Rhodes, Fed.Cas. 16,151 (1866), discussed supra, p.

92. B.H. Bristow to the Attorney-General, April 22nd, 1869, Attorney-Generals Papers, Nat. Archives, Group 60.

93. Blyew v U.S. 80 U.S. (13 Wall.) 581, and see Victor B. Howard, "The Black Testimony Controversy in Kentucky, 1866-1872" 58 Journal of Negro History (1973) for the argument that the case was instrumental in bringing pressure on the Kentucky legislature to change the law, which it did in 1872.

94. The Slaughterhouse Cases 83 U.S. 36 (1872). Michael Les Benedict, "Preserving Federalism: Reconstruction and the Waite Court," 1978 Supreme Court Review makes an interesting case for revising the view that the Court engaged in a counter-revolution against the original intentions of the framers. Although not in sympathy with the racial implications of the decision, he sympathises with the Court's dilemma in facing a novel situation in which states might lose their traditional regulatory power over a whole range of business which the framers might not have taken into account, like slaughterhouses. Nor does he think that the Court was against the idea of employing Congressional power to enforce black civil rights. The Justices - especially Bradley - acknowledged the power at least in dicta. It was the Fuller Court which closed the door the Waite Court had kept a little bit open.

95. Texas v Gaines Fed. Cas. 13, 847 (1874).

96. The Civil Rights Cases 109 U.S. 3 (1883).

97. Jones v Alfred Mayer Co. 392 U.S. 409 (1968). The historical record is ambiguous and rests upon inferences as to what they meant by custom. In addition to the literature cited in Note 23 Supra see Gerhard Caspar, "Jones v Mayer: Clio, Bemused and Confused Muse," 1968 Supreme Court Review; It may be of some importance that the Civil Rights Act drew its enforcement machinery from the Fugitive Slave Law which had been held to apply directly to individual infringements, in Prigg v Pennsylvania, 16 Peters (41 U.S.) 539 (1842). Mark de Wolfe Howe observed that if constitutional law had ended with that decision, there was "nothing in the nature of American federalism that disables Congress from controlling private conduct affecting the civil rights of others," "Federalism and Civil Rights," Massachusetts Historical Society Proceedings CXVIII (1965).

98. Hodges v United States 203 U.S. 1 (1906).

99. Brotherhood of Liberty, Justice and Jurisprudence: An Inquiry Concerning the Constitutional Limitations of the Thirteenth, Fourteenth and Fifteenth Amendments (N.Y., 1969 Reprint), pp.110-111.

100. Horace E. Flack, The Adoption of the Fourteenth Amendment (Baltimore, 1908) pp.50-51.

101. General U.S. Grant to E. Stanton, February 8th, 1867, Attorney-Generals Papers, Nat. Archives, Record Group 60.

102. Ibid., Attorney-General Henry Stanbery to President Johnson, January 21st, 1867.

Notes: Conclusion

1. This conclusion is not accepted by John S. Rosenberg, "Towards a New Civil War Revisionism," The American Scholar, Spring 1969. See Philip S. Paludan's rejoinder, "The American Civil War: Triumph Through Tragedy," 20 Civil War History 1974.

2. Orestes Brownson, The American Republic. Its Constitution, Tendencies and Destiny. (Louisville, 1969 Reprint) pp.2-3.

3. Frederick Douglass, "Reconstruction," Atlantic Monthly, December 1866.

4. Carl Schurz, "The True Problem," Atlantic Monthly, March 1867.

5. In George L. Stearns (comp.), The Equality of All Men Claimed and Defended (Boston, 1865) p.31.

6. For an argument against interpreting the Waite Court's work as a clean break see Michael Les Benedict, "Preserving Federalism: Reconstruction and the Waite Court," Supreme Court Review 1978.

7. Harold M. Hyman, A More Perfect Union (N.Y., 1973), Morton Keller, Affairs of State (Cambridge, 1977) and James C. Mohr, ed., Radical Republicans in the North.

8. Suzanne D. Lebsock, "Radical Reconstruction and the Property Rights of Southern Women," 43 Journal of Southern History 1977.

BIBLIOGRAPHY

Manuscripts

Salmon P. Chase Papers. Library of Congress.
The Papers of the Attorneys General. Record Group 60, National Archives.

Cases

Unites States Reports.
Federal Cases.
Federal Reports.
The Reports of individual State Supreme Courts, or Courts of Appeal.

Public Documents

Congressional Globe, 37th, 38th, and 39 Congresses.
Official Opinions of the Attorneys Generals of the United States. 40 vols. Washington: Government Printing Office 1791-1948.
Report of the Joint Committee on Reconstruction at the First Session, Thirty-Ninth Congress. Washington: Government Printing Office, 1866.
Richardson, James D., comp. A Compilation of the Messages and Papers of the Presidents. 10 vols. Washington: Government Printing Office, 1897.
Thorpe, Francis N., ed. The Federal and State Constitutions, Colonial Charters, and Other Organic Laws. 7 vols. Washington: Government Printing Office, 1909.
United States Statutes at Large.
United States, War Department. The War of the Rebellion: A Compilation of the Official Records of the Union and Confederate Armies. 128 vols. Washington: Government Printing Office, 1880-1901.

Newspaper

The Liberator.

Printed Sources - Books

Basler, Roy P., ed. Collected Works of Abraham Lincoln. 9 vols. New Brunswick: Rutgers University Press, 1953.
Bates, Edward. The Diary of Edward Bates, ed. Howard K. Beale. Washington: Government Printing Office, 1933.
Bishop, Joel P. Commentaries on the Criminal Law. Boston: Little, Brown, 1872.
Black, Henry C. A Treatise on the Laws and Practice Governing the Removal of Causes. St. Paul: West Publishing Co. 1898.
Blaine, James G. Twenty Years of Congress: from Lincoln to Garfield. 2 vols. Norwich: The Henry Bill Co., 1884-1886.
Boutwell, George S. Reminiscences of Sixty Years in Public Affairs. 2 vols. N.Y.: McClure, Phillips & Co., 1902.
———, Speeches and Papers Relating to the Rebellion and the Overthrow of Slavery. 2 vols. Boston: Little Brown & Co., 1867.
Brotherhood of Liberty. Justice and Jurisprudence: an Inquiry Concerning the Constitutional Limitations of the Thirteenth, Fourteenth and Fifteenth Amendments. N.Y. Negro Universities Press, 1969.
Browning, Orville H. The Diary of Orville Hickman Browning, ed. Theodore C. Pease and James G. Randall. 2 vols. Springfield: Illinois State Hist. Soc. Library, 1925.
Brownson, Orestes A. The American Republic. Its Constitution, Tendencies and Destiny. Louisville: Lost Cause Press, 1969.
Catterall, Helen T. Judicial Cases Concerning American Slavery and the Negro. 5 vols. Washington: Carnegie Institution, 1926-1937.
Chase, Salmon P. Inside Lincoln's Cabinet: The Civil War Diaries of

Salmon P. Chase, ed. David Donald. N.Y.: Longman, Green & Co., 1954.
Cole, Cornelius. Memoirs of Cornelius Cole. N.Y.: McLoughlin Bros., 1908.
Cooley, Thomas M. A Treatise on the Constitutional Limitations Which Rest Upon the Legislative Powers of the States of the American Union. Boston: Little, Brown & Co., 1871.
Cox, Samuel S. Eight Years in Congress from 1857 to 1865. N.Y.: D. Appleton & Co., 1865.
———, Union - Disunion - Reunion. Three Decades of Federal Legislation 1855-1885. Providence: Reid, 1886.
Dana, Charles A. Recollections of the Civil War. N.Y.: D. Appleton & Co. 1898.
De Forest, John W. A Union Officer in the Reconstruction, ed. James H. Croushore and David M. Potter. New Haven: Yale University Press, 1948.
Douglass, Frederick. Life and Times of Frederick Douglass. Hartford: Park Co., 1881.
Farrar, C.C.S. The War. Its Causes and Consequences. Cairo, Memphis & Paducak; Blelock & Co., 1864.
Farrar, Timothy. Manual of the Constitution of the United States of America. Boston: Little, Brown & Co., 1867.
Fisher, Sidney G. A Philadelphia Perspective. The Diary of Sidney George Fisher, ed. Nicholas B. Wainwright. Philadelphia: Historical Society of Pennsylvania, 1967.
Foner, Philip S. ed. The Life and Writings of Frederick Douglass. 4 vols. N.Y.: International Publishers, 1950-1955.
Hurd, Rollin C. A Treatise on the Right of Personal Liberty and the Writ of Habeas Corpus. Albany: W.C. Little & Co., 1858.
Julian, George W. Political Recollections 1840-1872. Chicago: Jansen, McClurg & Co., 1884.
———, Speeches on Political Questions. N.Y.: Hurd & Houghton, 1872.
Hendrick, Benjamin B., ed. The Journal of the Joint Committee of Fifteen on Reconstruction. 39th Congress, 1865-1867. N.Y.: Columbia University Press, 1914.
Lieber, Francis. Essays on Property and Labor as Connected with Natural Law and the Constitution of Society. N.Y.: Harper & Bros., 1841.
———, On Civil Liberty and Self-Government, ed. Theodore D. Woolsey. Philadelphia: J.B. Lippincott Co., 1911.
McClure, Alexander K. Recollections of Half a Century. Salem: Salem Press Co., 1902.
McCulloch, Hugh. Men and Measures of Half a Century. N.Y.: Scribner's, 1888.
McPherson, Edward. The Political History of the United States of America During the Great Rebellion. Washington: Solomons & Chapman, 1865.
———, The Political History of the United States of America During the Period of Reconstruction. Washington: Solomons & Chapman, 1875.
Mulford, Elias. The Nation: The Foundations of Civil Order and Political Life in the United States. N.Y.: Hurd & Houghton, 1870.
Nicolay, John G. and Hay, John. Abraham Lincoln, a History. 10 vols. N.Y.: The Century Co., 1917.
Parsons, Theophilus. The Political, Personal, and Property Rights of a Citizen of the United States. 2 vols. Chicago: Beach & Co., 1875.
Pierce, Edward L. Memoirs and Letters of Charles Sumner. 4 vols. London, 1878-1893.
Pomeroy, John N. An Introduction to the Constitutional Law of the United States. Boston & N.Y.: Houghton, Mifflin & Co., 1886.
Riddle, Albert G. Recollections of War Times: Reminiscences of Men and Events in Washington 1860-1865. N.Y.: Putnam's, 1895.
Schouler, James. Constitutional Studies, State and Federal. N.Y.: Dodd, Mead & Co., 1897.

Sherman, John. Recollections of Forty Years in the House, Senate, and Cabinet. 2 vols. Chicago: The Werner Co., 1895.

Strong, George T. The Diary of George Templeton Strong, ed. Alan Nevins and Milton H. Thomas. 4 vols. N.Y.: Macmillan, 1952.

Sumner, Charles A. Works. 15 vols. Boston: Lee & Shepherd, 1870-1873.

Tourgee, Albion W. A Fool's Errand, ed. John Hope Franklin. Cambridge: Belknap, 1961.

Welles, Gideon. The Diary of Gideon Welles, Ed. Howard K. Beale. N.Y.: Norton, 1960.

Whiting, William. War Powers Under the Constitution of the United States. Boston & N.Y.: Lee & Shepherd, 1871.

Printed Sources - Articles, Speeches, Pamphlets

(Anon.) "The Right to Confiscate and Emancipate," Monthly Law Reporter, 24 (September 1862), 645-656.

———, "The Power of Congress to Confiscate and Emancipate," Monthly Law Reporter, 24 (June 1862), 469-495.

———, "American Judges," Albany Law Review (March 1870).

———, "United States Provisional Court for the State of Louisiana," American Law Register, 13 (December 1864; March 1865).

Appleton, John. "Equality Before the Law in the Courts of the United States," The Law Magazine and Review, 17 (1864), 137-153.

Baldwin, Simeon E. "The Citizen of the United States," Yale Law Journal, 2 (February 1893).

———, "Recent Changes in Our State Constitutions," Journal of Social Science, Transactions of the American Association, 10 (1879).

Banks, Nathaniel P. An Address at the Customhouse, New Orleans, July 4, 1865. N.Y.: Harper & Bros., 1865.

Barrett, George C. "The Administration of Criminal Justice," Journal of Social Science, Transactions of the American Association, 2 (1870).

Cary, John W. "Limitations of the Legislative Power in Respect to Personal Rights and Private Property," Reports of the American Bar Association, XV (1892), 245-286.

Chamberlain, D.W. "The State Judiciary. Its Place in the American Constitutional System," in Constitutional History of the United States as Seen in the Development of American Law. N.Y.: 1889.

Curtis, B.R. Executive Power. Boston: Little, Brown & Co., 1862.

Curtis, George T. On Constitutional Liberty. N.Y.: McClellan Campaign Document No.7, 1864.

Dana, Richard. "Nullity of the Emancipation Edict," North American Review, 131.

Dillon, John F. "A Century of American Law," New York Bar Association Reports, 13 (1890).

Douglass, Frederick. "Reconstruction," Atlantic Monthly, XVIII (December 1866).

Ferris, Aaron A. "The Validity of the Emancipation Edict," North American Review, 131.

Field, David Dudley. "Centralization in the Federal Government," North American Review, CLXCIV (May 1881).

Fisher, Sidney George. "The Suspension of Habeas Corpus During the War of the Rebellion," Political Science Quarterly, 3 (September 1888).

Godkin, E.L. "The Constitution and Its Defects," North American Review (July 1864).

———, "The Lesson of the Crisis," The Nation, 4 (January 17th, 1867) 50–51.

Heiskell, J.B. "Conflict Between Federal and State Court Decisions," American Law Review, XVI (October 1882) 743–760.

Hurd, John C. "Theories on Reconstruction," American Law Review, 1 (January 1867).

Lowell, James R. "Reconstruction," North American Review (April 1865).

McQuillon, Eugene. "Some Observations on State Laws and Municipal Ordinances," Central Law Journal 64, 209.

Nott, C.C. "The Burden of the Supreme Court," The Nation, 10 (January 13th, 1870), 22–24.

Parker, Joel. "Constitutional Law," North American Review, XLIV (April, 1862).

———, "Habeas Corpus and Martial Law," North American Review 93.

Pierce, Edward L. "The Contrabands at Fortress Monroe," Atlantic Monthly, VIII (November 1861).

Sedgwick, A.G. "The Bar and the Judges," The Nation 9 (December 16th, 1869), 529–530.

Smith, Eugene. "Conflict of State Laws," Journal of Social Science, Transactions of the American Association, 19 (1884).

Stearns, George L. The Equality of All Men Before the Law Claimed and Defended: In Speeches by William D. Kelley, Wendell Phillips, and Frederick Douglass. Boston: Rand & Avery, 1865.

Tucker, John Randolph. Address Delivered Before the Phoenix and Philomathean Societies of William and Mary College, 3rd July, 1854. Richmond: 1854.

Washburn, Emory. "Reconstruction. The Duty of the Profession to the Times," Monthly Law Reporter, 26 (July 1864).

———, Lecture Before the Members of the Harvard Law School, January 11th, 1861. Boston: 1861.

———, "Limitations of Judicial Power," Journal of Social Science, Transactions of the American Association, 8 (1876).

Woolsey, T.D. "Nature and Sphere of Police Powers," Journal of Social Science, Transactions of the American Association, 3 (1871).

Secondary Materials – Books

Abbot, Richard. Cobbler in Congress: The Life of Henry Wilson, 1812–1875. Lexington: University of Kentucky Press, 1972.

Bauer, Elizabeth K. Commentaries on the Constitution, 1790–1860. N.Y.: Columbia University Press, 1952.

Beale, Howard K. The Critical Year: a Study of Andrew Johnson and Reconstruction. N.Y.: Ungar, 1958.

Belz, Herman. Reconstructing the Union: Theory and Practice During the Civil War. N.Y.: Cornell University Press, 1969.

———, A New Birth of Freedom: The Republican Party and Freedmen's Rights, 1861–1866. Westport: Greenwood, 1976.

———, Emancipation and Equal Rights. N.Y.: Norton, 1978.

Bentley, George R. A History of the Freedmen's Bureau. Philadelphia: University of Pennsylvania Press, 1955.

Berger, Raoul. Government by Judiciary: The Transformation of the Fourteenth Amendment. Cambridge: Harvard University Press, 1977.

Benedict, Michael L. A Compromise of Principle: Congressional Republicans and Reconstruction, 1863–1869. N.Y.: Norton, 1974.

Berlin, Ira. Slaves Without Masters: The Free Negro in the Antebellum South. N.Y.: Pantheon, 1974.

Berry, Mary F. Military Necessity and Civil Rights Policy: Black Citizenship and the Constitution, 1861-1868. Port Washington: Kennikat, 1977.
Bloomfield, Maxwell. Ameridan Lawyers in a Changing Society, 1776-1876. Cambridge: Harvard University Press, 1976.
Bogue, Alan. The Earnest Men: Republicans of the Civil War Senate. Ithaca, Cornell University Press, 1981.
Bowers, Claude G. The Tragic Era: The Revolution After Lincoln. Boston: Houghton, Mifflin & Co., 1929.
Brock, William R. An American Crisis: Congress and Reconstruction, 1865-1867. N.Y.: St. Martin's Press, 1963.
———, Investigation and Responsibility. Cambridge : Cambridge University Press, 1984.
Brodie, Fawn M. Thaddeus Stevens: Scourge of the South. N.Y.: Norton, 1959.
Burgess, John W. The Civil War and the Constitution, 1859-1865. N.Y.: Scribner's, 1901.
Castel, Albert. The Presidency of Andrew Johnson. Lawrence: Regents Press of Kansas, 1979.
Corwin, Edward S. Liberty Against Government: The Rise, Flowering and Decline of a Famous Juridical Concept. Baton Rouge: Louisiana State University Press, 1948.
Cover, Roger M. Justice Accused: Antislavery and the Judicial Process. New Haven: Yale University Press, 1975.
Cox, Lawanda and John, H. Politics, Principle and Prejudice, 1865-1866: Dilemma of Reconstruction America. N.Y.: Free Press of Glencoe, 1963.
———, Lawanda. Lincoln and Black Freedom: A Study in Presidential Leadership. Columbia: University of South Carolina Press, 1981.
Craven, Avery. Reconstruction: The Ending of the Civil War. N.Y.: Holt, Rinehart and Winston, 1969.
Crosskey, William W. Politics and the Constitution in the History of the United States. Chicago: University of Chicago Press, 1953.
Current, Richard. The Lincoln Nobody Knows. N.Y.: McGraw-Hill, 1958.
Curry, Leonard. Blueprint for Modern America: Nonmilitary Legislation of the First Civil War Congress. Nashville: Vanderbilt University Press, 1968.
Donald, David. Lincoln Reconsidered. N.Y.: Random House, 1961.
———, The Politics of Reconstruction 1863-1867. Baton Rouge: Louisiana State University Press, 1965.
———, Charles Sumner and the Rights of Man. N.Y.: Knopf, 1970.
Du Bois, W.E.B. Black Reconstruction. N.Y.: Harcourt, Brace, 1935.
Duker, William F. A Constitutional History of Habeas Corpus. Westport: Greenwood, 1980.
Dunning, William A. Reconstruction, Political and Economic, 1865-1877. N.Y.: Harper Bros., 1907.
Dusinberre, William. Civil War Issues in Philadelphia, 1856-1865. Philadelphia: University of Pennsylvania Press, 1965.
Elezar, Daniel J. The American Partnership: Intergovernmental Co-operation in the Nineteenth Century United States. Chicago: University of Chicago Press, 1962.
Emerson, Thomas I., Haber, David and Dorsen, Norman. Political and Civil Rights in the United States: A Collection of Legal and Related Materials. Boston: Little, Brown & Co., 1967.
Fairman, Charles. Mr. Justice Miller and the Supreme Court 1862-1890. Cambridge: Harvard University Press, 1939.
———, History of the Supreme Court of the United States, Vol.6, Reconstruction and Reunion, 1864-1888. N.Y.: MacMillan, 1971.

Fehrenbacher, Don E. The Dred Scott Case: Its Significance in American Law and Politics. N.Y.: 1978.

Ficklin, John R. History of Reconstruction in Louisiana. Baltimore: Johns Hopkins Press, 1910.

Flack, Horace Edgar. The Adoption of the Fourteenth Amendment. Baltimore: Johns Hopkins Press, 1908.

Foner, Eric. Free Soil, Free Labor, Free Men: The Ideology of the Republican Party Before the Civil War. N.Y.: Oxford University Press, 1970.

——, Politics and Ideology in the Age of the Civil War. N.Y.: Oxford University Press, 1980.

——, Nothing But Freedom: Emancipation and Its Legacy. Baton Rouge: Louisiana State University Press, 1983.

Frankfurter, Felix and Landis, James M. The Business of the Supreme Court: A Study in the Federal Judicial System. N.Y.: Macmillan, 1927.

Frederickson, George M. The Inner Civil War: Northern Intellectuals and the Crisis of the Union. N.Y.: Harper & Row, 1965.

Freyer, Tony. Harmony and Dissonance: The Swift and Eerie Cases in American Federalism. N.Y.: New York University Press, 1981.

Friedman, Lawrence. A History of American Law. N.Y.: Simon & Shuster, 1973.

Gawalt, Gerald W., ed. The New High Priests: Lawyers in Post-Civil War America. Westport: Greenwood, 1984.

Gerteis, Louis S. From Contraband to Freedman: Federal Policy Towards Southern Blacks, 1861-1865. Westport: Greenwood, 1975.

Gilette, William. Retreat from Reconstruction, 1869-1879. Baton Rouge: Louisiana State University Press, 1979.

Graham, Howard J. Everyman's Constitution. Madison: State Historical Society of Wisconsin, 1968.

Harris, Robert J. The Quest for Equality: The Constitution, Congress and the Supreme Court. Baton Rouge: Louisiana State University Press, 1960.

Harris, William C. The Day of the Carpetbagger: Republican Reconstruction in Mississippi. Baton Rouge: Louisiana State University Press, 1979.

Hesseltine, W.B. Lincoln's Plan of Reconstruction. Tuscaloosa: Confederate Publishing Co., 1960.

Horwitz, Morton R. The Transformation of American Law, 1780-1860. Cambridge: Harvard University Press, 1977.

Hurst, J. Willard. Law and Conditions of Freedom in the Nineteenth Century United States. Madison: University of Wisconsin Press, 1967.

Hyman, Harold M., ed. The Radical Republicans and Reconstruction, 1861-1870. Indianapolis & N.Y.: Bobbs-Merrill, 1967.

——, New Frontiers of the American Reconstruction. Urbana: University of Illinois Press, 1966.

——, A More Perfect Union. N.Y.: Knopf, 1973.

——, and Wiecek, William. Equal Justice Under Law: Constitutional Development 1835-1875. N.Y.: Harper & Row, 1982.

Jacobs, Clyde E. Law Writers and the Courts. Berkeley and Los Angeles: University of California Press, 1954.

James, Joseph B. The Framing of the Fourteenth Amendment. Urbana: University of Illinois Press, 1965.

Jellison, Charles A. Fessenden of Maine, Civil War Senator. N.Y.: Syracuse University Press, 1962.

Keller, Morton. Affairs of State: Public Life in Late Nineteenth Century America. Cambridge: Belknap, 1977.

Kettner, James H. The Development of American Citizenship, 1608-1870. Chapel Hill: University of North Carolina Press, 1978.

Konvitz, Milton R. A Century of Civil Rights. N.Y.: Columbia University Press, 1961.

Korngold, R. Thaddeus Stevens. Boston: Little, Brown & Co., 1950.

Kutler, Stanley I. Judicial Power and Reconstruction Politics. Chicago: University of Chicago Press, 1968.

Landynski, Jacob W. Search and Seizure and the Supreme Court: A Study in Constitutional Interpretation. Baltimore: Johns Hopkins Press, 1966.

Levy, Leonard W., ed. American Constitutional Law: Historical Essays. N.Y.: Harper, 1966.

———, The Law of the Commonwealth and Chief Justice Shaw. Cambridge: Harvard University Press, 1957.

———, Legacy of Suppression: Freedom of Speech and Press in Early American History. Cambridge: Belknap, 1960.

———, Origins of the Fifth Amendment: The Right Against Self-Incrimination. N.Y.: Oxford University Press, 1968.

Linden, Glenn M. Politics or Principle: Congressional Voting on the Civil War Amendments and Pro-Negro Measures, 1838-1869. Seattle: University of Washington Press, 1976.

Litwack, Leon. North of Slavery: The Negro in the Free States, 1790-1860. Chicago: Chicago University Press, 1961.

McCarthy, Charles H. Lincoln's Plan of Reconstruction. N.Y.: McClure, Phillips & Co., 1901.

McFeeley, William. Yankee Stepfather: General O.O. Howard and the Freedmen. New Haven: Yale University Press, 1968.

McKitrick, Eric. Andrew Johnson and Reconstruction. Chicago: University of Chicago Press, 1960.

McPherson, James M. The Struggle for Equality: Abolitionists and the Negro in the Civil War and Reconstruction. Princeton: Princeton University Press, 1964.

———, Ordeal by Fire: The Civil War and Reconstruction. N.Y.: Knopf, 1982.

McWhinney, Grady, ed. Grant, Lee, Lincoln and the Radicals: Essays in Civil War Leadership. Illinois: Northwestern University Press, 1964.

Miller, Perry. The Life of the Mind in America. N.Y.: Harcourt, Brace & World Inc., 1965.

Mohr, James C. Radical Republicans in the North: State Politics During Reconstruction. Baltimore: Johns Hopkins Press, 1976.

Morgan, Donald G. Congress and the Constitution: A Study of Responsibility. Cambridge: Belknap, 1966.

Nelson, William E. The Roots of American Bureaucracy, 1830-1900. Cambridge: Harvard University Press, 1982.

Nieman, Donald G. To Set the Law in Motion: The Freedmen's Bureau and the Legal Rights of Blacks, 1865-1868. Millwood, N.Y.: K.T.O., 1979.

Nichols, Roy F. American Leviathan. N.Y.: Harper & Row, 1966.

Olsen, Otto H. Carpetbagger's Crusade: The Life of Albion Winegar Tourgee. Baltimore: Johns Hopkins Press, 1965.

———, ed. Reconstruction and Redemption in the South. Baton Rouge: Louisiana State University Press, 1980.

Paludan, Philip. A Covenant with Death: The Constitution, Law and Equality in the Civil War Era. Urbana: University of Illinois Press, 1975.

Parish, Peter J. The American Civil War. London: Eyre Methuen, 1975.

Perman, Michael. Reunion Without Compromises: The South and Reconstruction, 1865-1868. Cambridge: Cambridge University Press, 1973.

Pole, J.R. The Pursuit of Equality in American History. Berkeley: University of California Press, 1978.

Quarles, Benjamin. Lincoln and the Negro. N.Y.: Oxford University Press, 1962.
Ramsdell, Charles. Reconstruction in Texas. N.Y.: Columbia University Press, 1910.
Randall, James G. Lincoln the President, 4 vols. N.Y.: Dodd, Mead & Co., 1945-1955.
———, Constitutional Problems Under Lincoln. N.Y. & London: D. Appleton & Co., 1926.
———, and David Donald. The Civil War and Reconstruction. Boston: D.C. Heath & Co., 1961.
Rawley, James A. The Politics of Union: Northern Politics During the Civil War. Hinsdale: Dryden, 1974.
Riddle, Albert G. The Life of Benjamin F. Wade. Cleveland: William W. Williams, 1886.
Riddleberger, Patrick. 1866: The Critical Year Revisited. Carbondale: Southern Illinois University Press, 1979.
Roche, John D. Courts and Rights: The American Judiciary in Action. N.Y.: Random House, 1961.
———, The Quest for the Dream: The Development of Civil Rights and Human Relations in Modern America. N.Y.: Macmillan, 1963.
Scott, Eben G. Reconstruction During the Civil War in the United States. Boston, N.Y.: Houghton, Mifflin & Co., 1895.
Sefton, James E. The United States Army and Reconstruction, 1865-1877. Baton Rouge: University of Louisiana State University Press, 1977.
Sewell, Ridhard H. John P. Hale and the Politics of Abolition. Cambridge: Harvard University Press, 1965.
Shapiro, Henry D. Confiscation of Confederate Property in the North. N.Y.: Cornell University Press, 1962.
Silver, David M. Lincoln's Supreme Court. Urbana: University of Illinois Press, 1956.
Simkins, Francis B. and Woody, Robert H. South Carolina During Reconstruction. Chapel Hill: University of North Carolina Press, 1932.
Stampp, Kenneth. The Era of Reconstruction, 1865-1879. N.Y.: Knopf, 1965.
———, and Litwack, Ledon, eds., Reconstruction: An Anthology of Revisionist Writings. Baton Rouge: Louisiana State University Press, 1969.
Stimson, Frederick J. The Law of the Federal and State Constitutions of the United States. Boston: 1908.
Swisher, Carl B. The History of the Supreme Court, Vol.5. The Taney Period, 1836-1864. N.Y.: Macmillan, 1974.
Tachau, Mary K. Bransteel. Federal Courts in the Early Republic, Kentucky, 1789-1816. Princeton: Princeton University Press, 1978.
TenBroek, Jacobus. The Antislavery Origins of the Fourteenth Amendment. Berkeley: University of California Press, 1951.
Thomas, Benjamin P. and Hyman, Harold M. Stanton: The Life and Times of Lincoln's Secretary of War. N.Y.: Knopf, 1962.
Thompson, C. Mildred. Reconstruction in Georgia, 1865-1872. N.Y.: Columbia University Press, 1915.
Trefousse, Hans L. Benjamin F. Wade: Radical Republican from Ohio. N.Y.: Twayne, 1963.
———, The Radical Republicans: Lincoln's Vanguard for Racial Justice. N.Y., Knopf, 1969.
Tushnet, Mark V. The American Law of Slavery, 1810-1860: Considerations of Humanity and Interest. Princeton: Princeton University Press, 1981.
Van Deusen, G. William Henry Seward. N.Y.: Oxford University Press, 1967.

Wagandt, Charles L. The Mighty Revolution: Negro Emancipation in Maryland, 1862–1864. Baltimore: Johns Hopkins Press, 1964.
Ware, Ethel K. A Constitutional History of Georgia. N.Y.: Columbia University Press, 1947.
Warren, Charles. The Supreme Court in United States History. 2 vols. Boston: Little, Brown & Co., 1960.
White, Benjamin. American Interpretations of Natural Law. Cambridge: Harvard University Press, 1931.
White, G. Edward. The American Judicial Tradition: Profiles of Leading American Judges. N.Y.: 1976.
White, Horace. The Life of Lyman Trumbull. Boston, N.Y.: Houghton, Mifflin & Co., 1913.
Wiecek, William. The Guarantee Clause of the United States Constitution. Ithaca: Cornell University Press, 1972.
———, Sources of Antislavery Constitutionalism in America, 1760–1848. Ithaca: Cornell University Press, 1977.
Wiggins, Warah W. The Scalawags in Alabama Politics. Alabama: University of Alabama Press, 1977.
Williams, T. Harry. Lincoln and the Radicals. Madison: University of Wisconsin Press, 1941.
Williamson, Joel. After Slavery: The Negro in South Carolina During Reconstruction, 1861–1877. Chapel Hill: University of North Carolina Press, 1965.
Willoughby, Westel W. The Constitutional Law of the United States. N.Y.: The Century Co., 1904.
Wood, Forrest G. Black Scare: The Racist Response to Emancipation and Reconstruction. Berkeley: University of California Press, 1968.
Wooster, Ralph. Politicians, Planters, and Plain Folk: Courthouse and Statehouse in the Upper South, 1850–1860. Knoxville: University of Tennessee Press, 1975.

Secondary Materials - Articles

Alexander, Thomas B. "The Civil War as Institutional Fulfillment." Journal of Southern History, February 1981.
Avins, Alfred. "The Fourteenth Amendment and Jury Discrimination: The Original Understanding," Federal Bar Journal, XXVII (1967).
Baggett, James A. "Origins of Upper South Scalawag Leadership," Civil War History, March 1983.
Belz, Herman. "The Constitution in the Gilded Age: The Beginnings of Constitutional Realism in American Scholarship," American Journal of Legal History, April 1969.
———, "The New Orthodoxy in Reconstruction Historiography" Reviews in American History, 1, 1973.
———, "The Freedmen's Bureau Act of 1865 and the Principle of No Discrimination According to Color," Civil War History, September 1975.
———, "Protection of Personal Liberty in Republican Emancipation Legislation of 1862," Journal of Southern History, August 1976.
Benedict, Michael L. "Preserving the Constitution: The Conservative Basis of Reconstruction," Journal of American History, 1974.
———, "Preserving Federalism: Reconstruction and the Waite Court," Supreme Court Review, 1978.
Bestor, Arthur. "The American Civil War as a Constitutional Crisis," American Historical Review, January 1964.

Blackard, W. Raymond. "The Demoralization of the Legal Profession in Nineteenth Century America," Tennessee Law Review 16, 1940.
Bloomfield, Maxwell. "Law vs. Politics: The Self-Image of the American Bar," American Journal of Legal History, October 1968.
Burt, Robert A. "Miranda and Title II: A Morganatic Marriage," Supreme Court Review, 1969.
Caspar, Gerhard. "Jones v Mayer: Clio, Bemused and Confused Muse," Supreme Court Review, 1968.
Corwin, Edward S. "The Higher Law Background of American Constitutional Law," Harvard Law Review 42, 1928.
———, "The Doctrine of Due Process of Law Before the Civil War," Harvard Law Review 24, 1911.
———, "The Dred Scott Decision in the Light of Contemporary Legal Doctrines," American Historical Review 17, 1911.
Cox, John H. and Lawanda. "Andrew Johnson and His Ghost Writers: An Analysis of the Freedmen's Bureau and Civil Rights Veto Messages," Mississippi Valley Historical Review, December 1961.
———, "General O.O. Howard and the Misrepresented Bureau," Journal of Southern History, November 1953.
Curry, Richard O. "The Civil War and Reconstruction, 1861-1877. A Critical Overview of Recent Trends and Interpretations," Civil War History, 1974.
Curtis, Michael Kent. "The Bill of Rights as a Limitation on State Authority: A Reply to Professor Berger," Wake Forest Law Review 16, 1980.
Doyle, Elisabeth Joan. "New Orleans Courts Under Military Occupation 1861-1865," Mid America, July 1960.
DuBois, W.E.B. "Reconstruction and its Benefits," American Historical Review XV, 1910.
Elazar, Daniel. "The Civil War and the Preservation of Federalism," Publius 1, 1970.
Fairman, Charles. "Does the Fourteenth Amendment Incorporate the Bill of Rights?: The Original Understanding," Stanford Law Review, December, 1949.
Farnham, Wallace D. "The Weakened Spring of Government: A Study in Nineteenth-Century American History," American Historical Review, April 1963.
Fishel, T. "Repercussions of Reconstruction: The Northern Negro, 1870-1883," Civil War History, 1968.
Flanagan, Dan. "Criminal Procedure in Slave Trials in the Antebellum South," Journal of Southern History, August 1974.
Frank, John P. and Munro, Robert F. "The Original Understanding of 'Equal Protection of the Laws,'" Columbia Law Review, February 1950.
Franklin, John H. "Mirror for Americans: A Century of Reconstruction History," American Historical Review, February 1980.
Frantz, L. "Congressional Power to Enforce the Fourteenth Amendment Against Private Acts," Yale Law Journal, 1964.
Graham, Howard J." "The Conspiracy Theory" of the Fourteenth Amendment," Yale Law Journal, 1938.
Hall, Kermit L. "The Civil War Era as a Crucible for Nationalizing the Lower Federal Courts," Prologue 7 Fall 1975.
———, "Social Backgrounds and Judicial Recruitment: A Nineteenth Century Perspective on the Lower Federal Judiciary," Western Political Quarterly, June 1976.
Hindus, Michael. "Black Justice Under White Law: Criminal Prosecutions of Blacks in Antebellum South Carolina," Journal of American History, December 1976.

Hollingsworth, Harold M. "George Andrews, Carpetbagger," Tennessee Historical Quarterly 28, 1969.
Howard, Victor. "The Black Testimony Controversy in Kentucky, 1866-1872," Journal of Negro History, April 1973.
Howe, Mark De Wolfe. "Federalism and Civil Rights, Massachusetts Society Proceedings, LXXVII, 1965.
Hume, Richard. "Carpetbaggers in the Reconstruction South: A Group Portrait of Outside Whites in the "Black and Tan" Constitutional Conventions," Journal of American History 64, 1977.
Hyman, Harold M. "Law and the Civil War," Civil War History, March 1968.
———, "Deceit in Dixie," Civil War History, March 1957.
———, "Lincoln and Congress: Why Not Congress and Lincoln?" Journal of the Illinois State Historical Society 68, 1975.
———, "Lincoln's Reconstruction: Neither Failure of Vision Nor Vision of Failure," The Third Annual R. Gerald McMurtry Lecture, Fort Wayne, Indiana, 1980.
Jones, Alan. "Thomas M. Cooley and "Laissez-faire Constitutionalism;" A Reconsideration," The Journal of American History 53, 1966-1967.
Larsen, Charles E. "Nationalism and States Rights in Commentaries on the Constitution After the Civil War," The American Journal of Legal History 3, 1959.
Lebsock, Suzanne D. "Radical Reconstruction and the Property Rights of Southern Women," Journal of Southern History, May 1977.
Lerche, Charles O. "Congressional Interpretations of the Guarantee of a Republican Form of Government," Journal of Southern History, May 1949.
Lucie, Patricia. "Confiscation: Constitutional Crossroads," Civil War History, 1977.
———, "On Being a Free Person and a Citizen by Constitutional Amendment," Journal of American Studies 12, 1978.
———, "Marriage and Law Reform in Nineteenth Century America," in Elizabeth M. Craik, ed., Marriage and Property, Aberdeen: Aberdeen University Press, 1984.
Lofton, William H. "Northern Labor and the Negro During the Civil War," Journal of Negro History, July 1949.
MacCreary, Peyton. "The Party of Revolution: Republican Ideas About Politics and Social Change, 1862-1867," Civil War History, December 1984.
May, J. Thomas. "The Freedmen's Bureau at the Local Level: A Study of a Louisiana Agent," Louisiana History IX, 1968.
Nash, A.E. Keir. "The Texas Supreme Court and Trial Rights of Blacks, 1845-1860," The Journal of American History, December 1971.
———, "A More Equitable Past? Southern Supreme Courts and the Antebellum Negro," North Carolina Law Review, 1969-1970.
Nelson, William E. "The Impact of the Antislavery Movement Upon Styles of Judicial Reasoning in Nineteenth Century America," Harvard Law Review, 1974.
Nerken, Ira. "A New Deal for the Protection of Fourteenth Amendment Rights: Challenging the Doctrinal Basis of the Civil Rights Cases' State Action Theory," Harvard Civil Rights, Civil Liberties Law Review, Spring 1977.
Nichols Roy F. "Federalism v. Democracy. The Significance of the Civil War in the History of United States Federalism," in Roscoe Pound, Charles H. McIlwain and Roy F. Nichols, Federalism as a Democratic Process, New Brunswick: Rutgers University Press, 1942.

Nieman, Donald G. "Andrew Johnson, the Freedmen's Bureau, and the Problem of Equal Rights, 1865–1866," Journal of Southern History, August 1978.

Note, "The New Thirteenth Amendment: A Preliminary Analysis," Harvard Law Review 82, 1969.

Oakes, James. "Failure of Vision: The Collapse of the Freedmen's Bureau Courts," Civil War History, 1979.

Olson, Otto H. "Reconsidering the Scalawagw," Civil War History, December 1966.

Paludan, Philip. "The American Civil War Considered as a Crisis in Law and Order," American Historical Review, October 1972.

———, "The American Civil War: Triumph Through Tragedy," Civil War History, 1974.

Pressly, Thomas J. "Bullets and Ballots: Lincoln and the Right of Revolution," American Historical Review, April 1962.

Randall, James G. "Some Legal Aspects of the Confiscation Bills," American Historical Review, October 1912.

———, "The Indemnity Act of 1863: A Study in Wartime Immunity of Government Officers," Michigan Law Review 20, 1922.

Simkins, Francis B. "New Viewpoints of Southern Reconstruction," Journal of Southern History, 1939.

Spector, Robert M. "Judicial Biography and the United States Supreme Court," American Journal of Legal History, January 1967.

Smallwood, James. "Charles E. Culver, A Reconstruction Agent in Texas: The Work of Local Freedmen's Bureau Agents and the Black Community," Civil War History, December 1981.

Smith, John D. "More Than Slaves, Less Than Freedmen: The "Slave Wages" Labor System During Reconstruction," Civil War History, September 1980.

Stampp, Kenneth M. "The Concept of a Perpetual Union," Journal of American History 65, 1978.

Trelease, A. "Who Were the Scalawags?" Journal of Southern History, November 1963.

Trussman, J. and TenBroek, J. "The Equal Protection of the Laws," California Law Review, September 1949.

Tushnet, Mark. "Approaches to the Study of the Law of Slavery," Civil War History, 1979.

Warren, Charles. "New Light on the History of the Federal Judiciary Act of 1789," Harvard Law Review 37, 1923–1924.

———, "Federal and State Court Interference," Harvard Law Review, January 1930.

———, "Federal Criminal Laws and the State Courts," Harvard Law Review, March 1925.

Weisberger, B.A. "The Dark and Bloody Ground of Reconstruction Historiography," Journal of Southern History, 1959.

Wiecek, William. "The Reconstruction of Federal Judicial Power, 1863–1876," American Journal of Legal History, 1969.

Dissertations

Cooke, John W. *Some Aspects of the Free Individual in the United States 1800-1860*. Unpublished Ph.D. Dissertation, Vanderbilt, Nashville, 1967.

Di Nunzio, Mario. *Lyman Trumbull, United States Senator*. Unpublished Ph.D. Dissertation, Clark University, 1964.

Hamilton, Howard D. *The Legislative and Judicial History of the Thirteenth Amendment*. Ph.D. Dissertation, University of Illinois, Urbana, 1950.

Henry, George S, Jr. *Radical Republican Policy Toward the Negro During Reconstruction 1862-1872*. Unpublished Ph.D. Dissertation, Yale University, 1963.

Hughes, David F. *Salmon P. Chase: Chief Justice*. Unpublished Ph.D. Dissertation, Princeton University, 1963.

Mitchell, Wendell. *Relations Between the Federal and State Courts*. Ph.D. Dissertation, Columbia University, 1949.

Syrett, John D. *The Confiscation Acts: Efforts at Reconstruction During the Civil War*. Unpublished Ph.D. Dissertation, University of Wisconsin, 1971.

AMERICAN LEGAL AND CONSTITUTIONAL HISTORY ★ A Garland Series of Outstanding Dissertations

Edited by
HAROLD HYMAN
William P. Hobby Professor of History,
Rice University

STUART BRUCHEY
Allan Nevins Professor of American
Economic History, Columbia University